THE CRIMINAL LAW OF SCOTLAND

THIRD EDITION

SUPPLEMENT

AUSTRALIA
LBC Information Services—Sydney

CANADA and USA
Carswell—Toronto

NEW ZEALAND
Brooker's—Auckland

SINGAPORE and MALAYSIA
Sweet & Maxwell Asia
Singapore and Kuala Lumpur

THE CRIMINAL LAW OF SCOTLAND

by

SIR GERALD H. GORDON
C.B.E., Q.C., LL.D.
Formerly Sheriff of Glasgow and Strathkelvin
and
Formerly Professor of Scots Law
at the University of Edinburgh

THIRD EDITION

SUPPLEMENT

Edited by

MICHAEL G. A. CHRISTIE
M.A., LL.B., Solicitor
Formerly Lecturer in Law
at the University of Aberdeen

Published under the auspices of
SCOTTISH UNIVERSITIES LAW INSTITUTE LTD

THOMSON
™
W. GREEN

Published in 2005 by W. Green & Son Ltd
21 Alva Street
Edinburgh EH2 4PS

Typeset by YHT Ltd, London
Printed and bound in Great Britain by
Athenaeum Press Ltd, Gateshead

No natural forests were destroyed to make this product;
only farmed timber was used and replanted

A CIP catalogue record for this book is available from the British Library

ISBN 0 414 01574 6

PREFACE

This supplement is intended to update the third edition to June 1, 2005, save that legislation passed prior (or occasionally subsequent) to that date has been treated as fully in force.

Sir Gerald Gordon has read all major revisions intended for the supplement, and has provided valuable comments and suggestions; but responsibility for the final state of the text, including the inevitable inaccuracies and omissions, remains solely that of the editor.

Michael Christie
June 2005

CONTENTS

Please note that there is no update to Chapters 27 (Concealment of Pregnancy) and 42 (Violation of Sepulchres).

TABLE OF CASES

Table of Cases

Table of Cases

xi

Table of Cases

Table of Cases

Table of Cases

TABLE OF STATUTES

Table of Statutes

Table of Statutes

Table of Statutes

Table of Statutes

Table of Statutes

Table of Statutes

Table of Statutes

Table of Statutes

Table of Statutes

Table of Statutes

Table of Statutes

TABLE OF STATUTORY INSTRUMENTS

PREFACE FOR THIRD EDITION

Pages vii to ix:

Under the heading *Scholarship and Criminal Cases* mention should now be made of the scholarly work of four distinguished law professors in preparing *A Draft Criminal Code For Scotland With Commentary*, published under the auspices of the Scottish Law Commission in September 2003. The authors (Professors Clive, Ferguson, Gane and McCall Smith) submitted their draft code to the Scottish Justice Minister in July of that year; and it is the considered opinion of those authors that Scots criminal law is ripe for codification. This publication demonstrates that interest in domestic criminal law is high and manifested at the highest academic level. The contents of the draft code are never less than thought provoking; and the Supplement refers to specific parts of the draft code wherever these are of particular interest relative to the contents of the third edition.

Page x:

n.28: In Ashworth's *Principles of Criminal Law* (4th ed., 2003) the appropriate page references are identical to those in the 3rd edition of his book.

Page xii:

The charge in *H.M. Advocate v. Grainger*, 1932 J.C. 40, would probably now be one of rape, following the re-assessment of the *actus reus* of that crime by a court of seven judges in *Lord Advocate's Reference No. 1 of 2001*, 2002 S.L.T. 466; but in *Spendiff v. H.M. Advocate*, 2005 S.C.C.R. 522 at 525G–526A, paras 5 and 6, the court observed that the Lord Advocate as master of the instance might still choose to charge indecent assault in circumstances of clandestine injury: see generally Chapter 33, below.

n.33: Force is not now a necessary element of rape: see *Lord Advocate's Reference No. 1 of 2001*, 2002 S.L.T. 466, and Chapter 33 below.

LIST OF ABBREVIATIONS

The following should be added to the List of Abbreviations in the third edition:

Draft Scottish Criminal Code

A Draft Criminal Code For Scotland With Commentary, prepared by Professors Eric Clive, Pamela Ferguson, Christopher Gane and Alexander McCall Smith, and published under the auspices of the Scottish Law Commission, September 2003.

And, the existing entry for "Smith and Hogan" should be amended to read as follows:

"Smith and Hogan

Criminal Law, J.C. Smith and B. Hogan, 10th ed., Sir John C. Smith (ed.), (London, 2002)."

CHAPTER 1

CRIMES, OFFENCES AND THE DECLARATORY POWER

It is not now strictly true that every fine carries with it the possibility of **1.02** imprisonment in default of payment. A person fined for an offence under s.107 (failure to comply with a requirement specified in, or a direction given under, a "parenting order") of the Antisocial Behaviour etc. (Scotland) Act 2004 (asp 8) cannot be imprisoned in default of payment of that fine: Criminal Procedure (Scotland) Act 1995, s.219(1) as amended, and s.219(1A) as inserted, by the 2004 Act (asp 8), Sched. 4, para. 5(4); for "parenting orders", see Part 9 (ss.102–110) of the 2004 Act (asp 8). A person fined under s.107 must be made the subject of a supervised attendance order if he fails to pay the fine (or any part or instalment thereof). It is true that a court may impose a period of imprisonment on a person who fails without reasonable excuse to comply with such an order; but imprisonment is then imposed for breach of that order: see s.235 of, and Sched. 7 to, the 1995 Act, both as amended by the 2004 Act (asp 8), Sched. 4, para. 5.

In the text of this paragraph, the reference to s.52(1) of the Children **1.03** (Scotland) Act 1995 should be replaced by a reference to s.52(2) and (2A) of that Act, as these subsections are amended/inserted by the Antisocial Behaviour etc. (Scotland) Act 2004 (asp 8), s.12(3).

n.5: Section 228 of the 1995 Act is also now amended by s.42(11)(a) of the Criminal Justice (Scotland) Act 2003 (asp 7); and the 1995 Act, s.245D, as substituted under Sched. 6, para. 3 to the Crime and Disorder Act 1998, is now amended by Sched. 4, para. 5(7) to the Antisocial Behaviour etc. (Scotland) Act 2004 (asp 8).

n.6: Section 52 of the Children (Scotland) Act 1995 is amended by the Antisocial Behaviour (Scotland) Act 2004 (asp 8), s.12(3).

n.7: Sections 56 and 65 of the Children (Scotland) Act 1995 are amended respectively by ss.137(2) and 12(4) of the Antisocial Behaviour etc. (Scotland) Act 2004 (asp 8).

A Draft Criminal Code for Scotland with Commentary, authored by four **1.05** distinguished Scottish law professors, was published in September 2003 under the auspices of the Scottish Law Commission.

n.34: Sections 10 and 11 of the Sexual Offences Act 1956 are repealed by **1.10** Sched. 7 to the Sexual Offences Act 2003. The 2003 Act does not use the term "incest"; but that Act does create offences where A "touches" B in a sexual manner (as defined in ss.25(6) and 26(6)), B is under 18 (where A

3

does not reasonably believe that B is 18 or over) or B is under 13 at the time, and A and B are "related" as provided for in s.27: see ss.25–29 of the 2003 Act.

n.36: Sexual "touching" between uncle and niece (or aunt and nephew) is now criminal in England under the provisions of ss.25–29 of the Sexual Offences Act 2003. Schedule 1 to the Marriage Act 1949 is now substituted by para. 17 of Sched. 27 to the Civil Partnership Act 2004, and s.1 of the 1949 Act (to which Sched. 1 refers) is amended by para. 13 of Sched. 27 to the 2004 Act.

1.12 n.39: Section 67(1) of the Criminal Justice Act 1993 is repealed by the Criminal Justice Act 2003, Sched. 37, Part 7, since s.285(3) of the 2003 Act increases the maximum penalty for an offence under s.1 of the Road Traffic Act 1988 from 10 to 14 years.

1.13 n.43: The maximum penalty for causing death by dangerous driving is now increased to 14 years by virtue of s.285(3) of the Criminal Justice Act 2003.

1.15 n.57: The declaratory power was exercised in *Watt v. Annan*, 1978 J.C. 84, in the view of Lord Justice-Clerk Gill (with whose opinion the four other members of the court agreed): see *Webster v. Dominick*, 2003 S.C.C.R. 525 at 537B, para. 28. It might also be argued that the majority decision in *Lord Advocate's Reference (No. 1 of 2001)*, 2002 S.L.T. 466, involved an exercise of the power since it involved enlargement of the ambit of rape in the face of an authority which had stood for some 143 years.

1.16 On the retrospective effect of judicial legislation, see the opinion of Lord McCluskey (dissenting) in *Lord Advocate's Reference (No. 1 of 2001)*, 2002 S.L.T. 466 at 483L–484E, para. 4.

n.60: *Chas. Sweenie* (1858) 3 Irv. 109 was overruled by the majority decision in *Lord Advocate's Reference (No. 1 of 2001)*, 2002 S.L.T. 466.

1.22 It has now been decided that "shamelessly indecent conduct" is not a crime at common law in Scotland: see *Webster v. Dominick*, 2003 S.C.C.R. 525.

1.25 and n.5: Notwithstanding the references to "clandestine injury to women" in the statutory provisions mentioned here, the overruling of *Chas. Sweenie* (1858) 3 Irv. 109 by the majority decision in *Lord Advocate's Reference (No. 1 of 2001)*, 2002 S.L.T. 466, entails that cases formerly chargeable as "clandestine injury" would now be indictable as rapes, since the victim in such cases would have given no active consent: see Chap. 33, as substituted *infra*.

n.5: Section 274 of the 1995 Act has been substituted under the provisions of s.7 of the Sexual Offences (Procedure and Evidence) (Scotland) Act 2002 (asp 9). The offences to which s.274 applies are now to be found in s.288C(2) of the 1995 Act, as inserted by s.1 of the 2002 Act (asp 9). The Sex Offenders Act 1997 has been repealed in its entirety by the Sexual Offences Act 2003, Sched. 7; Part 2 of the 2003 Act, from s.80 onwards, replaces the 1997 Act, and Sched. 3, paras 36–60, lists the Scottish offences to which Part 2 is applicable: see, in particular, paras 37 and 40.

The adoption of Macdonald's statement that "all shamelessly indecent **1.30** conduct is criminal" as a general principle by Lord Justice-General Clyde in *McLaughlan v. Boyd*, 1934 J.C. 19 at 23, was considered to be "obiter", "misguided" and "unsound" by Lord Justice-Clerk Gill in *Webster v. Dominick*, 2003 S.C.C.R. 525 at 533D, para. 18 and 540D, para. 46.

n.38: Section 13 of the Criminal Law (Consolidation) (Scotland) Act 1995 is amended by s.1(3) of the Sexual Offences (Amendment) Act 2000, s.10 of the Convention Rights (Compliance) (Scotland) Act 2001 (asp 7), and Sched. 5, Part 1 to the Mental Health (Care and Treatment) (Scotland) Act 2003 (asp 13).

n.40: For subsequent amendments of s.13, see the entry for para. 1.30, n.38, *supra*.

See the entries for paras 1.15 (n.57) and 1.30, *supra*; and see also the **1.31** entries for Chap. 36, *infra*. *Watt v. Annan*, 1978 J.C. 84, was overruled by *Webster v. Dominick*, 2003 S.C.C.R. 525, court of five judges; also overruled were "those cases in which the *ratio* of it has been followed": *Webster v. Dominick, supra*, Lord Justice-Clerk Gill (with whose opinion the other four members of the court agreed) at p.540D, para. 46. Since there is now no offence of "shameless indecency", the fact situations under the various cases mentioned in para. 1.31 are not criminal at all (at common law: see, *e.g. MacLean v. Bott*, 2003 S.C.C.R. 547, court of five judges) unless they can be brought within "lewd, indecent and libidinous practices" or "public indecency": see *Webster v. Dominick, supra*, and the entries for Chap. 36, *infra*.

n.62: At the end of the existing text for this note, add: "*Cf.* the Protection of Children and Prevention of Sexual Offences (Scotland) Act 2005 (asp 9), s.2(1) and (5)(b), and s.7 (encapsulating the offence of breach of a risk of sexual harm order)."

n.63: Section 5(4) [and (7)] of the Criminal Law (Consolidation) (Scotland) Act 1995, relative to time limits for prosecution, have been repealed by s.15 of the Protection of Children and Prevention of Sexual Offences (Scotland) Act 2005 (asp 9).

For an unusual charge of "attempt to defeat the ends of justice", which **1.32–1.36** involved the refusal of the appellant to co-operate with a warrant for an intimate medical examination, and in which the court held that the crime had not been made out, see *Vaughan v. Griffiths*, 2004 S.C.C.R. 537.

n.78: Section 13(b) of the Prisons (Scotland) Act 1989 is amended by **1.36** s.24(1) of the Criminal Justice (Scotland) Act 2003 (asp 7).

n.99a: Section 172(1)(c) (as substituted) of the Road Traffic Act 1988 is **1.38** amended by Sched. 1, Part 14, to the Statute Law Repeals Act 2004. Section 31 of the Fire Services Act 1947 is repealed by the Fire (Scotland) Act 2005 (asp 5), Sched. 4; see now s.85 (set out in the entry for para.

41.14, *infra*) of the 2005 Act. Section 43 of the Telecommunications Act 1984 is repealed by Sched. 19(1) to the Communications Act 2003; see now s.127(2) of the 2003 Act.

1.39 The ambit of breach of the peace has been somewhat restricted by the appeal court in *Smith v. Donnelly*, 2002 J.C. 65; the court's intention there was to ensure that the offence complied with the requirements of Art. 7 of the European Convention on Human Rights: see the entries for Chap. 41, *infra*.

n.1: *Steel v. United Kingdom* is reported at (1999) 28 E.H.R.R. 603, and *McLeod v. United Kingdom* at (1999) 27 E.H.R.R. 493.

1.43 n.12: Section 1(1)(c) of the Human Rights Act 1998 is amended by art. 2(1) of the Human Rights Act 1998 (Amendment) Order 2004 (S.S.I. 2004 No.1574).

n.15: In *Lord Advocate's Reference (No. 1 of 2000)*, 2001 S.L.T. 507 at 512L, para. 23, the Appeal Court stated that "[a] rule of customary international law is a rule of Scots law". This was said in the context of whether it was competent for a jury at a criminal trial to hear expert evidence on the content of customary international law, as that law was applicable to the United Kingdom and relevant to that case; it was also said in the context of the respondents' contention that the United Kingdom Government's deployment of a particular type of nuclear weapon was illegal as a matter of customary international law. The opinion of the Appeal Court does not deal directly with the question whether or under what circumstances—a crime clearly recognised under international law is to be recognised as a crime under Scots law, in the absence of statute or previous Scottish authority incorporating or supporting it (see, *e.g. Cameron v. H.M. Advocate*, 1971 J.C. 50 (piracy), and s.1 of the International Criminal Court (Scotland) Act 2001 (asp 13)); perhaps the most that can be said is that such a crime is capable of being recognised as part of Scots law. This is certainly the case under the law of England: see *R. v. Jones (Margaret)* [2004] 3 W.L.R. 1362 (C.A.) at 1373A, para. 24, where it is concluded: "There is no doubt ... that a rule of international law is capable of being incorporated into English law if it is an established rule derived from one or more of the recognised sources, that is a clear consensus, evidenced by the writings of scholars or otherwise, or by treaty." It was claimed in that case that English law should recognise the international crime of "aggression" as a crime in domestic law, "aggression" being one of the crimes over which the International Criminal Court has jurisdiction under Article 5.1 of the Rome Statute of the International Court (made on July 17, 1998: this Statute is conveniently set out in Appendix 3 of Kriangsok Kittichai-saree's *International Criminal Law* (Oxford, 2001) or in the Materials Volume of *The Rome Statute of the International Criminal Court: A Commentary* edited by Antonio Cassese, Paola Gaeta and John R.W.D. Jones (Oxford, 2002)); but the Court of Appeal found that there had been no international agreement as to the essential elements of "aggression", that the International Court had consequently not been able to exercise jurisdiction over that offence, and that it thus could not be said that there was any "firmly established rule of international law which establishes a crime of aggression which can be translated into domestic law as crime in domestic law": see *R. v. Jones (Margaret), supra*, at pp.1375B–1378D, paras 34–43.

(Text accompanying note 29.) The Scots courts have now extended rape **1.44** by overruling the case of *Chas. Sweenie* (1858) 3 Irv. 109: see *Lord Advocate's Reference (No. 1 of 2001)*, 2002 S.L.T. 466. The *actus reus* of rape now consists in a man's having vaginal sexual intercourse with a woman without her positive consent; the element of force, which *Sweenie* declared to be essential, has been abandoned, such that non-consensual intercourse with an insensible woman fulfils the *actus reus* of the crime: see the substituted Chap. 33, *infra*.

The courts have decided that shameless indecency is not a crime at **1.45** common law in Scotland: see *Webster v. Dominick*, 2003 S.L.T. 975, and relevant entries for Chap. 36, *infra*. For breach of the peace and its compliance with Art. 7 of the European Convention on Human Rights, see the entry for para. 1.39, *supra*.

CHAPTER 2

THE CONCEPT OF RESPONSIBILITY

2.04 n.6: The Draft Scottish Criminal Code uses "liability" in conjunction
with the adjective "criminal": see, *e.g.* Part 1 (General), clauses 3(2), 8(1),
9(1), 10, 11, 12, 13 and 14 of the Draft Criminal Law (Scotland) Bill.

2.13 n.39a: The Mental Health (Public Safety and Appeals) (Scotland) Act
1999 (asp 1) is repealed by Sched. 5, Part 1, to the Mental Health (Care
and Treatment) (Scotland) Act 2003 (asp 13): the 2003 Act (asp 13) sets
out the current regime for the admission to, and release from, hospital of
those suffering from "mental disorder" (as defined in s.328).

CHAPTER 3

THE CRIMINAL ACT

McKenzie v. Whyte (1864) 4 Irv. 570, was cited with approval by a full **3.02**
bench in *Webster v. Dominick*, 2003 S.C.C.R. 525, as authority for the
existence of the crime of "public indecency" (see the entries for Chap. 36,
infra). For the purposes of that offence, Lord Justice-Clerk Gill opined,
at p.542C–D, para. 58: "Whether a particular act is indecent will depend
on the circumstances of the case judged by social standards that will
change from age to age ... How such standards are applied in an individual case will depend on the time, place and circumstances of the
conduct complained of ...".

n.16: The reference to "Smith and Hogan" should now read: "(10th ed., **3.05**
2002, Sir J. Smith (ed.)), p.30".

In the text of this paragraph, at lines 2–3, it must be noted that rape is **3.06**
now defined, with rather less complexity, as sexual intercourse with a
female without her consent: see *Lord Advocate's Reference (No. 1 of
2001)*, 2002 S.L.T. 466; and, at line 12, the central element of rape, for
the purposes of the argument presented here, should probably now be
described as non-consensual sexual intercourse.

n.35: The reference to "Smith and Hogan" should now read: "(10th ed., **3.12**
2002, Sir J. Smith (ed.)), p.38".

n.36: There is now no exception in Scotland for murder: see the 1995 Act,
s.57, as amended by the Adults with Incapacity (Scotland) Act 2000 (asp
4), Sched. 5, para. 26(1), the Criminal Justice (Scotland) Act 2003 (asp 7),
s.2, and the Mental Health (Care and Treatment) (Scotland) Act 2003
(asp 13), Sched. 4, para. 8(3). The second sentence of this note should be
deleted, and the following substituted: "For the position in England, see
the Criminal Procedure (Insanity) Act 1964, s.5 (as substituted by the
Domestic Violence, Crime and Victims Act 2004, s.24(1))."

n.37: The Draft Scottish Criminal Code, in clause 25 of the Draft Bill, **3.13**
would establish a defence where any act or apparent act forming an
essential ingredient of the offence was without fault beyond the actor's
physical control; such an act would include a reflex movement, a spasm, a
convulsion, a bodily movement during unconsciousness (or sleep), the
result of his body (or part thereof) being used as an instrument by
another, or the result of subjection to natural forces or hypnosis: see also
clause 12—"Culpably self-induced state of mind".

n.49: The reference to "Smith and Hogan" should now read: "(10th ed., **3.13**
2002, Sir J. Smith (ed.)) p.40".

3.18 **n.62:** Murder is no longer treated as a special case: in any case, a mandatory compulsion order (authorising detention in a specified hospital) and restriction order apply only if the relevant court is satisfied on a balance of probabilities (on consideration of a report following an interim compulsion order) that the risk presented to public safety by the person in question's being at liberty is high: s.57(2)(a),(b) and (3) of the 1995 Act, as amended by the Criminal Justice (Scotland) Act 2003 (asp 7), s.2(h) and the Mental Health (Care and Treatment) (Scotland) Act 2003 (asp 13), Sched. 4, para. 8(3)(a), (b); otherwise, that court may choose which order to impose—including the option of making no order at all (see s.57(2)(e)).

3.19 **n.81:** For amendments to s.57(2) of the 1995 Act, see the entry for para. 3.18, n.62, *supra.*

3.22 **n.34:** See the entry for para. 3.19, n.81, *supra.*

3.25 In the text of this paragraph, at lines 5–6, for the words "Actual detention" to "murder", there should be substituted: "Actual detention in a hospital need not follow.[73]".

n.73: For amendments to s.57(2) and (3), see the entry for para. 3.18, n.62, *supra.*

In the text of this paragraph, at line 7, for the words "hospital order" there should be substituted the words "compulsion order": see the entry for n.73, *supra.*

3.26 **n.74:** The reference to "Smith and Hogan" should now read: "(10th ed., 2002, Sir J. Smith (ed.)), p.37".

3.31 **n.2:** In Ashworth's *Principles of Criminal law* (4th ed., 2003) the appropriate reference is to pp.113–114.

3.34 In *McCue v. Currie*, 2004 S.C.C.R. 200 at 206G–207A, para. 23, the Appeal Court held that the *mens rea* of culpable and reckless fire-raising must be determined by reference to the act of starting a fire and not by reference to something which took place thereafter: thus, where the appellant started a fire accidentally and was aware he had done so, he committed no crime by immediately leaving the scene and taking no steps whatever to extinguish the blaze or summon the fire-brigade. In so holding, the court (at p.205B–C, para. 15) agreed with counsel that the English case of *R. v. Miller* did not provide support for the proposition advanced in the 3rd edition of this book at para. 3.34(1). This was predicated on the submission that *R. v. Miller* was concerned with the terms of an English statutory provision (the Criminal Damage Act 1971, s.1(1) and (3)) which had no counterpart in Scotland. With great respect to the court's opinion, however, the decision in *Miller* depended on the general proposition that an omission to do what one has a legal duty to do is the equivalent of an act, such that where one is aware that one has created a situation of danger to another or his property, there is a legal duty to act in order to prevent or minimise that danger: see, *e.g.* the treatment of

Miller in Smith and Hogan (10th ed., 2002, Sir J. Smith (ed.)), at pp.66–67. *Cf.* the Draft Scottish Criminal Code, clause 14(c).

n.12: In Ashworth's *Principles of Criminal law* (4th ed., 2003) the appropriate reference is to pp.111–112.

Cf. the Draft Scottish Criminal Code, clauses 14 and 51(2).   **3.38**

n.77: In Brownlie's *Principles of International Law* (6th ed., 2003) the **3.41** appropriate reference is to p.299.

n.78: In Brownlie's *Principles of International Law* (6th ed., 2003) the appropriate reference is to pp.301–302.

n.80: Section 16B of the Criminal Law (Consolidation) (Scotland) Act 1995—that section being maintained in force notwithstanding the repeal of, *inter alia*, s.8 of the Sex Offenders Act 1997 by the Sexual Offences Act 2003, Sched. 7—is amended by the Criminal Justice (Scotland) Act 2003 (asp 7), s.19(2)(c), so as to confer jurisdiction on sheriff courts: *cf. McCarron v. H.M. Advocate*, 2002 S.L.T. 866, opinion of the court at p.868I–J, para. 8, relative to a qualifying crime committed in Spain.

At the end of this footnote, the following should be added: "See also the Criminal Justice (Scotland) Act 2003 (asp 7), s.69, relative to bribery at common law and certain analogous statutory offences allegedly committed outwith the United Kingdom by United Kingdom nationals, Scottish partnerships or bodies incorporated in any part of the United Kingdom."

n.82: In Brownlie's *Principles of International Law* (6th ed., 2003) the appropriate reference is to p.299.

n.86: In Brownlie's *Principles of International Law* (6th ed., 2003) the **3.42** appropriate reference is to pp.299–300.

n.90: In Brownlie's *Principles of International Law* (6th ed., 2003) the appropriate reference is to p.299.

n.96: In the third last line of this footnote, a closing bracket should be **3.43** inserted after "para. 2.26".

n.98: For s.16B of the Criminal Law (Consolidation) (Scotland) Act 1995, see the entry for para. 3.41, n.80, *supra*. In Brownlie's *Principles of International Law* (6th ed., 2003) the appropriate reference is to p.309.

n.1: In Brownlie's *Principles of International Law* (6th ed., 2003) the appropriate reference is to pp.302–303.

n.83: The reference to "Smith and Hogan" should now read: "(10th ed., **3.48** 2002, Sir J. Smith (ed.)), pp.295–296".

n.92: After the reference to the 9th ed. of "Smith and Hogan", there **3.49** should be inserted: "; on the more modern English law, see the 10th ed., 2002, Sir J. Smith (ed.), at p.309".

n.93: For the more modern English law, see "Smith and Hogan" (10th ed., 2002, Sir J. Smith (ed.)), p.341 at "a)".

n.96: The Sex Offenders Act 1997 is repealed by the Sexual Offences Act 2003, Sched. 7: see now the 2003 Act, s.72.

n.99: In line 3 of this footnote, for "para. 80" read: "para. 8".

CHAPTER 4

THE PROBLEM OF CAUSATION

n.16: See also *Borwick v. Urquhart*, 2003 S.C.C.R. 243.   **4.06**

n.26: The law as advanced in *Brown v. H.M. Advocate*, 1993 S.C.C.R.   **4.12**
382, has changed in consequence of the decision in *McKinnon v. H.M.
Advocate*, 2003 S.C.C.R. 224 (court of five judges)—a decision which
goes far to support the position outlined in the text of para. 4.12 of the
3rd edition. *Brown* had required the Crown to establish, in a case
involving antecedent concert, that each accused had had in contemplation, at the time of a fatal stabbing, an act of such wicked recklessness as
to make him as responsible for murder as the person who actually killed
the deceased; but, in *McKinnon*, the court preferred the views expressed
by Hume and in *Docherty v. H.M. Advocate*, 1945 J.C. 89, *viz.* that what
mattered primarily was what was foreseeable when (*e.g.*) knives were
knowingly carried (see *Peden v. H.M. Advocate*, 2003 S.C.C.R. 605) by
some members of a group of persons who had an antecedent common
purpose of robbery, and one of that group fatally stabbed the victim in
the course of that robbery: see in particular the opinion of the court in
McKinnon at pp.238C–239B, paras 29–32. When there is spontaneous,
rather than antecedent, concert what was said in *Brown* probably still
represents the law: see *Docherty v. H.M. Advocate*, 2003 S.C.C.R. 772.

n.12: In Ashworth's *Principles of Criminal Law* (4th ed., 2003) the   **4.43**
appropriate references are to pp.128–129, and 130 at (ii).

CHAPTER 5

ART AND PART

5.01 **n.2:** See also *Mackinnon v. H.M. Advocate*, 2003 S.C.C.R. 224, L.J.-G. Cullen (opinion of a court of five judges), at pp.237G–238A, para. 27; and *Vogan v. H.M. Advocate*, 2003 S.C.C.R. 564, where the appellant struck no blows against the victim but his conviction for attempted murder by art and part was upheld by the Appeal Court.

5.03 **n.14:** The reference to Smith & Hogan should read: "(10th ed., 2002, Sir J. Smith (ed.)), pp.173–174."

5.04 **n.16:** The reference to Smith & Hogan should read: "(10th ed., 2002, Sir J. Smith (ed.)), pp.142–143 and 173–174."

5.05 Text of this paragraph at p.149 (of the 3rd edition), line 12: although s.13(4) of the Criminal Law (Consolidation) (Scotland) Act 1995 continues to refer to "shameless indecency", there is now no common law offence of that name: *Webster v. Dominick*, 2003 S.L.T. 975.

Text of this paragraph at p.149 (of the 3rd edition), lines 13 and 16: for the word "eighteen" read "sixteen", on account of amendments to s.13 of the Criminal Law (Consolidation) (Scotland) Act 1995 by s.1(3) of the Sexual Offences (Amendment) Act 2000.

nn.23 and 24: *Cf.* the Draft Scottish Criminal Code, clause 17(6)(b), (c).

n.25: The Appeal Court has decided that there is now no common law crime known as "shameless indecency": see *Webster v. Dominick*, 2003 S.L.T. 975.

5.11 Text of this paragraph at p.154 (of the 3rd edition): for the avoidance of doubt, the Salmon Fisheries (Scotland) Act 1868 is repealed by the Salmon and Freshwater Fisheries Etc. (Scotland) Act 2003 (asp 15), Sched. 4, Part 2.

5.16 Text of this paragraph at lines 18–19: it is no longer certain whether guilt, as stated here, is "subject to variations in individual *mens rea*"; that statement was advanced in terms of dicta in *Brown v. H.M. Advocate*, 1993 S.C.C.R. 382—dicta which were, at least in respect of antecedent concert, disapproved of by a court of five judges in *McKinnon v. H.M. Advocate*, 2003 S.C.C.R. 224 at 237C, para. 24. In *McKinnon*, Lord Justice-General Cullen (in delivering the opinion of the court) said at pp.236F–237A, para. 22: "If the court [in *Brown*] should be understood as stating that in a case of antecedent concert it is necessary for the jury to be satisfied as to what was contemplated by each accused at the time of the attack [*i.e.* for conviction of murder in *Brown*, where the actual killer was unidentified, that each accused had in contemplation as part of the joint enterprise in which he was participating an act of the necessary degree of wicked recklessness such as, as happened in the case, that the deceased would be stabbed to the heart], we consider that this approach was unwarranted. This is quite apart from the fact that, in referring to the contemplation of the murderous act such as that which actually happened, the court appears to have postulated an over-exacting standard."

The court in *McKinnon* (where the facts disclosed not a typical spontaneously concerted brawl but rather killing in furtherance of an antecedent plot) concluded as follows, at p.239A–B, para. 32:

> "[A]n accused is guilty of murder art and part where, first, by his conduct, for example his words or actions, he actively associates himself with a common criminal purpose which is or includes the taking of human life or carries the obvious risk that human life will be taken, and, secondly, in the carrying out of that purpose murder is committed by someone else. It is for the Crown to prove in relation to each individual accused, inter alia, that there was a purpose of that character and scope and that the particular accused associated himself with that purpose. Where he is not proved to have associated himself with that purpose or is proved to have participated in some less serious common criminal purpose in the course of which the victim dies, the accused may be guilty art and part of culpable homicide, whether or not any other person is proved guilty of murder."

These conclusions seem also capable (when taken along with what the court had to say relative to *mens rea* and to the carrying of weapons: see the entry for para. 5.39, n.55, *infra*) of application to cases of spontaneous concert.

Gallacher was not referred to in the leading case of *McKinnon v. H.M.* **5.35** *Advocate*, 2003 S.C.C.R. 224, which was a case involving antecedent concert; but Lord Justice-General Cullen (delivering the opinion of the court of five judges in *McKinnon*) does make some observations which tend to support the conclusions of the earlier case: see L.J.-G. Cullen at pp.237G to 238E, paras 27–30 (esp. paras 29 and 30), and *cf.* pp.238E to 239 A, para. 31 where the position relative to the carrying of weapons is summarised.

n.46: After the reference to *Quinn v. H.M. Advocate*, the following should **5.36** be inserted: "*Vogan v. H.M. Advocate*, 2003 S.C.C.R. 564:".

n.55: After the references to *H.M. Advocate v. Fraser and Rollins* and *Wm* **5.39** *and Helen Harkness*, the remaining text of this note should be replaced by the following.

"Whether the guilt of any party is of murder or culpable homicide depends on the nature and scope of the common criminal purpose. If A voluntary joins B in a plot, from the nature and scope of which it is obvious or foreseeable that death may ensue if the plot is implemented, A may be convicted of murder if B, in the course of implementing their common criminal purpose, kills C and exhibits the wicked recklessness which that crime requires in doing so. This would follow, for example, if A knows that weapons will be carried and used to effect serious personal injury in furtherance of the plot—the weapons being of the sort which can readily effect death, *e.g.* firearms, knives or machetes. The individual *mens rea* of A at the time of the killing is of no consequence here: *McKinnon v. H.M. Advocate*, 2003 S.C.C.R. 224 (court of five judges), L.J.-G. Cullen at pp.236D to 237C, paras 21–24 (where dicta *per contra* in *Brown v. H.M. Advocate*, 1993 S.C.C.R. 382, are disapproved—at least in relation to cases of antecedent concert). Since A's guilt depends on what is foreseeable given the nature and scope of the common criminal purpose, he may not be guilty of murder even if lethal weapons were to be carried in furtherance of that purpose, if the agreement had been that those weapons were to be used only for intimidating their victim or to do him minor injury; in that case, if B were to murder C during the implementation of the plot, A may be guilty of culpable homicide rather than murder—depending in turn on whether it was reckless in all the circumstances for A to participate in such a purpose with such weapons: *McKinnon v. H.M. Advocate, supra cit.*, L.J.-G. Cullen at pp.238D to 239A, paras 30–31. If it appears from the evidence that C was killed by a single blow, but it cannot be established whether A or B delivered that blow, the outcome is the same: each will be guilty of murder or culpable homicide, depending on the view taken of the circumstances of the killing—whether it showed wicked recklessness or something less—and the nature and scope of the common criminal purpose; the individual *mens rea* of each accused at the time of the killing is again of no consequence: *McKinnon v. H.M. Advocate, supra cit.*, L.J.G. Cullen at p.238B–C, para. 28.

Where, on the other hand, there is no prior plot but rather a spontaneous outburst of violence in which A and B attack C and C is killed unintentionally, the situation is one of spontaneous concert and is not necessarily resolved in the same way as stated above. The nature and scope of the concert is here determined by the circumstances of the attack itself; and the responsibility of each assailant may be assessed separately, to the extent of the recklessness *vis á vis* the death of C shown by his own acts of participation. In particular, if there are striking differences between the participation of A and B in the assault, it is permissible to reflect this in the verdicts against each: thus, if A's actions are of a minor nature in relation to those of B, a discriminatory verdict may be justified whereunder A is convicted of culpable homicide and B of murder: see *Melvin v. H.M. Advocate*, 1984 S.C.C.R. 113, Lord Cameron at p.117, Lord Avonside at p.118 and Lord Stott at p.118; *Malone v. H.M. Advocate*, 1988 S.C.C.R. 498, L.J.-G. Emslie at p.508; *Docherty v. H.M. Advocate*, 2003 S.C.C.R. 772. Cf. *Codona v. H.M. Advocate*, 1996 S.C.C.R. 300, where the appellant's liability for culpable homicide was not discussed owing to the lack of evidence to show that she had in fact participated in the fatal assault."

5.40 n.58: This note should be deleted, in view of the disapproval of dicta in *Brown* by the court in *Mckinnon*: see the entry for para. 5.16, *supra*.

5.41 In the text of this paragraph, at line 15 on p.170 of the 3rd edition, for "the", read "she".

Also in the first text paragraph here, the following should be substituted for what begins on p.170 with "It is not the carrying" and ends on p.171 with "requires to be part of the plan":

"The carrying of weapons capable of causing death and the likelihood of their use may certainly imply the requisite foreseeability of death or serious injury on the part of all participants; but such implication may be tempered by the circumstances 'including the way in which it was envisaged that the weapons were to be or might be used. There is no rule of law that the jury must convict. In particular it is not a rule of law that homicide in the pursuance of the commission of a crime involving the use of violence is necessarily a murder. The jury may conclude that they are not satisfied, in regard to an individual accused, that it was obvious that weapons were being carried or at any rate that such weapons might be used to kill the victim. If, for example, one of two accused is carrying a stick or even a penknife which, so far as the other accused is concerned, is intended to frighten a shopkeeper whom they intend to rob, the latter might well not be guilty of murder perpetrated by the former even though he had reason to anticipate that such a weapon would or might be used for such limited purpose. Much will depend on whether the participant is reckless as to the consequences of proceeding."[62]"

n.62: The following should be substituted for the existing text in the 3rd edition: "*McKinnon v. H.M. Advocate*, 2003 S.C.C.R. 224, at pp.238F to 239A, para. 31, *per* L.J.-G. Cullen (delivering the opinion of a court of five judges)."

In the second text paragraph, on p.171 of the 3rd edition, at line 2, for "contemplation" there should be substituted "implication", and at lines 8 and 11 for "contemplated" there should be substituted "envisaged"

n.64: Delete the first sentence of this note, and substitute the following: "What is to be envisaged is probably assessed objectively: see *McKinnon v. H.M. Advocate*, 2003 S.C.C.R. 224." And, at the end of the remaining text of this note, add the following: "But the English approach was considered to be unhelpful by the court in *McKinnon v. H.M. Advocate, supra cit.*, at p.230F, para. 7, on the ground of the obvious differences between the laws of Scotland and England."

n.66: Delete the existing text of this note, and substitute the following: **5.42** "See *McKinnon v. H.M. Advocate*, 2003 S.C.C.R. 224, L.J.-G. Cullen (delivering the opinion of a court of five judges) at pp.238E to 239B, paras 31–32."

The text of this paragraph from the last sentence on p.171 to the end of that paragraph on p.172 of the 3rd edition (together with existing footnotes, 69 and 70) should be deleted, and the following substituted:

"Whether he is guilty of murder or not will be determined by his own *mens rea* at the time of the causing of death; but the position of the other members of the group is otherwise determined. Each such other member may be liable to conviction for murder if the jury takes the view on the evidence that it was reckless of him to continue his participation in the plot in the knowledge that a gun was being carried, since what was being carried was a weapon obviously capable of producing serious injury if used.[67a] It seems that it is the foreseeability of its being so used which is the determinative factor, and that that foreseeability is itself to be determined in the case of each participant at the time he agreed to be a party to the plot, or at the time he continued his participation in the knowledge that such a weapon was to be carried.[67b]

From the above discussion, it would probably go too far to say that if A becomes a party to a criminal operation, he takes the risk of any offence his colleagues in crime might commit in the furtherance of that operation, provided that such an offence was reasonably foreseeable—in other words that A may be convicted of an offence he neither desired nor contemplated[68]; but the fairly recent decision of a full bench in *McKinnon v. H.M. Advocate*[69] favours a position for Scots law, at least in relation to antecedent concert, which is close to the above.[70]"

n.67a: For the existing text, substitute the following: "And, of course, a person who uses a weapon to cause serious injury almost certainly exhibits the wicked recklessness for murder if his victim dies."

Add the following new footnote, **n.67b:** "See *McKinnon v. H.M. Advocate*, 2003 S.C.C.R. 224, L.J.-G. Cullen (delivering the opinion of a court of five judges) at p.239A–B, para. 32, and *cf.* the example set out by him at pp.238F to 239A, para. 31."

n.69: For the existing text, substitute the following: "2003 S.C.C.R. 224."

n.70: For the existing text, substitute the following: "See 2003 S.C.C.R. 224, L.J.-G. Cullen (delivering the opinion of a court of five judges) at p.237C–D, paras 24–25, where the views of Hume (especially at i, 268–9 and 270) and Lord Moncrieff in *Docherty v. H.M. Advocate*, 1945 J.C. 89 at 95–96 (quoted by Lord Cullen at p.233E–F, para.14) are accepted as correct, and the contrary views of L.J.-G. Hope in *Brown v. H.M. Advocate*, 1993 S.C.C.R. 382, declared as non-authoritative, at least relative to cases of antecedent concert.

5.43 n.72: The reference to Smith & Hogan should read: "(10th ed., 2002, Sir J. Smith (ed.)), pp.160 *et seq.*"

5.45 The following should be substituted for the penultimate sentence on p.173 of the 3rd edition: "It now seems clear that he would have been guilty of murder if he had known that serious violence was contemplated.[77a]"

Add the following new footnote, **n.77a**: "See *McKinnon v. H.M. Advocate*, 2003 S.C.C.R. 224, L.J.-G. Cullen (delivering the opinion of a court of five judges) at p.237A–B, para. 23, although the passage referred to envisages the use of weapons."

5.48 n.88: *Brown v. H.M. Advocate*, 1993 S.C.C.R. 382, was overruled by *McKinnon v. H.M. Advocate*, 2003 S.C.C.R. 224, to the extent that the former case required evidence that the accused contemplated that another with whom he was in concert would use violence to the degree of wicked recklessness required by murder at the time of a killing, in addition to evidence that death was foreseeably within the scope of the common criminal purpose, in order for the accused to be guilty of murder by antecedent concert. *Melvin*'s case is unaffected by *McKinnon*: see L.J.-G. Cullen in *McKinnon* at p.237E–F, para. 26.

Quoad the text of this paragraph in the 3rd edition, the passage from **5.52** Lord Moncrieff's opinion in *Docherty v. H.M. Advocate*, 1945 J.C. 89 at 95–96, is employed by a full bench in *McKinnon v. H.M. Advocate*, 2003 S.C.C.R. 224, in support of their view of the law relative to antecedent concert: see *McKinnon* at pp.233D to 234B, para. 14, and also at p.237C, para. 25 where L.J.-G. Cullen in delivering the opinion of the court concludes: "There is no reason to think that what was said by Hume and by Lord Moncrieff in *Docherty* does not or should not represent a correct statement of the law in regard to guilt of murder on the basis of antecedent concert."

n.98: Dicta in *Brown* were disapproved of, in so far as they related to antecedent concert, by a full bench in *McKinnon v. H.M. Advocate*, 2003 S.C.C.R. 224: see L.J.-G. Cullen (delivering the opinion of the court) at p.237C, para. 24 of *McKinnon*. Thus, the possibility remains that *Brown* provides the modern rule, or part of the modern rule, for spontaneous concerts or brawls which result in death—whether weapons were used or not.

See the entries for para. 5.52, *supra*. **5.56**

In line 1 (on p.182 of the 3rd edition) of this paragraph, there should be inserted between "must" and "take" the words "probably still", to make allowance for what was said (specifically in relation to antecedent concert, but often wide enough to cover a brawl situation) by the court of five judges in *McKinnon v. H.M. Advocate*, 2003 S.C.C.R. 224.

The opinion of a full bench in *McKinnon v. H.M. Advocate*, 2003 **5.57** S.C.C.R. 224 (see the entry for para. 5.52, n.98, *supra*, for the court's treatment of *Brown*) does not mention the earlier unreported cases either, possibly (since these cases appear to have been cited by the Crown in *McKinnon*) because *McKinnon* is primarily concerned with antecedent concert; but *McKinnon* does cite with approval what was said by Lord Moncrieff in *Docherty*: see the entry relative to the text of para. 5.52, *supra*; and if what was said by Lord Moncrieff were to be applied by the Appeal Court in a modern case involving a brawl situation, then the approach taken by the court in *Brown* would probably cease to be applicable to any type of concert.

In so far as the use of weapons is concerned, it has been affirmed that where a knife is used by A in a brawl-type attack made by A and B upon C, B having used a piece of wood to strike the victim, the Crown must show that B actually knew that A had a knife in order that B should be convicted art and part of aggravated assault where the injuries constituting the aggravation were inflicted solely by the use of that knife; telling the jury that they might so convict B if B knew or ought to have known that A had a knife was considered to be a misdirection (although B's knowledge might, as is usual in Scots law, be established by inference from the facts and circumstances): *Peden v. H.M. Advocate*, 2003 S.C.C.R. 605. Assault, of course, cannot be committed unintentionally; but *Peden* was followed in the murder case of *Dempsey v. H.M. Advocate*, 2005 S.C.C.R. 169, where the court's opinion at pp.173G–174A, para. 11, includes the following: "In the particular circumstances of this case, where it was alleged that there had been spontaneous concert and the Crown case was that the appellant must have seen [his co-accused] using a knife on the deceased, we are of the opinion that the appellant could have been convicted of murder only if the jury were satisfied that it could be inferred from the evidence they accepted that the appellant knew that [his co-accused] had a knife and was using it on the deceased, and that with that knowledge he had continued with the joint attack on the deceased." In both these cases, of course, it was established in the evidence (by admission or otherwise) which of the two accused had carried and used the weapon used to kill the victim.

CHAPTER 6

INCHOATE CRIMES

n.1: The reference to Smith & Hogan should read: "(10th ed., 2002, Sir J. **6.01** Smith (ed.)), pp.328–349".

n.72: The reference to Smith & Hogan should read: "(10th ed., 2002, Sir **6.19** J. Smith (ed.)), pp.333–338".

The Draft Scottish Criminal Code, in clause 18, deals with the problem in **6.20** this way: "(1) A person who, intending to commit an offence, embarks on, but does not complete, the commission of the offence is guilty of an attempt to commit the offence." The accompanying commentary states that the "test in [clause] 18 (whether the accused has moved from preparing to commit a crime to actually embarking on the commission of that crime) is similar to the common law distinction between preparing and starting to perpetrate" but also criticises theories of attempt which draw the line at a very late stage. It seems, therefore, that the Draft Criminal Code is intended to allow the courts to "draw the line" at a similar stage to that thought to be followed by the modern common law (see para. 6.43 of the 3rd edition).

n.84: The reference to Smith & Hogan should read: "(10th ed., 2002, Sir **6.21** J. Smith (ed.)), p.335".

The Draft Criminal Code for Scotland, in clause 18, deals with repen- **6.29** tance in this way: "(2) Sub[clause] (1) [see the entry for para. 6.20, *supra*] does not apply if the attempt was voluntarily abandoned, as a result of repentance, before all the acts necessary for the commission of the offence were done."

n.9: The reference to Smith & Hogan should read: "(10th ed., 2002, Sir J. **6.30** Smith (ed.)), pp.342–343"; and the reference to Ashworth's *Principles of Criminal law* should read: "(4th ed., 2003), pp.467–468".

n.76: The reference to para. 5.11 should read: "para. 5.10". **6.48**

n.80: The reference to Smith & Hogan should read: "(10th ed., 2002, Sir **6.49** J. Smith (ed.)), pp.343–349"; and the reference to Ashworth's *Principles of Criminal Law* should read: "(4th ed., 2003), pp.453–455".

n.98: In line 2 of this footnote, the first "that" should be deleted. **6.52**

n.7: The reference to Smith & Hogan should read: "(10th ed., 2002, Sir J. **6.53** Smith (ed.)), p.343".

6.57 In *Cochrane v. H.M. Advocate*, 2002 S.L.T. 1424, it was held that a charge of conspiring with C and M to break into a house was irrelevant since it was not a crime *per se* to break into a house; and it was also held that it was not possible to cure this defect by inferring from what C and M were alleged to have done in furtherance of the conspiracy (*viz.*, break into the house in question and there commit robbery) that the charge was one of conspiring to break into that house and rob the complainer: see 2002 S.L.T. 1424, opinion of the court at 1426I–K, para. 15.

6.70 n.6: The references to Smith & Hogan should read: "(10th ed., 2002, Sir J. Smith (ed.)), p.298" (instead of pp.277–278) and "pp. 295–297" of that edition (instead of pp.272–273)".

6.71 n.15: The reference to Smith & Hogan should read: "(10th ed., 2002, Sir J. Smith (ed.)), p.295".

Chapter 7

THE CRIMINAL MIND

n.8: In *Drury v. H.M. Advocate*, 2001 S.L.T. 1013 at 1016J, para. 11, Lord **7.05**
Justice-General Rodger indicated that perhaps the most obvious way of
completing Macdonald's definition of voluntary murder involved the
application of the word "wicked" to the "intent to kill"; thus, for conviction of murder, either a wicked intent to kill or wicked recklessness
would have to be established: see also the opinion of the Lord Justice-
General at p.1018F–H, para. 18, where he considers the effect of provocation on the essential requirements for murder: *cf.* the opinion of
Lord Mackay of Drumadoon, at p.1033I–J, para. 10, where no criticism
is advanced of the "standard direction on assault", which refers to "evil
intent" as being of the essence of the crime, but where it is stated that
"[m]urder requires a wickedness, over and above the evil intent that may
suffice for an assault or culpable homicide".

n.11: The felony-murder doctrine seems to have been re-introduced to the
law of Trinidad and Tobago in 1997: see *Khan v. State of Trinidad and
Tobago* [2004] 2 W.L.R. 692 (PC).

n.13: The relevant dicta in *Brown v. H.M. Advocate*, 1993 S.C.C.R. 382, **7.06**
were disapproved in *McKinnon v. H.M. Advocate*, 2003 S.C.C.R. 224
(court of five judges): see, in particular, the opinion of the court at
p.237C, para. 24.

n.24: At the end of this footnote, the following should be added: "*Cf.* **7.09**
further, the Draft Scottish Criminal Code, clause 8, which, so far as
relevant to the present discussion, reads:

'(1) The general rule is that a person is criminally liable—

(a) for an act, only if the person intended to perform that act;
(b) for causing a result, only if the person intended to cause that
result.

(2) The enactment defining an offence may, however, provide in
relation to the offence or any element of it that recklessness or some
other state of mind suffices ...'.

For the meaning of 'intention' in the Draft Code, see the entry for para.
7.18, *infra*."

n.37: The reference to Smith & Hogan should read: "(10th ed., 2002, Sir **7.13**
J. Smith (ed.)), Chap. 5, pp.70 *et seq.*"; and the reference to Ashworth's
Principles of Criminal Law should read: "(4th ed., 2003), pp.173 *et seq.*".

7.18 **n.52:** The reference to Ashworth's *Principles of Criminal Law* should read: "(4th ed., 2003), pp.173–180".

The Draft Scottish Criminal Code favours an extended definition of intention. Clause 9 of the Draft Code includes the following:

> "(1) For the purpose of criminal liability, and without restricting the ordinary meaning of intention—
>
> > (a) a person is treated as intending a result of his or her act if, at the time of the act, the person foresees that the result is certain or almost certain to occur;".

"Almost" certain may or may not be equivalent to "virtual certainty"; but the rule seems as evidentially based as the current English rule. The example used in the Draft Code's commentary, in justification of the extended definition of intention, narrates that a man, in attempting to escape pursuit, "may deliberately drive a car through a fence. He might argue that damaging the fence was not his intention. His intention was to escape and the fence was just in the way". The problems with this example are that it is difficult to see why deliberately driving through a fence should not be seen as an example of intention in its ordinary significance, and, that the crime in question is presumably "criminal damage to property"—which in the Draft Code, at clause 81 (and indeed under common law malicious mischief), is satisfied by intention or recklessness.

7.19 **n.68:** The reference to Ashworth's *Principles of Criminal Law* should read: "(4th ed., 2003), pp.177–178".

7.34 Section 12(1) of the Children and Young Persons (Scotland) Act 1937 is amended by the Criminal Justice (Scotland) Act 2003 (asp 7), s.51(5), such that the references to "assault" and "assaulted" are deleted.

7.45 **n.32:** The reference to Ashworth's *Principles of Criminal Law* should read: "(4th ed., 2003), pp.181–182"; and the reference to Smith & Hogan should read: "(10th ed., 2002, Sir J. Smith (ed.)), p.85". It should be noted, however, that both these works were published before the decision of the House of Lords in *R. v. G* [2004] 1 A.C. 1034: see the entry for n.34, *infra*.

n.34: The reference to Ashworth's *Principles of Criminal Law* should read: "(4th ed., 2003), p.187".

The dominance of "advertant" recklessness in England has recently been enhanced: in *R. v. G* [2004] 1 A.C. 1034, the House of Lords changed its mind as to the availability of an objective form of recklessness in relation to s.1 of the Criminal Damage Act 1971. The House held that the objective form favoured by Lord Diplock and the majority of the court in *R. v. Caldwell* [1982] A.C. 341 (H.L.) represented a misinterpretation of Parliament's intentions relative to that section of the Act. Lord Bingham of Cornhill (with whom Lords Browne-Wilkinson and Hutton agreed) also criticised the *Caldwell* approach as being contrary to principle (*cf.* the opinion of Lord Bingham of Cornhill at p.1055C–D, para. 32, with that of Lord Rodger of Earlsferry at pp.1064E–1065H, paras 65 to 70) and potentially productive of injustice; the criticism by judges and academics also contributed to the decision that *Caldwell* should be departed from. An objective form of recklessness is not now accepted in England, therefore, in respect of s.1 of the 1971 Act—except in relation to self-induced intoxication (see the opinion of Lord Bingham of Cornhill at p.1055C–D, para. 32); but, since the House expressly did not depart from its own prior decisions (see *R. v. Lawrence (Stephen)* [1982] A.C. 510 (H.L.); *R. v. Reid* [1992] 1 W.L.R. 793 (H.L.)) in respect of "reckless driving" (an offence which does not now exist: see para. 7.46, n.40, of the 3rd edition), it may be that there are some statutory offences involving recklessness, to which a subjective approach is not to be applied under English law: see *R. v. G*, Lord Bingham of Cornhill at p.1054D–E, para. 28.

In the Draft Scottish Criminal Code, the treatment of recklessness is **7.49** quasi-objective: see clause 10 of the draft Code bill.

n.49: The reference to Ashworth's *Principles of Criminal Law* should read: "(4th ed., 2003), p.158 *et seq.*".

n.50: In *Drury v. H.M. Advocate*, 2001 S.L.T. 1013 at 1016J, para. 11, Lord Justice-General Rodger opined that in murder, Macdonald's definition was incomplete in that it did not adequately describe the relevant intention; Lord Rodger continued that "[i]n truth, just as the recklessness has to be wicked so also must the intention be wicked". This was said, however, without reference to *Scott v. H.M. Advocate*, 1995 S.C.C.R. 760, and does not imply that recklessness and intention can, or should be, conflated as states of mind, or that recklessness should be viewed subjectively.

n.58: The reference to Ashworth's *Principles of Criminal Law* should **7.50** read: "(4th ed., 2003), p.181".

In line 10 of the text of this paragraph, for "acceptabe" read: **7.51** "acceptable".

The view that juries will make the "right" inference in appropriate cases even under a regime of subjective recklessness seems to be accepted by the House of Lords in *R. v. G* [2004] 1 A.C. 1034: see the opinions of Lord Bingham of Cornhill at p.1057C–E, para. 39, and Lord Steyn at p.1063C–D, para. 58.

In England, the account of recklessness favoured by the House of Lords **7.52** in *R. v. Caldwell* [1982] A.C. 341, was departed from by the House in *R. v. G* [2004] 1 A.C. 1034. Whilst it may go too far to state that the English approach to recklessness is now wholly subjective, a subjective approach is now unlikely to be departed from very often: see the entry for para. 7.45, n.34, *supra*, for the case of *R. v. G*.

n.69: *Elliott v. C* [1983] 1 W.L.R. 939, is impliedly overruled by the decision of the House of Lords in *R. v. G* [2004] 1 A.C. 1034. In *R. v. G*, the convictions of two boys (one aged 11 and the other 12) for arson contrary to s.1(1) and (3) of the Criminal Damage Act 1971 were quashed since the convictions had been based on the principle established in *R. v. Caldwell* [1982] A.C. 341 (H.L.). Part of the reason for departing from *Caldwell* in *R. v. G* was that, in determining whether a defendant had been reckless as to whether property was destroyed or damaged, *Caldwell* required that the standard of the reasonable adult should be used—thus promoting injustice in cases such as *Elliott v. C*, where the youth and personal characteristics of the appellant, which almost certainly made it impossible for her to appreciate the risks, had been ignored. If a reasonable adult would have appreciated the risks, these being obvious to an ordinary adult person, then the particular defendant was in effect deemed to be reckless if he or she had given no thought to the risks: see, in particular, *R. v. G*, the opinion of Lord Bingham of Cornhill, at p.1055C–G, paras 32–33. *R. v. Reid* [1992] 1 W.L.R. 793 (H.L.), is not overruled by *R. v. G*—see the opinion of Lord Bingham of Cornhill there at p.1054D, para. 28. (See also the entry for para. 7.45, n.34, *supra*.)

n.73: The reference to "Gane and Stoddart" should now read: "*A Casebook on Scottish Criminal Law* (3rd ed., Edinburgh, 2001) at paras 4.05 and 10.25."

n.74: The reference to "Gane and Stoddart" should now read: "*A Casebook on Scottish Criminal Law* (3rd ed., Edinburgh, 2001) at para. 10.25."

7.54 *Quoad* Macdonald's definition of murder, *cf.* the entry for para. 7.49, n.50, *supra*.

7.56 For criticism of the view that provocation reduces a charge of murder to one of culpable homicide, see *Drury v. H.M. Advocate*, 2001 S.L.T. 1013, Lord Justice-General Rodger at p.1018D–H, paras 17–18.

Also in *Drury v. H.M. Advocate, supra*, at p.1020J, para. 24, Lord Justice-General Rodger indicates his preference for the expression "the ordinary man or woman" rather than "the reasonable man".

n.84: Whether Scots law is prepared to admit particular characteristics of the accused in any assessment of provocation remains moot: *cf. Drury v. H.M. Advocate*, 2001 S.L.T. 1013, Lord Justice-General Rodger at p.1022D–E, para. 29. For the situation in English law, see also *R. v. Weller* [2004] 1 Cr.App.R. 1 (CA), especially the opinion of the court at p.7, paras 16–17.

7.58 With respect to Macdonald's definition of murder, quoted on p.287 of the 3rd edition, Lord Justice-General Rodger observed in *Drury v. H.M. Advocate*, 2001 S.L.T. 1013 at 1016J, para. 11, that that definition was incomplete and that an obvious way of completing it was by adding "wickedly" to the "intended to kill" part of it. (See also the opinions of Lord Johnston at p.1029F–G, para. 18, Lord Nimmo Smith at p.1031A, para 3, and Lord Mackay of Drumadoon at p.1033G–H, para.9.)

n.1: *Cf.* also the Draft Scottish Criminal Code, clause 8 ("General rules on state of mind required") which makes intention the primary *mens rea* element, and clause 10 which defines "recklessness" for those Code or statutory offences which expressly require that element.

nn.3 and **6:** Indecent exposure is now criminal if it amounts to lewd, indecent and libidinous practices, or public indecency: on these offences, see *Webster v. Dominick*, 2003 S.L.T. 975, and the entries for Chap. 36, *infra*. The indecent exposure case of *Usai v. Russell*, 2000 J.C. 144, would now be charged as one of public indecency rather than shameless indecency (the latter having been discredited as an offence at common law by the court in *Webster v. Dominick, supra*); but in *Usai v. Russell*, it was held, at p.147H, that "the *mens rea* necessary for committing the crime of shameless indecency can properly be inferred in circumstances where the accused person was in fact observed behaving as the appellant did behave, where the likelihood was that there would be persons who would observe what was being done and where the appellant was recklessly indifferent as to whether or not he was observed". It must be assumed that reckless indifference would also be sufficient for public indecency involving such indecent exposure as was established in this case.

n.13: The English definition of rape has now changed: see the Sexual Offences Act 2003, s.1.

The circularity of the dictum of Lord Justice-Clerk Aitchison in *Paton v.* **7.59** *H.M. Advocate*, 1936 S.L.T. 298 and 299 (*i.e.* the use of the word "criminal") was noted in *Transco Plc v. H.M. Advocate*, 2004 S.L.T. 41, by Lord Hamilton (with whose opinion Lord McLean agreed) at p.54C, para. 37, and by Lord Osborne (who also takes issue with Lord Justice-Clerk Aitchison's use of the word "negligence") at p.44D–F, para. 4.

In *Transco Plc v. H.M. Advocate*, 2004 S.L.T. 41, the opinions of Lord Osborne and Lord Hamilton (with whom Lord McLean agreed) stress that gross negligence, as an objective standard of carelessness, is insufficient *per se* for conviction of "lawful act" culpable homicide; what matters *in finem* is that the accused should be shown to have had the requisite state of mind for that type of culpable homicide. The opinions reject the view of English law in *R. v. Adomako* [1995] 1 A.C. 171 (H.L.)—that a finding of gross negligence is sufficient for the equivalent English crime of manslaughter—as applicable to Scotland since Scots law requires evidence of *mens rea* in such an offence: see *Transco Plc*, opinion of Lord Hamilton at pp.54L–55B, para. 40, and 55I–K, para. 44, and opinion of Lord Osborne at pp.45F–46C, para. 8. It is not clear from the opinions, however, what precise *mens rea* is required for this type of culpable homicide, save that it involves some form of knowledge (perhaps some actual awareness of risks, in the sense rejected as appropriate to the (then) statutory offence of reckless driving by the court in *Allan v. Patterson*, 1980 J.C. 57, and as quoted, and commented upon, by Lord Hamilton in *Transco Plc* at p.54I–L, para. 39), or awareness of the factors (*e.g.* the potential for corrosion of long-buried underground gas pipes) which obviously create certain risks if no remedial action is taken in respect of them: see the opinion of Lord Hamilton in *Transco Plc* at p.55L, para. 45. It is clear, however, that the "actual" state of mind of the accused may be determined by inference from objective facts, and that that state of mind should relate to a complete indifference to the consequences for the safety of others or to an utter disregard for their safety: see, in particular, the opinion of Lord Hamilton in *Transco Plc* at pp.54D–G, paras 37–38, and 55J, para. 44.

n.17: *Cf.* the culpable homicide indictment in *Transco Plc v. H.M. Advocate*, 2004 S.L.T. 41, quoted in part by Lord Hamilton at pp.52J–53A, para. 33, where the accused's alleged failings were said to involve "a complete and utter disregard for the safety of the public and in particular for the safety of [the occupants of a particular house who had been killed in an explosion there]".

n.20: The reference to Smith & Hogan should read: "(10th ed., 2002, Sir J. Smith (ed.)), p.471"; and the reference to A. Ashworth's *Principles* should read: "(4th ed., 2003), p.349". Rape is now defined rather differently in England: see the Sexual Offences Act 2003, s.1.

7.60 n.29: *Cf. Transco Plc v. H.M. Advocate*, 2004 S.L.T. 41, which is discussed in the entry for para. 7.59, *supra*.

n.32: Dicta of Lord Justice-General Hope in *Brown v. H.M. Advocate*, 1993 S.C.C.R. 382 at 391F–392A, were disapproved in *McKinnon v. H.M. Advocate*, 2003 S.C.C.R. 224 (court of five judges), at 236E–237C, paras 22–24, at least *quoad* antecedent concert: see the entry for para. 5.39, n.55, *supra*. It would seem, therefore, that there is little room for culpable homicide where the accused foresaw the use of lethal weapons to cause serious personal injury.

n.33: The Draft Scottish Criminal Code defines murder as follows:

"37(1)—A person who causes the death of another person with the intention of causing such a death, or with callous recklessness as to whether such a death is caused, is guilty of murder."

In the commentary to the above clause, it is suggested, *inter alia*, that "callous recklessness" be taken as meaning "extreme disregard for human life". This may well have advantages over the present common law definition; but it is possible, were the Code to be enacted, that "callous recklessness" would be treated in practice as no different from "wicked recklessness", since the authors of the Code intend that murder should continue to have a "special type of recklessness ... more than ordinary recklessness" (commentary on the Code, at p.84), "ordinary recklessness" being defined in clause 10.

7.61 *Cf. Transco Plc v. H.M. Advocate*, 2004 S.L.T. 41, in relation to the *mens rea* of involuntary culpable homicide: see the entries for para. 7.59, *supra*.

For criticism of the test of recklessness in *Allan v. Patterson*, 1980 J.C. 57 (relative to the former statutory offence of reckless driving) as being applicable also to common law offences involving recklessness (or, at least, to culpable homicide), see *Transco Plc v. H.M. Advocate*, 2004 S.L.T. 41 at 54H–L, para. 39, opinion of Lord Hamilton (with whom Lord McLean agreed).

n.50: See also charge (1) in *Borwick v. Urquhart*, 2003 S.C.C.R. 243.

The definition of rape in English law is now rather different. Section 1 **7.62** (headed "Rape") of the Sexual Offences Act 2003 provides:

"(1) A person (A) commits an offence if—

    (a) he intentionally penetrates the vagina, anus or mouth of another person (B) with his penis,

    (b) B does not consent to the penetration, and

    (c) A does not reasonably believe that B consents.

(2) Whether a belief is reasonable is to be determined having regard to all the circumstances, including any steps A has taken to ascertain whether B consents.

(3) Sections 75 and 76 [presumptions about consent] apply to an offence under this section."

n.73: See also *Lord Advocate's Reference (No. 1 of 2001)*, 2002 S.L.T. 466; *McKearney v. H.M. Advocate*, 2004 S.C.C.R. 251; *Cinci v. H.M. Advocate*, 2004 S.C.C.R. 267.

n.75: *R. v. Caldwell* [1982] A.C. 341, was departed from by the House of Lords in *R. v. G* [2004] 1 A.C. 1034: see the entry for para. 7.45, n.34, *supra*. The reference to Ashworth's *Principles of Criminal Law* should read: "(4th ed., 2003), p.187", but what is written there must now be read subject to *R. v. G, supra*.

and **n.88:**   **7.65**
Rape is now differently defined in English law: see the entry for para. 7.62, *supra*.

R. v. Caldwell [1982] A.C. 341, was departed from by the House of Lords **7.67** in *R. v. G* [2004] 1 A.C. 1043: see the entry for para. 7.45, n.34, *supra*.

n.92: Rape is now differently defined in English law: see the entry for para. 7.62, *supra*.

In *Lord Advocate's Reference (No. 1 of 2001)*, 2002 S.L.T. 466 at 473H, **7.68** para. 29, Lord Justice-General Cullen (after quoting from Lord Justice-General Hope's opinion in *Jamieson v. H.M. Advocate*, 1994 S.L.T. 537 at 541C–E) stated as follows: "It may be noted that the implication of the court's decision in *Jamieson* was to distinguish between the man who failed to think about, or was indifferent as to, whether the woman was consenting (which might be described as subjective recklessness), and the man who honestly or genuinely believed that the woman was consenting but had failed to realise that she was not consenting when there was an obvious risk that this was the case. The latter might be described as objective recklessness. This distinction was not examined in the course of the discussion in the present reference." Although there was thus no debate on the point, somewhat surprisingly Lord Justice-General Cullen went on to include the following at the end of his opinion (at p.76A–B, para. 44): "In my view this court should hold that . . . (iii) *mens rea* on the part of the man is present when he knows that the woman is not consenting or at any rate is reckless as to whether she is consenting. Standing the decision in *Jamieson* and in the absence of discussion of this topic in the present reference, 'reckless' should be understood in the subjective sense to which I have referred earlier in this opinion."

7.74 **n.13:** The reference to Ashworth's *Principles of Criminal Law* should read: "(4th ed., 2003), pp.193–196".

7.77 With respect to "gross negligence" and culpable homicide, see the entry for para. 7.59, *supra*.

7.79 **n.31:** The reference to Smith & Hogan should read: "(10th ed., 2002, Sir J. Smith (ed.)), p.330".

For the current, and rather different, definition of rape in English law, see the Sexual Offences Act 2003, s.1 (set out in the entry for para. 7.62, *supra*).

n.35: The reference to Smith & Hogan should read: "(10th ed., 2002, Sir J. Smith (ed.)), pp.330–331".

n.36: The reference to Smith & Hogan should read: "(10th ed., 2002, Sir J. Smith (ed.)), pp.331–333".

n.37: The reference to Smith & Hogan should read: "(10th ed., 2002, Sir J. Smith (ed.)), p.330".

n.38: The reference to Smith & Hogan should read: "(10th ed., 2002, Sir J. Smith (ed.)), pp.348–349".

7.82 **n.58:** The reference to Smith & Hogan should read: "(10th ed., 2002, Sir J. Smith (ed.)), p.156".

CHAPTER 8

MENS REA IN STATUTORY OFFENCES AND CORPORATE RESPONSIBILITY

In *Sheldrake v. D.P.P.* [2004] 3 W.L.R. 976 (H.L.) at 1009F–1010A, Lord **8.04** Rodger of Earlsferry (referring to the opinion of the European Court of Human Rights in *Salabiaku v. France* (1988) 13 E.H.R.R. 379 at 389, para. 27) found nothing in the European Convention on Human Rights to prevent the Contracting States from criminalising "a simple objective fact" without criminal intent or negligence; his Lordship also concluded that such criminalising does not (as such) violate any relevant Convention right.

n.45: Subsections (1) and (2) of s.8 of the Criminal Law Consolidation **8.09** (Scotland) Act 1995 are repealed by the Criminal Justice (Scotland) Act 2003 (asp 7), s.19(2)(a): no equivalent provisions are enacted by the 2003 Act.

n.81: The "Zebra" Pedestrian Crossings Regulations 1971 (S.I. 1971 No. **8.16** 1524) and the "Pelican" Pedestrian Crossings Regulations 1987 (S.I. 1987 No. 16) were revoked by reg. 2(1) and Sched. 2, Part II, para. 2 of the Zebra, Pelican and Puffin Pedestrian Crossings Regulations 1997 (S.I. 1997 No. 2400): consequently, the reference here should be to the 1997 Regulations, and to regs 25 and 26 thereof.

n.7: Section 111A of the Social Security Administration Act 1992 is **8.21** extensively amended by s.16(1), (2) of the Social Security Fraud Act 2001; but provided that the reference is restricted to s.111A(1)(a), (b) and (4), its usefulness as an example will remain. In a similar fashion, and for much the same reason, the reference in this note to s.112 of the 1992 Act should be restricted to s.112(1). The original reference to s.112(1A) should be deleted.

The penultimate text paragraph on p.326 of the 3rd Edition refers to s.22 **8.22** of the Post Office Act 1953; but that Act was repealed in its entirety by the Postal Services Act 2000, Sched. 9. The 2000 Act contains no counterpart of s.22.

n.32a: The missing footnote 32a should have read: "[1948] 1 K.B. 695." **8.24**

Text and **n.36:** The Mental Health (Scotland) Act 1984 is repealed in its **8.25** entirety by the Mental Health (Care and Treatment) (Scotland) Act 2003 (asp 13), Sched. 5, Part 1. The 2003 Act contains no offence equivalent in wording to s.106 of the 1984 Act—*i.e.* no offence which refers to the unlawfulness of sexual intercourse with a mentally disordered person: *cf.* s.313 of the 2003 Act ("Persons providing care services: sexual offences");

s.313(5)(a)(ii) is amended by the Civil Partnership Act 2004, Sched. 28, para. 70—but the amendment should have related to s.313(3)(a)(ii).

n.37: The Post Office Act 1953 is repealed in its entirety by the Postal Services Act 2000, Sched. 9. The 2000 Act contains no counterpart of s.53; but such offences as it does contain do not use the word "unlawful" or any of its correlatives: see, *e.g.* ss.83 and 84 of the 2000 Act.

8.26 See also *Arnott v. McFadyen*, 2002 S.C.C.R. 96, which confirms that it is not necessary for the Crown to prove that the accused knew the indecent photograph he possessed was that of a child (*i.e.* of a person under the age of 16), in order that he might be convicted of an offence contrary to the Civic Government (Scotland) Act 1982, s.52A (possessing an indecent photograph of a child), which was inserted by the Criminal Justice Act 1988, s.161(1).

n.24: The Post Office Act 1953 is repealed in its entirety by the Postal Services Act 2000, Sched. 9. The 2000 Act contains no counterpart of s.28 of the 1953 Act.

8.32 n.84: The Mental Health (Scotland) Act 1984 was repealed in its entirety by the Mental Health (Care and Treatment) (Scotland) Act 2003 (asp 13), Sched. 5, Part 1. *Cf.* the wording of s.106(2) of the former Act and that of ss.311(5) and 313(3)(a)(i) of the 2003 Act.

8.33 n.89: The reference to "Smith and Hogan" should now read: "(10th ed., 2002, Sir J. Smith (ed.)), Chap. 6 (pp.108–114)."

8.35 n.1: The reference to Ashworth's *Principles of Criminal Law* should now read: "(4th ed., 2003), p.171."

8.36 n.20: See also *Henvey v. H.M. Advocate*, 2005 S.L.T. 384.

8.38 n.32: The reference to "Smith and Hogan" should now read: "(10th ed., 2002, Sir J. Smith (ed.)), pp.329–331."

8.39 n.34: The reference to "Smith and Hogan" should now read: "(10th ed., 2002, Sir J. Smith (ed.)), at pp.156–157."

8.43 Under s.1 of the Breastfeeding etc. (Scotland) Act 2005 (asp 1), it is an offence deliberately to prevent or stop a person in charge of a child from feeding milk to that child in a public place or in licensed premises; and s.2, which is headed "Vicarious liability", provides:

> "(1) Anything done by a person in the course of that person's employment [as defined in subs. (4)] shall, in any proceedings brought under this Act, be treated for the purposes of this Act as done also by that person's employer, whether or not it was done with the employer's knowledge or approval.
> (2) Anything done by a person as agent for another person with the authority (whether express or implied and whether precedent or subsequent) of that other person shall, in any proceedings brought

under this Act, be treated for the purposes of this Act as done also
by that other person."

A defence is allowed under subsection (3) to an employer who proves that
he took such steps as were reasonably practicable to prevent his employee
from committing an offence under s.1 of the Act.

n.65: The Betting, Gaming and Lotteries Act 1963 is repealed in its
entirety by the Gambling Act 2005, s.356(3)(f) and Sched. 17.

Where the statutory provision in question contained the words "no **8.49**
person shall use, drive or cause or permit to be driven" (rather than "no
person shall use, or cause or permit to be used"), a Divisional Court in
England held that it was not compelled by authority to favour the
orthodox restricted meaning of "use": see *Richmond L.B.C. v. Martin*
[2000] R.T.R. 79, where *West Yorkshire Trading Standards Service v. Lex
Vehicle Leasing Ltd* [1996] R.T.R. 70, was distinguished.

n.51b: This footnote should have been numbered "50b".   **8.58**

In the English case of *Lloyd-Wolper v. Moore* [2004] R.T.R. 507 (C.A.) **8.79**
(No. 30), the ability of insurers to recover what they were required to pay
in respect of uninsured losses depended upon whether the defendant had
"permitted the use of the vehicle which gave rise to the liability": see the
Road Traffic Act 1988, s.151(8)(b). Although this was not a criminal case,
the Court of Appeal decided that "permitting" carried the same significance under that section as it did under s.143 of the 1988 Act. That
significance, according to Lord Justice Pill with whom Sir William
Aldous agreed, is as follows (see p.517, para 25):

> "A permission which would arise only subject to and upon the ful-
> filment of a condition is not a permission until that condition is
> fulfilled. However, a permission is given for the purposes of the
> section when there is an honest, although mistaken, belief as to the
> circumstances of the person to whom permission is given. A per-
> mission does not cease to be a permission for the purposes of the
> statute because, in good faith, the person giving it believes that the
> person to whom it is given is covered by the policy when in fact that
> person is not."

As the reasons why the defendant's son was not covered by the policy
were that he had in fact passed a driving test when he was 16 and thus
held no valid driving licence, and that the policy (effected by the defendant) limited driving by the son for social or pleasure purposes to a
vehicle of a smaller engine capacity than was being driven on the material
occasion, it might have been argued that if the defendant did not actually
know these particular circumstances then he ought to have known them.
The opinions of the Court of Appeal, however, far from supporting any
such argument, cite with approval the law as laid down in the earlier cases
of *Lyons v. May* [1948] 2 All E.R. 1062, *Newbury v. Davis* [1974] R.T.R.
367, and *Baugh v. Crago* [1975] R.T.R. 453. The Court of Appeal also
held that it would make no difference if the defendant's belief that his son
was covered by the relevant policy of insurance was based on a

misrepresentation (as to age) made by his son: see the opinion of Lord Justice Pill at p.518, para 28.

8.83 n.87: The reference to "Smith and Hogan" should now read: "(10th ed., 2002, Sir J. Smith (ed.)), pp.122–123."

8.89 n.27: Corporate bodies now include "limited liability partnerships" under the Limited Liability Partnerships Act 2000. Section 1(2) of the Act provides: "A limited liability partnership is a body corporate (with legal personality separate from that of its members) which is formed by being incorporated under this Act". Such a partnership is a novel legal entity which is closer to an incorporated company than an ordinary partnership: see, *e.g.* s.15 ("Application of company law etc.") of the Act.

8.90 n.38: The reference to Ashworth's *Principles of Criminal Law* should now read: "(4th ed., 2003), pp.119–120"; and, the reference to "Smith and Hogan" should now read: "(10th ed., 2002, Sir J. Smith (ed.)), p.207."

n.39: The reference to "Smith and Hogan" should now read: "(10th ed., 2002, Sir J. Smith (ed.)), pp.205–206."

n.40: The procedure contained in s.70 of the 1995 Act has been modified by s.10(6) of the Criminal Procedure (Amendment) (Scotland) Act 2004 (asp 5) in relation to trial in the absence of a body corporate.

8.99 The approach favoured in *Meridian Global Funds Management Asia Ltd v. Securities Commission* [1995] 3 W.L.R. 413, was not found helpful by the court in *Transco Plc v. H.M. Advocate*, 2004 S.L.T. 41 (see entry for paras 8.103–8.107, *infra*).

8.103– 8.107 It has now been clearly determined in Scots law that a corporate body can competently be prosecuted for a common law crime (which, of course, requires *mens rea*) provided the essentials of the "directing mind and will" theory of corporate responsibility can be met—the directing mind and will theory, as expounded in *Tesco Supermarkets Ltd v. Nattrass* [1972] A.C. 153, being the theory preferred by the law of Scotland; the approach set out in *Meridian Global Funds Management Asia Ltd v. Securities Commission* [1995] 3 W.L.R. 413, has been considered to be "of no assistance", and the "aggregation theory" has been rejected as "contrary to the basic tenets of Scots criminal law": see *Transco Plc v H.M. Advocate*, 2004 S.L.T. 41, opinion of Lord Hamilton (with whom Lord MacLean concurred) at pp.59L–60K, paras 62–64.

In *Transco Plc v. H.M. Advocate*, a charge of culpable homicide was brought against a company responsible for the distribution of gas to consumers via a system of pipes. The company was a "public gas transporter" with statutory duties and responsibilities for developing and maintaining a safe system of gas distribution. It was alleged that between 1986 and 1999 the company had established a series of engineering and management committees, and a number of posts, to take decisions on all aspects of safe distribution, and that the company had thus acquired knowledge and awareness through those committees and posts of the risks to life and limb posed by the propensity for rapid corrosion exhibited by a particular type of metal pipe. It was further alleged that the company, in the face of its knowledge and awareness of such risks, and with complete and utter disregard for the safety of human life, had failed to create or maintain any adequate or effective safety policy or strategy, with the result that one such metal pipe for which the company was responsible had become so badly corroded that an explosion was occasioned whereby four people were killed. (There were also alternative charges under provisions of the Health and Safety at Work Act 1974.)

Lord Hamilton, with whom Lord MacLean agreed, reviewed the prior Scottish authorities and concluded that a corporate body could competently be charged with a common law crime, and with culpable homicide in particular, provided, of course, that Scots law had "on some intelligible and recognised basis, acknowledged a mode by which the relevant human characteristics of the *actus reus* and the *mens rea* of a particular common law offence [could] be attributed to a corporate body": *Transco Plc v. H.M. Advocate*, 2004 S.L.T. 41 at 58B–C, para. 56. The prior authorities reviewed by Lord Hamilton included *Purcell Meats (Scotland) Ltd v. McLeod*, 1987 S.L.T. 528, which had simply proceeded on the basis that a company could be found guilty of attempted fraud, and *Dean v. John Menzies (Holdings) Ltd*, 1981 J.C. 23, where, whilst the majority of the court had determined that a charge of shameless indecency against a company was incompetent, it had not been decided that a corporate body could not competently be charged with common law offences in general. (Whether the actual determination in *Dean v. John Menzies (Holdings) Ltd* had correctly been made or not is now academic, since in *Webster v. Dominick*, 2003 S.L.T. 975, a full bench decided that there was no such offence as shameless indecency at common law in Scotland. *Dean v. John Menzies (Holdings) Ltd* may arguably provide authority for the view that there are some common law offences which by their nature, rather than by reason of sentencing considerations, are unsuited to corporate criminal liability; but *Transco Plc v. H.M. Advocate* gives little support for such argument—especially as Lord Hamilton (at p.58D, para. 56) refers to Lord Cameron's "powerful dissenting opinion" in the former case: in any event, it is plain from *Transco Plc* (see *infra*) that the *mens rea* relative to the crime in question must be that of actual human beings, and that it is their states of mind which are to be attributed to the company—provided that these human beings are of sufficient status within the ranks of the company itself.) Lord Hamilton was careful to point out that if a firm decision as to the amenability of a company to prosecution for common law crimes in general were to be considered something of a novelty in Scots law, then that was a novelty whose advent had clearly been signalled by the earlier authorities he had reviewed—thus ensuring no conflict between that decision and the jurisprudence of the European Court of Human Rights anent legitimate development of the law within the meaning of Art. 7(1) of the European Convention on Human Rights: see, *e.g. SW v. United Kingdom* (1995) 21 E.H.R.R. 363 at 399, para. 36.

The question remained whether Scots law should be considered to have adopted an intelligible mode of attribution such as to make corporate criminal liability an objective reality. Lord Hamilton's opinion confirms that the position taken by the House of Lords (or at least by Lord Reid) in *Tesco Supermarkets Ltd v. Nattrass* [1972] A.C. 153, *is* the mode of attribution preferred by Scots law. Thus, if a company is to be made criminally liable, the acts (or failures to act) and the *mens rea* (knowledge or awareness in *Transco Plc* itself) appropriate to the crime in question are to be attributed to that company on the "directing mind and will" basis. There must, therefore, be an individual or even a group of individuals who, at the relevant time, acted as the mind and will of the company; his, or their collective, conduct and state of mind is thus attributed to the company. In *Transco Plc* itself, the Crown were unable to point to such a particular individual who was, or such a particular group of individuals who were, the actor or actors, or the person or persons who failed to act, with the required breadth of knowledge or awareness. The Crown's argument was in fact that over the years, from 1986 to 1999, successive individuals and committees within the organisation had acquired various parts of what would eventually become the entire requisite knowledge or awareness—those parts being attributed to the company as and when the individuals and groups acquired them; thus, on the eve of the fatal explosion, the company might be said to have accumulated from a number of sources all of the various parts which made up the requisite knowledge—such that "when other individuals or groups subsequently having and exercising the directing mind and will of the company acted (or failed to act), the company is [to be] treated as having so acted (or failed to act) with the accumulated states of knowledge and awareness of all those hitherto having and exercising the directing mind and will" (*per* Lord Hamilton, at p.60F–G, para. 63). The Crown's argument, therefore, was an application of the aggregation theory, which Lord Hamilton rejects as contrary to the Scots law approach to corporate criminal liability. In particular, since the "directing mind and will" approach assumes that a corporate body "has no mind or memory . . . [it] cannot be treated as itself retaining knowledge or awareness" (*per* Lord Hamilton, at p.60H, para. 63).

Lord Osborne's opinion in *Transco Plc* accepts that corporate criminal liability rests on the attributive theory, and that the rule of attribution in Scots law is that of the "directing mind and will" as set out in *Tesco Supermarkets Ltd v. Nattrass*; Lord Osborne also accepts that the Crown's argument was in effect one which espoused the illegitimate "aggregation" theory. Where his opinion appears to differ from that of Lord Hamilton is in the attribution to a company of the collective acts and mind of a group or committee. Although Lord Osborne envisages that the directing mind and will may reside in more than one person (see his opinion at p.51E–F, para. 23), he insists that each and all such persons must possess the necessary state of mind, and that "committees" and "posts" cannot as such exercise the mind and will of the company, since only human persons are capable of that: committees and posts, apart from the human beings who form them, are no more able to act or have a mind than the company itself (see his opinion at p.51H–I, para. 24). Lord Hamilton (with whom Lord MacLean agreed), on the other hand, is prepared to accept a group decision (in relation to an act or omission) and a group state of mind—whilst conceding that nice questions may arise if not all within the group had agreed with the decision, or if within the group some had had different states of knowledge to others (see Lord Hamilton's opinion, at p.60D–E, para. 62). That apart, however, *Transco Plc v. H.M. Advocate* provides considerable clarification of the law.

How is it to be determined, however, whether a particular person or group of persons is the directing mind and will of the corporate body at any particular time? Lord Hamilton in *Transco Plc v. H.M. Advocate* seems to favour the criterion of delegation. As he states: "... the articles of a company incorporated under the Companies Acts commonly provide that its business shall be managed by the directors. These directors, acting collectively, may delegate their powers and responsibilities to a greater or lesser degree to one or more of their number or to employees or agents of the company": see p.60B, para. 62. Delegated authority (possibly limited to express authority) is thus required. Lord Osborne (at p.48C–D, para. 13) quotes extensively from Lord Reid's opinion in *Tesco Supermarkets Ltd v. Nattrass*—which opinion also refers to the delegation of functions of management by the board of directors; but Lord Osborne also refers to other dicta, from that case and from more modern English cases, where a wider range of persons might be seen as the directing mind and will—in particular, those persons who, much more generally, may be said to occupy such a position in the control of the company as to be capable of being characterised as its directing mind and will, at least in relation to the acts and states of mind which inform the criminal prosecution in question (see, *e.g.* Lord Osborne's opinion at p.51F–G, para. 23, where he quotes from Lord Reid). The conclusion seems to be that, within a corporate body, persons other than the directors and other than those with express delegated responsibilities *may* nevertheless be considered as of sufficient status within that body to be counted as its directing mind and will *quoad* the particular criminal liability under examination; and that the identification of such persons is probably an *ad hoc* matter, depending on the precise circumstances of each case.

See the entry for para. 8.89, n.27, *supra*, on "limited partnerships".   **8.103**

The decision in *Transco Plc v. H.M. Advocate*, 2004 S.L.T. 41 (see the **8.104** entry *supra* for paras 8.103–8.107), in which the "directing mind and will" theory of attribution is applied to corporate liability for common law crimes, must also apply to statutory offences where some form of *mens rea* is required to be shown.

It has been decided by a full bench that shameless indecency is not an **8.106** offence at common law in Scotland: see *Webster v. Dominick*, 2003 S.L.T. 975.

In the third last line of the text of this paragraph on p.394 of the 3rd **8.107** edition, for "though", the word "through" should be substituted.

n.40: Several modern statutes also make provision for Scottish partner- **8.109** ships: see, *e.g.* the Human Tissue Act 2004, s.49; and the Breastfeeding etc. (Scotland) Act 2005 (asp 1), s.3.

CHAPTER 9

ERROR

9.03 In *Lord Advocate's Reference (No. 1 of 2001)*, 2002 S.L.T. 466 (court of seven judges), at p.476B, para. 44, Lord Justice-General Cullen stated that *"mens rea* on the part of the man is present when he knows that the woman is not consenting or at any rate is reckless as to whether she is consenting. Standing the decision in *Jamieson* [*v. H.M. Advocate*, 1994 J.C. 88] and in the absence of discussion of this topic in the present reference 'reckless' should be understood in the subjective sense to which I have referred earlier in this opinion." His earlier view was that subjective recklessness was to be understood as a failure to think about, or indifference to, whether the woman was consenting: see p.473G, para. 29. As the members of the court who agreed with the Lord Justice-General (*viz.* Lady Cosgrove and Lords Nimmo Smith, Wheatley and Menzies) must also be taken to accept the caveat with which the *mens rea* of rape was expressed by Lord Cullen, what is meant by recklessness as to consent in rape, let alone reckless error as to consent, remains unsettled until discussed fully in an appropriate case.

9.06 n.12: The decision of the seven-judge court in *Lord Advocate's Reference (No. 1 of 2001)*, 2002 S.L.T. 466, confirms that Scots law has in effect followed (to the extent indicated in n.12) the former English law as to the definition of rape. For the current, and rather different, English definition of rape, see the Sexual Offences Act 2003, s.1.

9.09 n.17 (and accompanying text example on p.398 of the 3rd edition): The example which begins "If A has sexual intercourse with B" is no longer appropriate, since the case of *Chas. Sweenie* (1858) 3 Irv. 109, was overruled by a seven-judge court in *Lord Advocate's Reference (No. 1 of 2001)*, 2002 S.L.T. 466. Thus, A, in the example, would now be guilty of rape in the circumstances postulated: see Chap. 33, *infra*.

9.13 That accidents are not punished by the criminal law is probably too obvious to require authority; but that that is indeed the position in law is confirmed by *McCue v. Currie*, 2004 S.L.T. 858 at 862G, para. 25.

9.16 n.56: The reference to "Smith and Hogan" should now read: "(10th ed., 2002, Sir J. Smith (ed.)), pp.97–99; *cf.* pp.100–101".

9.20 Relative to the first text paragraph on p.407 of the 3rd edition: sexual intercourse between an uncle and niece is now criminal in England—see the Sexual Offences Act 2003, ss.64 and 65.

9.21 As a result of observations made by Lords Marnoch, Philip and Clarke in *Brown v. H.M. Advocate*, 2002 S.L.T. 809, it now seems that entrapment is not so much a form of defence as something much more fundamental affecting the legitimacy of the prosecution itself. According to Lord Marnoch, at p.812J–K, para. 11:

"... the nature of the unfairness complained of in a case of entrapment is that an accused has been pressurised by the state into committing a criminal act which, but for that pressure, would never have seen the light of day. Accordingly, the focus of that unfairness lies in the fact of the prosecution itself. To prosecute such a case is to my mind just as oppressive to the citizen as to prosecute him in the face of inordinate delay or extravagant pre-trial publicity or, indeed any one of the many and varied situations covered by the plea in bar of trial based on oppression."

For Lord Marnoch, therefore, entrapment informs a plea in bar of trial, or an objection to the continuance of proceedings, on the basis of oppression—the onus of establishing oppression being with the defence (see pp.812L–813A, para. 12). He accepts, however, that entrapment may also be seen as an abuse of process—which is Lord Philip's position. Lord Philip, at p.815J, para. 14 states:

"In entrapment cases, the abuse of state power is so fundamentally unacceptable that it is not necessary to investigate whether the accused has been prejudiced or has been the victim of any form of unfairness. Indeed one can envisage cases of entrapment where it might be difficult to conclude that an accused had been truly (as opposed to theoretically) prejudiced or the victim of unfairness."

Lord Clarke takes a view similar to that of Lord Philip, as can be seen in the following extract from his opinion (at p.816D, para. 2): "For my part ... I would not wish to confine the court's power, and indeed, duty, in appropriate circumstances, to prevent the continued prosecution of a charge which had been brought about by entrapment, to cases where it could be said that there was oppression, as traditionally defined in Scots law [*i.e.* where it would not be possible to ensure a fair trial by appropriate directions to a jury], or, more generally, when unfairness to the accused could be seen to be involved."

All three judges were influenced in their opinions by the views expressed by the House of Lords in the case of *R. v. Looseley* [2001] 1 W.L.R. 2060. The distinction, referred to in para. 9.21 of the 3rd edition, between legitimate and illegitimate police activity would still, of course, require to be carefully drawn (see, *e.g.* the opinion of Lord Clarke in *Brown* at p.816L, para. 4).

n.75: The Scottish cases cited here are superseded by the observations expressed by Lords Marnoch, Philip and Clarke in *Brown v. H.M. Advocate*, 2003 S.L.T. 809.

In the first text paragraph on p.409 of the 3rd edition, in line 4, after the **9.26** words "or not" there should be inserted "it".

Relative to the final text paragraph on p.410 of the 3rd edition, and **nn.89** and **90**, the account of English law given here remains the orthodox view, so far as self-defence is concerned; but the law relating to sexual offences has changed. In particular, the Sexual Offences Act 2003 has repealed the Indecency With Children Act 1960 and the Sexual Offences Act 1956. The 2003 Act has redefined rape such that the offence requires penetration of B's vagina, anus or mouth by A's penis, where B does not consent to the penetration, and A does not reasonably believe that B consents: see s.1 of the Act. The same requirement of reasonableness of belief applies in s.2 (assault by penetration), s.3 (sexual assault), s.4 (causing a person to engage in sexual activity without consent), and s.9 (sexual activity with a child who is over 13 but under 16 years of age): see also ss.10–11, 12–19 and 25–26. It seems, therefore, that the legislature is not in sympathy with the position adopted by the English courts in relation to beliefs by the defendant as to a victim's age or consent; where it has had the opportunity to do so, Parliament has invariably preferred the "reasonable belief" approach.

n.90: See also *R. v. K* [2001] 3 W.L.R. 471 (H.L.)—indecent assault on a girl aged 14, contrary to s.14 of the now repealed Sexual Offences Act 1956.

9.27 n.95: This footnote should be moved to the foot of the list of footnotes on p.410 of the 3rd edition.

9.32 n.33: In *Lord Advocate's Reference (No. 1 of 2001)*, 2002 S.L.T. 466 at 473H, para. 29, Lord Justice-General Cullen noted that the implication of the decision in *Jamieson v. H.M. Advocate*, 1994 S.L.T. 537, "was to distinguish between the man who failed to think about, or was indifferent as to, whether the woman was consenting (which might be described as subjective recklessness), and the man who honestly or genuinely believed that the woman was consenting but had failed to realise that she was not consenting when there was an obvious risk that this was the case". He described the latter as "objective recklessness", but conceded that the court had not been addressed on the issue of recklessness in relation to the *mens rea* of rape at all.

Following the decision in *Lord Advocate's Reference (No. 1 of 2001)*, it has been held, in *McKearney v. H.M. Advocate*, 2004 S.L.T. 739, that in cases of non-forcible rape, a jury must be directed to consider whether the accused might honestly have believed in the complainer's consent—in all such cases (*per* Lord Justice-Clerk Gill at p.741H–I, para. 12) or possibly just in such cases where the evidence provides a proper basis upon which the jury might accept that he so believed (*per* Lord McCluskey at p.748F, para. 35; but, *cf.* what Lord McCluskey also states at pp.743H–744B, para. 25).

9.33 n.39: The Betting, Gaming and Lotteries Act 1963 is repealed in its entirety by the Gambling Act 2005, s.356(3)(f) and Sched. 17.

CHAPTER 10

INSANITY

n.4: For a contemporary account of the insanity defence in other jur- **10.02**
isdictions, see Scottish Law Commission, "Discussion Paper on Insanity
and Diminished Responsibility" (Disc. Paper No. 122, January 2003),
App. E, Part 1.

n.8: The Mental Health (Scotland) Act 1984 and the Mental Health **10.03**
(Public Safety and Appeals) (Scotland) Act 1999 (asp 1) are both repealed
by the Mental Health (Care and Treatment) (Scotland) Act 2003 (asp 13),
Sched. 5, Part 1. The 2003 Act ties its provisions to the more general
concept of "mental disorder", which is defined in s.328 as follows:

> "(1) Subject to subsection (2) below, in this Act 'mental disorder'
> means any—
>
> > (a) mental illness;
> > (b) personality disorder; or
> > (c) learning disability,
>
> however caused or manifested; and cognate expressions shall be
> construed accordingly.
>   (2) A person is not mentally disordered by reason only of any of
> the following—
>
> > (a) sexual orientation;
> > (b) sexual deviancy;
> > (c) transsexualism;
> > (d) transvestism;
> > (e) dependence on, or use of, alcohol or drugs;
> > (f) behaviour that causes, or is likely to cause, harassment,
> >   alarm or distress to any other person;
> > (g) acting as no prudent person would act."

The above definition in s.328 is used for the purposes of the Criminal
Procedure (Scotland) Act 1995: see s.307(1) of the 1995 Act, as amended
by the 2003 Act, Sched. 4, para. 8(16)(d).

For criticism of the continued use of the word "insanity" and discussion **10.05**
of a suitable alternative word, see the Scottish Law Commission's *Report
on Insanity and Diminished Responsibility*, Scot Law Com No. 195, July
2004, paras 2.19–2.23.

In the first text paragraph on p.420 of the 3rd edition, the words from "A
person is liable" in line 1, to "and yet liable to conviction." at the end of
that paragraph should be deleted, and the following substituted:

41

"A person who has such a disorder is liable under the Mental Health (Care and Treatment) (Scotland) Act 2003 (asp 13) to be detained in a hospital under a 'compulsory treatment order' provided other qualifying conditions are met (see ss.63–66). The change in terminology was no doubt brought about partly for euphemistic reasons and for the sake of the 'image' of mental illness, but even if persons liable to detention under the 2003 Act are just persons who would formerly have been described as certifiably insane,[15] the modern legislation apparently distinguishes the requirements of 'civil' detention from the requirements of insanity in the criminal law.[16] For section 59A of the 1995 Act contemplates the situation of a person who has been convicted of an offence but who might well fulfil the grounds for detention under the 2003 Act—*i.e.* that he has a mental disorder and meets other qualifying criteria[17]; such a situation empowers the court to order his detention in a specified hospital under a 'hospital direction'. The legislation, therefore, arguably subscribes to the view that a person may be 'medically insane' and yet liable to conviction.[18]"

n.13: The existing text of this note should be deleted, and the following substituted:

"See the Mental Health (Care and Treatment) (Scotland) Act 2003 (asp 13), s.328 (which is set out in n.8, *supra*). It is noteworthy, however, that disposals by a court involving detention in a hospital of those acquitted on the ground of insanity, or found unfit to plead on that ground, depend upon 'mental disorder' rather than 'insanity': see, *e.g.* ss.57 (as amended in particular by the Adults with Incapacity (Scotland) Act 2000 (asp 14), Sched. 5, para. 26(1)(c), the Criminal Justice (Scotland) Act 2003 (asp 7), s.2(b); and the 2003 Act (asp 13), Sched. 4, para. 8(3)(a)–(d)) and 57A (inserted by the 2003 Act (asp 13), s.133)—'compulsion orders'; s.59 (as amended by the 2003 Act (asp 13), Sched. 4, para. 8(5))—'restriction orders'; and, s.59A (as substituted by the 2003 Act (asp 13), Sched. 4, para. 8(c))—'hospital directions'."

n.14: The note should be deleted.

n.15: There should be inserted in line 2 of this note, after "Act 1984", the following: "which was in turn superseded by the 2003 Act (asp 13)."

n.16: In line 4 of this note, the word "now" should be deleted; and, in line 5, after "Act 1984", there should be inserted: ", itself now superseded by the Mental Health (Care and Treatment) (Scotland) Act 2003 (asp 13)".

n.17: In line 2 of this note, after "s.6(1)" the following should be inserted: "and is now substituted by the 2003 Act (asp 13), Sched. 4, para. 8(6). The conditions under which a hospital direction may be made under s.59A(3)(a)–(d) of the 1995 Act, and the conditions which have to be satisfied for the granting of a compulsory treatment order under s.64(5)(a)–(e) of the 2003 Act (asp 13), are not exactly the same; but the similarity of approach in core essentials supports the argument in the text."

n.18: Lines 1 to 5 of this note, which refer to s.58 of the 1995 Act, should be deleted since, by virtue of amendments made by the Adults with Incapacity (Scotland) Act 2000 (asp 4), Sched. 5, para. 26(2) and by the 2003 Act (asp 13), Sched. 4, para. 8(4), that section is applicable only to the making of guardianship orders.

In line 7, the words "is restricted simply" should be deleted and the word "applies" substituted.

n.20: The following new paragraph should be added after the end of the existing text:

"As far as criminal law is concerned, then, the appropriate term is 'insanity' and the significance of 'insanity' is left to the common law and the courts. The Scottish Law Commission, however, has recently recommended that the term 'insanity' should no longer be used by the criminal law, and that a statutory definition should replace the relevant common law (see *Report on Insanity and Diminished Responsibility*, Scot Law Com No. 195, July 2004). In the Commission's draft 'Criminal Responsibility and Unfitness for Trial (Scotland) Bill', clause 1 substitutes the following for the existing special defence of insanity:

'(1) A person is not criminally responsible for conduct constituting an offence, and is to be acquitted of the offence, if the person was at the time of the conduct unable by reason of mental disorder to appreciate the nature or wrongfulness of the conduct.

(2) But a person does not lack criminal responsibility for such conduct if the mental disorder in question consists only of a personality disorder which is characterised solely or principally by abnormally aggressive or seriously irresponsible conduct.'

Clause 5 provides for the abolition of the common law rules; and clause 8 provides that 'conduct' includes acts and omissions, whilst 'mental disorder' is effectively to be given the meaning it carries in s.328(1) of the 2003 Act (asp 13)—save that the reference there to subsection (2) of s.328 is not to apply."

For s.328 of the 2003 Act (asp 13), see the entry for para. 10.03, *supra*.

On p.427 of the text of the 3rd edition, in the penultimate line, for "that" **10.11** read "what".

n.68: *Cf.* the Scottish Law Commission's *Report on Insanity and Dimin-* **10.15** *ished Responsibility*, Scot Law Com No. 195, July 2004, paras 2.31–2.51, and the Commission's draft "Criminal Responsibility and Unfitness for Trial (Scotland) Bill" at clause 1 (set out, *quoad* relevant to the present discussion, in the entry for para. 10.05, n.20, *supra*).

Cf. what is suggested in this paragraph with the formulation favoured by **10.21** the Scottish Law Commission: see the entry for para. 10.05, n.20, *supra*.

In the text of this paragraph, on p.434 of the 3rd edition, in line 7, the word "hospital", where it first occurs, should be deleted and the word "compulsion" substituted; in line 16, there should be inserted between the words "hospital" and "order" the following: "direction or compulsion"; in line 17, there should be inserted between the words "result" and "would", the following: ", in respect of a compulsion order,"; and, in line 20, the word "hospital" should be deleted.

n.82: The reference to the Mental Health (Scotland) Act 1984 should be deleted, and a reference to the Mental Health (Care and Treatment) (Scotland) Act 2003 (asp 13) substituted. (The 1984 Act is repealed in its entirety by the 2003 Act, Sched. 5, Part 1.)

n.84: Section 57 of the 1995 Act must now be read subject to the significant amendments made, in particular, by the Mental Health (Care and Treatment) (Scotland) Act 2003 (asp 13), Sched. 4, para. 8(3)(a)–(d).

n.85: The existing text of this note should be deleted, and the following substituted:

"See the 1995 Act, s.57A (as inserted by the Mental Health (Care and Treatment) (Scotland) Act 2003, asp 13, s.133)—which is not applicable where the sentence for the offence of which the person in question has been convicted in the High Court or a sheriff court is one 'fixed by law'— and s.59A (as added by the Crime and Punishment (Scotland) Act 1997, s.6(1) and now substituted by the 2003 Act, asp 13, Sched. 4, para. 8(6))."

For s.58 of the 1995 Act, see the entry for para. 10.05, n.18, *supra*.

n.87: Section 59A of the 1995 Act must be read as substituted by the Mental Health (Care and Treatment) (Scotland) Act 2003 (asp 13), Sched. 4, para. 8(6).

10.22 *et* *seq.* For another account of the history of the insanity defence in Scots law, see Victor Tadros, "Insanity and the Capacity for Criminal Responsibility" (2001) 5 E.L.R. 325, at pp.329–340.

10.40 **n.80:** *Cf.* also the recommendation of the Scottish Law Commission, set out in the entry for para. 10.05, n.20, *supra*. See also Victor Tadros, "Insanity and the Capacity for Criminal Responsibility" (2001) 5 E.L.R. 325.

10.42 The Scottish Law Commission, in Part 4 of its *Report on Insanity and Diminished Responsibility* (Scot Law Com No. 195, July 2004), has recommended that the common law test for "insanity in bar of trial" be replaced by a statutory test for "unfitness for trial". What is proposed is incorporated in the Commission's draft "Criminal Responsibility and Unfitness for Trial (Scotland) Bill", which, so far as relevant, would insert the following new provision in the 1995 Act:

> **"Unfitness for trial**
> **53F.**—(1) A person is unfit for trial if it is established on the balance of probabilities that the person is incapable, by reason of a mental or physical condition, of participating effectively in a trial.
> (2) In determining whether a person is unfit for trial the court shall have regard to—

(a) the ability of the person to—

    (i) understand the nature of the charge;

    (ii) understand the requirement to tender a plea to the charge and the effect of such a plea;

    (iii) understand the purpose of, and follow the course of the trial;

    (iv) understand the evidence that may be given against the person;

    (v) instruct and otherwise communicate with the person's legal representative; and

(b) any other factor which the court considers relevant.

(3) The court shall not find that a person is unfit for trial by reason only of the person being unable to recall whether the event which forms the basis of the charge occurred in the manner described in the charge.

(4) In this section 'the court' means—

    (a) as regards a person charged on indictment, the High Court or the sheriff court;

    (b) as regards a person charged summarily, the sheriff court."

Russell v. H.M. Advocate, 1946 J.C. 37, was followed in *Hughes v. H.M.* **10.44**
Advocate, 2002 J.C. 23.

n.90: In line 2 of this note, for "s.54(5)" there should be read: "s.54(6)".

n.99: Section 54(1)(b) of the 1995 Act is amended by the Criminal Procedure (Amendment) (Scotland) Act 2004 (asp 5), Sched., para. 13, to take account of findings made at or before a "First Diet" or "Preliminary Hearing".

n.6: Section 57(3) of the 1995 Act no longer excepts murder: see the entry **10.45**
for n.7, *infra*.

n.7: Section 57 must now be read subject to the amendments made by the Adults with Incapacity (Scotland) Act 2000 (asp 4), Sched. 5, para. 26(1)(c), the Criminal Justice (Scotland) Act 2003 (asp 7), s.2(b), and the Mental Health (Care and Treatment) (Scotland) Act 2003 (asp 13), Sched. 4, para. 8(3)(a)–(d).

CHAPTER 11

DIMINISHED RESPONSIBILITY

11.01 to In the leading case of *Galbraith v. H.M. Advocate*, 2002 J.C. 1, a bench of
11.02 five judges made it quite plain that diminished responsibility does affect
legal responsibility and thus guilt (see the opinion of the court at p.16E,
para. 41; p.16H–I, para. 42; pp.17G–18A, para. 44), contrary to what was
argued in the 3rd edition. The reduction in the accused's responsibility is
reflected in a corresponding reduction in the penalty which might
otherwise have been imposed for the criminal act or omission in question
(see opinion of the court at p.18A–B, para. 45, where it is, of course,
accepted that in a murder case, an appropriate reduction can be achieved
only if the accused is convicted of culpable homicide rather than of
murder; but diminished responsibility is plainly not simply "a special case
of the rule that personal factors mitigate sentence". The court in *Galbraith* has also clarified the law of diminished responsibility and, in doing
so, has considerably widened its scope; accordingly, it is no longer true
that the concept is restricted to mental illness or disease (see the entry for
para. 11.22A, *infra*).

Under the Scottish Law Commission's proposals, diminished responsibility would be treated as if it were a special defence for the purposes of
s.78 of the 1995 Act: see paras. 5.50–5.53 of the Commission's *Report on
Insanity and Diminished Responsibility* (Scot Law Com No. 195, July
2004).

For the relationship between provocation and diminished responsibility, see the entry for para. 11.03, *infra*.

11.03 It now appears that provocation is not a mitigating factor in voluntary
murder, but rather a significant matter to be weighed in determining
whether the accused had the necessary "wicked" intent to kill: see *Drury
v. H.M. Advocate*, 2001 S.L.T. 1013, especially the opinion of Lord
Justice-General Rodger at p.1018C–I, paras 17–19. In *Galbraith v. H.M.
Advocate*, 2002 J.C. 1, the court did not mention the approach taken to
provocation in the earlier case of *Drury*; it seems, therefore, that provocation affects the establishment of wickedness *quoad* the *mens rea* of
murder, whilst diminished responsibility affects responsibility in a more
general way: both pleas, if successfully established, lead to a conviction of
culpable homicide rather than murder—but what other relationship there
is between them is uncertain.

n.24: In *Galbraith v. H.M. Advocate*, 2002 J.C. 1 at 18C, para. 45, the
court declined to comment on the correctness of Lord Brand's direction
to the jury in *H.M. Advocate v. Blake*, 1986 S.L.T. 661 at 663C (see also
Lord Brand at pp.662K and 663B), since the court had heard no detailed
submissions relative to it. As diminished responsibility reduces the
responsibility of the accused, however, rather than merely acting as a

mitigating factor, the approach of Lord Brand would seem justified on principle.

n.26: See the entry for para. 11.03, n.24, *supra.*   **11.04**

An obstacle perhaps to convicting of reckless fire-raising, on a charge of wilful fire-raising, on the ground of diminished responsibility is presented by the opinion of the court in *Byrne v. H.M. Advocate*, 2000 S.L.T. 233 at 239F, that "A charge of wilful fire-raising does not contain an implicit alternative charge of culpable and reckless fire-raising."

In *Galbraith v. H.M. Advocate*, 2002 J.C. 1, the court's opinion at p.18A–   **11.05**
B, para. 45, states: "Because the individual is not fully responsible in law for what he does when his mental state is substantially impaired, the law mitigates the punishment which it deems appropriate for his criminal acts." The court then proceeds to narrate that on a charge of murder (which carries a fixed sentence) an accused person whose plea of diminished responsibility is established must be convicted of culpable homicide—"a lesser crime for which the judge may determine the level of punishment". It is not entirely clear from this whether the reduction of responsibility entailed by the plea is simply to be reflected in mitigation of sentence (in which case diminished responsibility applies generally in the criminal law, the "reduction" from murder to culpable homicide being exceptional to accommodate flexibility in sentencing), or whether diminished responsibility as a "doctrine" is applicable only to murder, or whether the reduction in the category of the crime charged is a "where possible" requirement as well as mitigation of sentence. The court in *Galbraith* did not impugn Lord Brand's directions to the jury in *H.M. Advocate v. Blake*, 1986 S.L.T. 661 at 663B (*viz.* "In a case of murder if diminished responsibility is established the crime is reduced from murder to culpable homicide. So in a case of attempted murder, if diminished responsibility is established, the crime is reduced from attempted murder to assault."); and, therefore, the extent and effect of diminished responsibility's applicability to crimes other than murder remains uncertain.

The Scottish Law Commission in its *Report on Insanity and Diminished Responsibility* (Scot Law Com No. 195, July 2004) recommends that diminished responsibility should not be extended beyond cases of murder (see paras 3.43–3.49, where arguments in favour of extension are considered and rejected). The Commission accepts at para. 3.46, however, that where in non-murder cases "there are mitigating circumstances which in a murder case would constitute diminished responsibility, these can be the subject of a plea in mitigation and be reflected in the actual sentence handed down by the court."

n.41: Section 59A of the 1995 Act is now found in Sched. 4, para. 8(6) to   **11.06**
the Mental Health (Care and Treatment) (Scotland) Act 2003 (asp 13). In its substituted form, that section permits the High Court or a sheriff court to impose a "hospital direction" on a person, other than a child (as defined in s.307(1) of the 1995 Act), convicted on indictment of an offence punishable by imprisonment. Such a direction authorises the admission and detention of the convicted person in a specified hospital "in addition to any sentence of imprisonment which [the court] has the power or the duty to impose." Future release from that hospital is subject to the

provisions of Part 11, ss.205–217, of the 2003 Act. Before a court can make a hospital direction, however, it must be satisfied that the convicted person has a mental disorder; that medical treatment which would be likely to prevent that disorder worsening or alleviate any of its symptoms or effects is available for that person; that if that person were not provided with such treatment there would be significant risk to his health, safety or welfare, or to the safety of any other person; that the making of such a direction is necessary; and in all the circumstances, including the nature of the offence, the antecedents of the convicted person, and any alternative means of dealing with him, that the making of such a direction is appropriate. "Mental disorder" for the purposes of the 1995 Act has the same meaning as that term carries in s.328 of the 2003 Act—see the 1995 Act, s.307(1), as amended by the 2003 Act, Sched. 4, para. 8(16)(d). [Section 328 is set out in the entry for paragraph 10.03, n.8, *supra*.]

It is now unnecessary to consider the conditions for "civil" admission to a hospital, since s.59A, as substituted, is self-contained relative to qualifying criteria; but those criteria are similar to (although not completely identical with) the criteria required for a "compulsory treatment order" under ss.57 and 64 of the 2003 Act.

11.08 In consequence of changes in the law, the existing text of this paragraph should be deleted, and the following substituted:

"A more important change, at least prior to the full bench decision in *Galbraith v. H.M. Advocate*, 2002 J.C. 1, was the passing of the Mental Health (Scotland) Act 1960, s.55. The equivalent modern provisions are to be found in the 1995 Act, at sections 53 (as substituted by section 131 of the Mental Health (Care and Treatment) (Scotland) Act 2003 (asp 13)) and 57A (as inserted by section 133 of the 2003 Act). If a person is convicted in the High Court or a sheriff court of an offence punishable with imprisonment but where the sentence for that offence is not fixed by law (*i.e.* convicted of an offence other than murder[43]), and the court is satisfied that that person has a mental disorder, and is further satisfied that certain conditions are met (in the case of section 57A) or has reasonable grounds to believe (in the case of section 53) that certain conditions are likely to be met, it may make an interim compulsion order under section 53 or a compulsion order under section 57A. The conditions common to both sections specify that medical treatment, likely to prevent the mental disorder worsening or to alleviate any of its symptoms or effects, is available for the convicted person; that if such treatment were not provided for that person, there would be significant risk to his health, safety of welfare, or to the safety of any other person; and, that the making of the order is necessary. The court must also be satisfied in all the circumstances, including the nature of the offence and any alternative means of dealing with him, that it is appropriate to make such an order.

Under an interim compulsion order, the convicted person must be detained in a specified hospital; but such an order can only be made if the court is further satisfied that there are reasonable grounds for believing that the convicted person's mental disorder is such that it would be appropriate to make a disposal consisting of a compulsion order authorising his detention under section 57A(8)(a) together with a restriction order (see the 1995 Act, s.59, as amended by the 2003 Act,

Sched. 4, para. 8(5)(a)–(c), and Sched.5, Part 1), or a hospital direction (see the 1995 Act, s.59A, as substituted by the 2003 Act, Sched. 4, para. 8(6)). A compulsion order, on the other hand, may authorise detention of the convicted person in a specified hospital (provided the additional requirements of s.57A(5) are satisfied) with or without a restriction order; if a compulsion order is combined with a restriction order, however, then the measures authorised by the compulsion order are to be without limit of time (see s.57A(7)).

The effect of an interim compulsion order is, and of a compulsion order may be, that a convicted person is detained in a hospital *instead* of being dealt with in any other way.[44]

Prior to the decision in *Galbraith v. H.M. Advocate, supra*, when it was assumed that diminished responsibility depended upon a finding that the accused had a mental illness or disease, almost everyone to whom the doctrine applied would have been a person to whom the statutory provisions (in their earlier manifestation) would also have applied. And thus, the most appropriate way of dealing with such a person would have been the making of an appropriate order (now under sections 53 and 57A of the 1995 Act): where today compulsion orders are made (with or without restriction orders), the revocation of such orders is subject to the complex procedures in Part 10 of the 2003 Act (see ss.182–204). It is not now necessary, however, that a finding of diminished responsibility depends upon the existence of a mental illness; and the widening of the reach of diminished responsibility in *Galbraith*[45] makes it possible to envisage a wide range of possible disposals of those convicted of culpable homicide on the grounds of diminished responsibility—depending upon the type of mental abnormality from which the accused suffered."

n.43: For the avoidance of doubt, the text of this note is to be retained as it was in relation to para. 11.08 in the 3rd edition.

n.44: At the beginning of the text of this note, the following should be inserted: "Section 57A(15) makes plain that a compulsion order cannot be combined with any conventional form of disposal, such as prison or a fine."; in line 2 of this note, after s.6, there should be inserted: ", and now substituted by virtue of Sched. 4, para. 8(6) to the 2003 Act (asp 13)"; and in lines 4–5, delete the words: ", and para. 11.09, *infra*".

n.45: Delete the existing text of this note, and substitute: "See para. 11.22A, *infra*."

This paragraph, together with notes 46–49, are to be deleted: both the **11.09** High Court (in *Galbraith v. H.M. Advocate*, 2002 J.C. 1) and the Scottish Law Commission seem agreed that diminished responsibility—in its wide form (see para. 11.22A, *infra*)—should continue, and in statutory form— if the Commission's proposals are accepted and enacted by the Scottish Parliament: see *Report on Insanity and Diminished Responsibility*, Scot Law Com No. 195, July 2004, Part 3, and App. A (Draft Criminal Responsibility and Unfitness to Plead (Scotland) Bill, clause 3).

In view of the widening of diminished responsibility in *Galbraith v. H.M.* **11.18** *Advocate*, 2002 J.C. 1 (see para. 11.22A, *infra*), amendments require to be made here: in the first text paragraph, on p.463 of the 3rd edition, in line

7, for "has been" read: "was"; in line 8, for "The modern" read: "That"; and from line 9 to the end of that paragraph, verbs should be read as if they were in the past tense.

11.19 In the first text paragraph, on p.464 of the 3rd edition, in line 1, after "The most important", there should be inserted: "twentieth century"; and with respect to what appears in lines 2–3, it should be noted that in *Galbraith v. H.M. Advocate*, 2002 J.C. 1, at 11D, para. 25, the court pointed out that the first judicial use of the term "diminished responsibility" occurred in *Kirkwood v. H.M. Advocate*, 1939 J.C. 36 at 37, *per* Lord Justice-General Normand.

Also in the first text paragraph on p.464 of the 3rd edition, in line 5, for "have been" there should be substituted: "were, prior to the decision in *Galbraith v. H.M. Advocate*, 2002 J.C. 1 (see para. 11.22A, *infra*),"; and in line 6, for "come" read: "came".

In the first text paragraph (following the quotation) on p.465 of the 3rd edition, in line 2, for "is" read: "was"; and in the penultimate line, the word "modern" should be deleted.

In the second text paragraph on p.465 of the 3rd edition, in line 2, for "has become" there should be substituted: ", prior to *Galbraith v. H.M. Advocate*, 2002 J.C. 1, became".

In the final text paragraph on p.465 of the 3rd edition, in line 3, for "has itself become the authoritative origin of the modern", there should be substituted: "became the authoritative origin of the twentieth century".

In the first text paragraph on p.466 of the 3rd edition, in line 1, for "is" there should be substituted: ", prior to *Galbraith v. H.M. Advocate*, 2002 J.C. 1, was".

n.2: The facts in *H.M. Advocate v. Savage*, 1923 J.C. 49, are rehearsed in greater detail by the court in *Galbraith v. H.M. Advocate*, 2002 J.C. 1 at 14C–15A, paras 34–36; from these facts, it appears that the jury was asked to consider diminished responsibility on the basis that the accused had been intoxicated at the time of the killing, had lost control and was possibly therefore only partially responsible for his conduct. As the court points out in *Galbraith*, at p.15C–F, para. 38, such treatment of self-induced intoxication was possible at the time of *Savage*, but not following *Brennan v. H.M. Advocate*, 1977 J.C. 38 (see Chapter 12 of the 3rd edition); the court accordingly considered it surprising that what was said in *Savage* should continue to have been upheld as *the* classic formulation of diminished responsibility notwithstanding *Brennan* (see *Galbraith*, at pp.15F–16A, para. 39).

n.6: The following amendments should be made to the text of this note: in line 8, for "emphasise" read: "emphasised"; in line 11, for "is" read: "was"; in line 12, for "are now", read: "were then"; and at the end, the following should be inserted: "In fact, of course, change was introduced by the High Court in the full bench case of *Galbraith v. H.M. Advocate*, 2002 J.C. 1 (see para. 11.22A, *infra*), which the Scottish Law Commission proposes should be entrenched (with some amendment) in statutory form: see the Scottish Law Commission's *Report on Insanity and Diminished Responsibility* (Scot Law Com No. 195, July 2004), at paras 3.3 to 3.50. For the convenience of the Scottish Parliament, the Commission has drafted a "Criminal Responsibility and Unfitness for Trial (Scotland) Bill, as App. A of the Report: see, in particular, clauses 3 and 5.

11.20 In the second text paragraph on p.467 of the 3rd edition, in line 3, for "does" read: "did"; in lines 11–12, for "The most recent", substitute: "Late twentieth century"; in line 12, for "suggest" read: "suggested", and for "is" read: "was"; and, in line 13, for "must" read: "had to".

n.13: *Connelly v. H.M. Advocate*, 1990 S.C.C.R. 504 and *Williamson v. H.M. Advocate*, 1994 S.C.C.R. 358, are overruled by *Galbraith v. H.M. Advocate*, 2002 J.C. 1. See para. 11.22A, *infra*.

n.14: See the entry for para. 11.20, n.13, *supra*.

11.21 In the first text paragraph on p.467 of the 3rd edition, in line 3, insert between "the" and "law" the words: "twentieth century"; in line 4, for "It is" read: "In that century, it was"; and, in line 6, for "purports", read: "purported".

With respect to the remainder of the text after the first text paragraph, it should be noted that the court in *Galbraith v. H.M. Advocate*, 2002 J.C. 1 (see para. 11.22A, *infra*) took the view that *Carraher v. H.M. Advocate*, 1946 J.C. 108, was authority for the second of the propositions set down on p.467, and that the exclusion of psychopathic personality from diminished responsibility should continue (see *Galbraith*, opinion of the court at p.17C–E, para. 43, and at p.21H, para. 54). That the court in *Galbraith* did not seek to challenge any part of what was said in *Carraher* suggests that the latter case was not seen as closing the categories within which diminished responsibility operates; but the full bench in *Galbraith* was not, of course, in any position to review any part of a previous full-bench decision.

It should also be noted that the Scottish Law Commission in its *Report on Insanity and Diminished Responsibility* (Scot Law Com No. 195, July 2004), after due consideration of the matter at paras 3.24–3.33, concluded that there was no justification for the exclusion of psychopathic personality from diminished responsibility, and recommended that such exclusion be removed from the law (at para. 3.34). In the Commission's draft "Criminal Responsibility and Unfitness for Trial (Scotland) Bill" (see App. A of the *Report*), that recommendation would be implemented by the simple device of introducing a statutory definition of diminished responsibility (see clause 3), which does not expressly exclude psychopathic personality, and simultaneously abolishing the common law rules relative to the plea (see clause 5).

11.22 In the text of this paragraph on p.469 of the 3rd edition, in line 1, for "Recent" substitute: "Subsequent twentieth century", and for "have" read: "did"; in line 2, for "sought" read: "seek", and delete "has"; in line 4, for "have" read: "had"; in line 5, for "has been" read: "was"; and in line 7, for "falls" read: "fell", and for "is" (in both places where it occurs) read: "was".

n.34: See the entry for para. 11.20, n.13, *supra*; and, delete the text from "In Williamson" to the end of the note.

At the end of paragraph 11.22, the following new headings, footnotes and paragraph (11.22A) should be inserted:

"THE MODERN LAW

Galbraith v. H.M. Advocate[37a]

11.22A *Galbraith v. H.M. Advocate* sets out the modern common law rules on diminished responsibility. The general rule is that 'diminished responsibility applies in cases where, because the accused's ability to determine and[37b] control his actings is impaired[37c] as a result of some mental abnormality, his responsibility for any killing can properly be regarded as correspondingly reduced. The accused should, accordingly, be convicted of culpable homicide rather than murder.'[37d] The mental abnormality has to be one 'that is recognised by the appropriate science',[37e] but need not amount to a mental illness[37f] or border on insanity.[37g] Indeed, the opinion of the court puts the matter this way: 'For a variety of reasons ... an adult's mind may be affected, either permanently or for a certain period, in such a way that it does not work like the mind of a normal adult. The law takes account of this. In extreme cases, the person's mind can be affected so extensively that the law treats him as being insane and, therefore, as not being responsible at all for his acts and omissions. In other cases, the operation of the person's mind is affected to a lesser degree so that he remains able to determine or control his acts and omissions but his ability to do so is impaired and is not that of a normal adult. Where a person's mind is so affected to a substantial degree, according to our law he is not to be treated as fully responsible for his acts and omissions: his responsibility is diminished.'[37h]

The above description is very wide, as is shown by the very varied ways in which the required mental abnormality may be brought about.[37i] These include external factors (such as sun stroke, chronic drinking,[37j] accident, injury, shock, the taking of therapeutic drugs, or sexual or other abuse), congenital factors (such as low intelligence), organic factors (such as brain tumours, thyroid disorders), physical illnesses (such as hypoglycaemia, fevers and palsies) depressive illnesses, and other recognised conditions (such as schizophrenia)—provided that they impair the accused's ability to determine or control his acts or omissions to a substantial degree.

What the court in *Galbraith* had in mind as 'impairment' for the purposes of diminished responsibility includes (but is not limited to) a significant distortion of the way in which a normal person would perceive 'physical acts and matters', the onset of delusions, and an adverse effect on ability 'to form a rational judgment as to whether a particular act is right or wrong or to decide whether to perform it':[37k] there has to be, in general terms, recognition 'that the individual is to be pitied since, at the relevant time, he was not as normal people are. There was unfortunately something far wrong with him, which affected the way he acted.'[371]

The decision in *Galbraith* effectively reverses the trend set by the twentieth century cases, and provides at common law[37m] an account of diminished responsibility which is both flexible and wide. There are, nevertheless, restrictions: in particular, the effects of normal human failings and emotions (such as anger and jealousy) do not qualify at all[37n]; and, for policy reasons, certain mental abnormalities are disallowed. Those which have so far been recognised as belonging to this 'disallowed' class are psychopathic personality disorder (following *Carraher v. H.M. Advocate*, 1946 J.C. 108) and drunkenness to any degree brought on by the voluntary consumption of alcohol or drugs or the sniffing of glue (following *Brennan v. H.M. Advocate*, 1977 J.C. 38).[37o]

n.37a: 2002 J.C. 1 (court of five judges).

n.37b: In other passages from the court's opinion, "and" becomes "or": see, *e.g.* p.17H–J, para. 44; p.20F, para. 52; and, p.21D–E, para. 54.

n.37c: The impairment has to be substantial: see the opinion of the court at pp.17G–18A, para. 44, set out below.

n.37d: 2002 J.C. at p.16E, para. 41.

n.37e: *ibid.*, at p.21F, para. 54.

n.37f: See *Galbraith*, at p.20G, para. 52. In so far as *Connelly v. H.M. Advocate*, 1990 S.C.C.R. 504 and *Williamson v. H.M. Advocate*, 1994 S.C.C.R. 358 required mental illness or mental disease as an essential element of diminished responsibility, these cases were disapproved: see *Galbraith* at p.20G, para. 52; and in so far as *Connelly v. H.M. Advocate* required that the passage from Lord Justice-Clerk Alness's direction to the jury in *H.M. Advocate v. Savage*, 1923 J.C. 49 at 51 (quoted at para. 11.19, *supra*) should be, read as a whole, taken as a definitive description of the requirements of diminished responsibility, it was overruled: see *Galbraith*, at pp.13D–14A, paras 30–32.

n.37g: See *Galbraith*, at p.18E, para. 46.

n.37h: *Galbraith*, at pp.17G–18A, para. 44.

n.37i: See *Galbraith*, at pp.20B–21B, paras 52–53.

n.37j: *i.e.* in the sense of bringing on delirium tremens.

n.37k: *Galbraith*, at p.19F–G, para. 51.

n.37l: *ibid.*, at p.19H, para. 51.

n.37m: *Cf.* the discussion by, and recommendations of, the Scottish Law Commission in its *Report on Insanity and Diminished Responsibility* (Scot Law Com No. 195, July 2004), paras 3.1–3.51. The Commission recommends the retention of diminished responsibility in statutory form, but with certain departures from the common law position; in particular, the 'rule', that diminished responsibility cannot be pled if the accused's mental condition falls within the insanity defence, should cease to apply; psychopathic personality disorder should not continue to be outwith the ambit of the plea; and, self-induced intoxication, although not itself sufficient for, should cease to be a total bar to, diminished responsibility provided that the requirements of the plea can be met *aliunde*.

n.37n: *ibid.*, at pp.19I–20A, para. 51, where the court quotes with approval from Lord Justice-Clerk Cooper in *H.M. Advocate v. Braithwaite*, 1945 J.C. 55 at 57–58.

n.37o: Opinion of the court in *Galbraith*, at p.17B–E, para. 43."

11.23 This paragraph, and nn. 38 to 44 fall to be deleted, since the Mental Health (Scotland) Act 1984 is repealed in its entirety by the Mental Health (Care and Treatment) (Scotland) Act 2003 (asp 13), Sched. 5, Part 1; s.328(1) of the 2003 Act provides that mental illness, personality disorder and learning disability are separate sub-classes of the general class of "mental disorder" (and, thus, does not maintain that personality disorders are types of mental illness); and the full bench decision in *Galbraith v. H.M. Advocate*, 2002 J.C. 1, has now confirmed that psychopathic personality disorder is not to be received as diminished responsibility at common law. (The Scottish Law Commission in its *Report on Insanity and Diminished Responsibility*, Scot Law Com No. 195, July 2004, has recommended that psychopathic personality disorder should not be excluded from the plea, for the reasons which the Commission advances at paras 3.24 to 3.33.)

11.24 This paragraph, and n.45, fall to be deleted, since the treatment of intoxication relative to diminished responsibility is covered by *Galbraith v. H.M. Advocate*, 2002 J.C. 1: see para. 11.22A, *supra*. (The Scottish Law Commission in its *Report on Insanity and Diminished Responsibility*, Scot Law Com No. 195, July 2004, does not recommend that the temporary effects of self-induced intoxication (as opposed to "chronic intoxication", which the Commission more accurately refers to as "alcohol or drug dependency" at para. 3.37 of its *Report*) should be a sufficient mental abnormality to meet the requirements of diminished responsibility; but it does recommend that acute self-induced intoxication should not be a bar to the plea, where the essentials for that plea can be established *aliunde*: see paras 3.35–3.42.)

11.25 The heading in block capital letters immediately above this paragraph in the 3rd edition should be amended to read:

"A Note on Learning Disability"

In the first text paragraph of para. 11.25, at p.472 of the 3rd edition, in line 4, for "mental handicap" there should be substituted: "learning disability"; in line 5, for "Since such handicap" there should be substituted: "To the extent that a learning disability"; in line 6, for "is mentally handicapped" there should be substituted: "has such a disability"; in line 8, for "is normally" there should be substituted: "would normally be"; in line 9, for "are" read: "were"; in line 10, there should be inserted after "trial", "—and this should also be the case in respect of severe learning disability"; in lines 12–13, the words "mentally handicapped" should be deleted; in line 13, after "person" there should be inserted: "with a learning disability"; in lines 14–15, for "mental handicap" there should be substituted: "learning disability"; in line 17, for "mental deficiency" there should be substituted: "learning disability"; and in line 23, for "mental handicap" there should be substituted: "learning disability".

In the second text paragraph of this paragraph, at p.472 of the 3rd edition, the first sentence should be deleted, and the following substituted: "Following the full bench decision in *Galbraith v. H.M. Advocate*,[49] there is no doubt that learning disability may constitute diminished responsibility.[50]"

The second text paragraph (which begins: "The Mental Health (Scotland) Act 1984"), on p.473 of the 3rd edition, should be deleted, since the 1984 Act is entirely repealed by the Mental Health (Care and Treatment) (Scotland) Act 2003 (asp 13), Sched. 5, Part 1, and the complex new provisions of the 2003 Act, and those that that Act inserts into the 1995 Act, are beyond the scope of this Supplement.

n.47: The existing text of this note should be deleted, and the following substituted: "Mental Health (Care and Treatment) (Scotland) Act 2003 (asp 13); the same applies to the 1995 Act: see s.307(1), where (as amended by the 2003 Act, Sched. 4, para. 8(16)) the meaning of 'mental disorder' is to be that of s.328(1) of the 2003 Act."

n.49: The existing text of this note should be deleted, and the following substituted: "2002 J.C. 1; see para. 11.22A, *supra*."

nn.53–55: These footnotes should be deleted (following deletion of the text to which they relate).

CHAPTER 12

INTOXICATION

12.03 n.8: The reference to Ashworth's *Principles of Criminal Law* should now read: "(4th ed., 2003), p.213."

12.06 n.18: The following should be added at the end of this note: "; *Galbraith v. H.M. Advocate*, 2002 J.C. 1 (court of five judges) at 20C, para. 52.

n.19: The following should be added at the end of this note: "; *Galbraith v. H.M. Advocate*, 2002 J.C. 1 (court of five judges) at 17B–C, para. 43.

n.20: The following should be added at the end of this note: "*Cf.* Scottish Law Commission's *Report on Insanity and Diminished Responsibility* (Scot Law Com No. 195, July 2004), at paras 3.35–3.42."

12.12 n.70: *Metropolitan Police Commr v. Caldwell* [1982] A.C. 341 was departed from, and effectively overruled, by *R. v. G.* [2004] 1 A.C. 1034 (H.L.). The ambit of objective recklessness in English criminal law is, therefore, now negligible; the reference to Ashworth's *Principles of Criminal Law* should now read: "(4th ed., 2003), p.187", but that edition was completed before the decision in *R. v. G.*

12.14 n.84: The reference to "Smith and Hogan" should now read: "(10th ed., 2002, Sir J. Smith (ed.)), p.242."

n.85: The reference to Ashworth's *Principles of Criminal Law* should now read: "(4th ed., 2003), p.214", and the reference to "Smith and Hogan" should now read: "(10th ed., 2002, Sir J. Smith (ed.)), at p.243."

n.87: The reference to "Smith and Hogan" should now read: "(10th ed., 2002, Sir J. Smith (ed.)), at p.243."

n.88: The references to "Smith and Hogan" should now read: "(10th ed., 2002, Sir J. Smith (ed.)), at pp.243, and 243–244."

n.91: The reference to "Smith and Hogan" should now read: "(10th ed., 2002, Sir J. Smith (ed.)), at pp.83–88; but see the entry for para. 12.12, n.70, *supra*."

n.92: The references to Ashworth's *Principles of Criminal Law* should now read: "(4th ed., 2003), at pp.215 and 214, respectively." The quotation in the text, for which p.215 is now the reference, is slightly amended in the 4th ed., so as to read: "In most cases it is far fetched to argue that a person in the process of getting drunk is aware of the type of conduct he or she might later indulge in".

Relative to the final sentence of the text of this paragraph, *cf.* the Draft **12.21**
Scottish Criminal Code, which, in clause 12, simply asserts that a person,
in a temporary state of mind which is culpably self-induced and which
precludes the intention or other mental element required for an offence, is
to be regarded as having that intention or mental element: a temporary
state of mind is to be regarded as "culpably self-induced" if it is caused by
a voluntary taking by that person of alcohol or any other drug or substance, or by a voluntary failure to take any medication or precautionary
measures, when the person knew, or ought to have known, that the
taking or failure to take was likely to lead to loss of self-control. The
authors of the Draft Code, however, exclude from the ambit of that
clause offences "of presence with intent to commit an offence [clause 94]
or possession of tools with intent to commit an offence [clause 95]", on
the basis that these offences "depend almost entirely on intent and, if the
person was to be regarded under [clause 12] as having the intention
necessary to commit the offences, their scope would be unacceptably
wide" (commentary to clause 12, at p.35).

Cf. the Draft Scottish Criminal Code, clause 12 (which is considered, **12.23**
quoad relevant, in the entry for para. 12.21, *supra*).

CHAPTER 13

NECESSITY, COERCION AND SUPERIOR ORDERS

n.1: The reference to "Smith and Hogan" should now read: "(10th ed., 2002, Sir J. Smith (ed.)), at pp.251 *et seq.*, and the reference to Ashworth's *Principles of Criminal Law* should now read: "(4th ed., 2003), pp.221 *et seq.*".

13.02 n.5: The approach adopted in the Model Penal Code has not commended itself to the Scottish courts: see the necessity case of *Lord Advocate's Reference (No. 1 of 2000)*, 2001 J.C. 143 at 162B–E, para. 55.

13.06 n.11: That Lord Hailsham's views in *R. v. Howe* [1987] 1 A.C. 417, are in general accepted in Scotland is supported by the opinion of the court in *Lord Advocate's Reference (No. 1 of 2000)*, 2001 J.C. 143 at 158C–I, paras 41–42: see also the opinion of the court at p.162E, where it is confirmed that the law of Scotland in relation to necessity is to be found in *Moss v. Howdle*, 1997 J.C. 123.

13.08 n.17: See also *Lord Advocate's Reference (No. 1 of 2000)*, 2001 J.C. 143.

13.09 In *Cochrane v. H.M. Advocate*, 2001 S.C.C.R. 655 at 666F, para. 20, the court stated that "[c]oercion or compulsion is not a defence which the law regards with particular favour", having already concluded (see p.666B–C, para. 17) from the authorities, particularly *Moss v. Howdle*, 1997 J.C. 123, that Scots law proceeded on the basis "that there was no relevant difference between coercion or duress per minas and duress of circumstances or necessity" such that the same objective test fell to be applied in both.

n.20: In line 4 of this note, on p.505 of the 3rd edition, for the reference to "s.34(3)" of the Road Traffic Act 1988, there should be substituted a reference to "s.34(4)" of that Act, since the original s.34 was itself substituted by the Countryside and Rights of Way Act 2000, Sched. 7, para. 5: the relevant wording remains the same; and, also in line 4 of the note, it should be noted that s.30 of the Fire Services Act 1947 is repealed by the Fire (Scotland) Act 2005 (asp 5), Sched. 4. Section 25 of the 2005 Act now provides:

> "(1) An employee of a relevant authority [as defined in s.6] who is authorised in writing by the authority for the purposes of this section (an 'authorised employee') and on duty may—
>
> > (a) if the employee reasonably believes that a fire has broken out, do anything the employee reasonably believes to be necessary for the purposes of—
> >
> > > (i) extinguishing [as defined in s.52] the fire; or

      (ii) protecting life or property;

  (b) if the employee reasonably believes that a road traffic accident has occurred, do anything the employee reasonably believes to be necessary for the purpose of—

      (i) rescuing people; or
      (ii) protecting them from serious harm;

  (c) if the employee reasonably believes that an emergency [as defined in s.52] other than a fire or road traffic accident has occurred, do anything the employee reasonably believes to be necessary for the purpose of carrying out any function conferred on the authority in relation to the emergency; and
  (d) do anything the employee reasonably believes to be necessary for the purpose of preventing or limiting damage to property resulting from action taken as mentioned in paragraph (a), (b) or (c).

  (2) An authorised employee may in particular under subsection (1)—

  (a) enter premises or a place (by force if necessary);
  (b) move a vehicle without the consent of its owner;
  (c) force open and enter a lockfast vehicle;
  (d) close a road [as defined in s.52];
  (e) stop and regulate traffic;
  (f) restrict the access of persons to premises or a place."

In relation to fires, similar (but not identical) powers are granted to constables by s.26 of the 2005 Act.

n.54: The reference to Ashworth's *Principles of Criminal Law* should now read: "(4th ed., 2003), at p.222".   **13.17**

Relative to what is stated in the text paragraph which follows the quotation on p.513 of the 3rd edition, *cf.* the speech of Lord Bingham of Cornhill (with which Lords Steyn, Rodger of Earlsferry and Brown of Eaton-under-Heywood agreed) in *R. v. Z* [2005] 2 W.L.R. 709 (H.L.) which strongly suggests that the law applicable to the defence of duress should not be relaxed and, in particular, that genuineness of belief is not sufficient if not backed by reasonable grounds: see Lord Bingham's speech at pp.717H, para. 21 at (4), 718G, para. 22, and 719E–F, at para. 23.   **13.18**

n.55: At the end of this note, the following should be added: "*Cf. R. v. Z* [2005] 2 W.L.R. 709 (H.L.) at 716E, para. 19, where Lord Bingham of Cornhill said, without qualification, 'The only criminal defences which have any close affinity with duress are necessity, where the force or compulsion is exerted not by human threats but by extraneous circumstances, and, perhaps, marital coercion under section 47 of the Criminal Justice Act 1925.' The case concerned duress, however; and Lord Bingham does not suggest in what he says that necessity is a general defence in English law: see also Lord Bingham's remarks, at p.720E, para. 25, concerning the Canadian case of *Perka v. The Queen* [1984] S.C.R. 232."

13.19 n.73: The reference to "Smith and Hogan" should now read: "(10th ed., 2002, Sir J. Smith (ed.)), at p.713". Relative to s.5(2)(b) of the Criminal Damage Act 1971, as also to the defence of duress of circumstances, *cf. R. v. Jones (Margaret)* [2005] 1 Q.B. 259 (C.A.).

13.21 That *Moss v. Howdle*, 1997 J.C. 123, declares the law of Scotland on necessity is affirmed by the opinion of the court in *Lord Advocate's Reference (No. 1 of 2000)*, 2001 J.C. 143 at 162E, para. 55.

It now seems clear, from observations made by the court in *Lord Advocate's Reference (No. 1 of 2000)*, 2001 J.C. 143 at 157H–159C, paras 40–43, that Scots law follows English law in the matter of testing objectively what the accused did in response to a situation of danger: thus, "the defence will only be available if a sober person of reasonable firmness, sharing the characteristics of the actor, would have responded as he did"—an observation which is repeated twice, at p.158I, para. 42, and at p.159A, para. 43. The test contained in that observation applies equally to coercion; and it is in coercion cases, particularly in *Cochrane v. H.M. Advocate*, 2001 S.C.C.R. 655, that that test—particularly what is meant by "sharing the characteristics of the actor"—has been explained: see the entries for para. 13.29, *infra*.

It also seems clear that the actor must have had, at the material time, reason to think that his actions had some prospect of removing the perceived danger, in the sense that "[i]f there were no prospect that the conduct complained of would affect the danger anticipated the relationship between the danger and the conduct would not be established": *Lord Advocate's Reference (No. 1 of 2000)*, *supra*, at pp.159H–160A, para. 46; but, "if the action could achieve no more than, say, a postponement or interruption of danger (so that it is only averted for a time) or some lessening of its likelihood (without removing the danger even temporarily) the assessment of any necessity would be less simple [than in the court's example of the destruction of a runaway vehicle in an attempt to save those endangered by it]": opinion of the court at p.160B, para. 46. The implications of this additional requirement are not further developed in the case; but the reference to "some prospect of success" suggests that the intention is not to discourage, for example, would-be interveners or rescuers from doing what they reasonably can in situations of immediate danger. There is, however, a general requirement of proportionality, in that the "conduct carried out must be broadly proportional to the risk": opinion of the court, at p.160C, para. 47.

n.78: In *Lord Advocate's Reference (No. 1 of 2000)*, 2001 J.C. 143 at 157A–B, para. 37, the court stated that "immediate" was to be construed in its "ordinary sense"; but the court also indicated, at p.157D, para. 37: "One might not weigh the conduct of the rescuer or intervener in too fine a balance, and there may be marginal cases of difficulty. But making allowance for human judgment in the heat of the moment, the danger to which the individual claims to respond must have the character of immediacy." This suggests that although the test for "immediacy" of the danger is objective, it is not rigidly so.

Also, in the *Lord Advocate's Reference (No. 1 of 2000)*, *supra*, at p.159D–F, para. 44, the court rejected the submission of the Crown that the person(s) reasonably believed to be exposed to danger of death or serious harm must be identifiable and must have some relation to the actor—in the sense that in a crowd of persons so exposed, intervention amounting to a crime would be justified only if the actor had a "companion" in that crowd. Indeed, the court stated, at p.159E–F, para. 44, that were it necessary to define such a "companion", it would extend to "anyone who could reasonably be foreseen to be in danger of harm if action were not taken to prevent the harmful event." The court further emphasised, at p.159F–G, para. 45, that it did not matter that those reasonably believed to be in danger of death or serious harm were in a place physically remote from the *locus* of the alleged criminal act; provided that such persons were "within the reasonably foreseeable area of risk", that was enough.

n.81: In *Lord Advocate's Reference (No. 1 of 2000)*, 2001 J.C. 143 at 155H–I, para. 34, the court confirmed that necessity could be a defence to a charge of damaging the property of another (malicious mischief) provided the essentials of the defence were satisfied, and that, as had been held in *Moss v. Howdle*, 1997 J.C. 123, it did not matter how the requisite danger arose: indeed, as the court stated at pp.155I–156A, para. 34, in "the context of damage to property the danger may arise from accident or carelessness which may cause some physical thing to become dangerous. A vehicle rolling out of control towards a crowd might be intercepted by someone other than the owner or driver as the only way of preventing death or injury, even if the actions carried out caused damage to the vehicle. The contingency giving rise to the danger again appears to be immaterial."

n.84: An honest, but unreasonable, belief is now unlikely to be sufficient under English law: see the entry for para. 13.18, *supra*, pertaining to the recent case of *R. v. Z* [2005] 2 W.L.R. 709 (H.L.).

n.86: After the reference to "*Moss v. Howdle*, 1997 J.C. 129G", there should be added: "see also *Lord Advocate's Reference (No. 1 of 2000)*, 2001 J.C. 143 at 157G, para. 39, where the court put the rule in this way: '... the defence is only available where there is so pressing a need for action that the actor has no alternative but to do what would otherwise be a criminal act under the compulsion of the circumstances in which he finds himself'."

n.92: See also *Lord Advocate's Reference (No. 1 of 2000)*, 2001 J.C. 143. **13.22**

n.94: The Draft Scottish Criminal Code would apply necessity (as broadly defined) and coercion (as also broadly defined) to all crimes— save that these defences would be applicable to the taking of human life "only if that is done to save human life": see clauses 24(3) and 29(3)—the latter having slightly different wording from the former.

n.96a: *Perka v. The Queen* [1984] 2 S.C.R. 232, is also referred to in *Lord Advocate's Reference (No. 1 of 2000)*, 2001 J.C. 143 at 157D–G, paras 38 and 39.

That duress operates as an excuse is accepted in English law: see *R. v. Z* **13.26** [2005] 2 W.L.R. 709 (H.L.), speech of Lord Bingham of Cornhill (with which Lords Steyn, Rodger of Earlsferry and Brown of Eaton-under-Heywood agreed) at p.716B–C, para. 18.

13.27 In line 1 of the text on p.518 of the 3rd edition, the word "called" should be deleted.

13.29 At the end of the existing text of this paragraph, on p.521 of the 3rd edition, the following new text should be added:

"In *Cochrane v. H.M. Advocate*, 2001 S.C.C.R. 655 at 666B–C, para. 17, Lord Justice-General Rodger (with whom Lords Marnoch and Cowie agreed) noted that in *Moss v. Howdle*, 1997 J.C. 123 and *Lord Advocate's Reference (No. 1 of 2000)*, 2001 J.C. 143, the court had proceeded on the basis that there was no relevant distinction to be drawn between coercion and necessity so far as the general rules were concerned; Lord Rodger concluded, therefore, that the response of the accused to a situation of necessity or coercion should be subject to the same objective test—*viz.* as expressed in English law and referred to in *Lord Advocate's Reference (No. 1 of 2000)*, *supra*, at pp.158I, para. 42 and 159A, para. 43, that the defence would only be available if a sober person of reasonable firmness, sharing the characteristics of the accused, would have responded as the accused had done. This raised the question as to which characteristics of the accused should be taken into account for the purposes of the test, and it was held in *Cochrane v. H.M. Advocate, supra*, at p.667C–D, para. 21, that these were limited to the age, sex and physical handicap (if any) of the accused: as the test referred to 'a person of reasonable firmness', inclusion of a characteristic such as low intelligence which made the accused more compliant, or unusual propensity for compliance, in the face of threats, was not possible, since otherwise such inclusion would 'be inconsistent with, would indeed annihilate, the essential characteristic of reasonable firmness' (see p.667E, para. 22), unless, it seems, the accused was also suffering from 'a recognised mental illness or psychiatric condition' which made the sufferer more susceptible to pressure or threats: see p.671B–E, para. 30, where reference is made to the court's earlier quotation, with approval, of a passage from the Court of Appeal's opinion in *R. v. Bowen* [1997] 1 W.L.R. 372. In so quoting with approval from *R. v. Bowen, supra*, the court in *Cochrane v. H.M. Advocate, supra*, refused to find applicable the opinion of the House of Lords in *R. v. Smith (Morgan)* [2001] 1 A.C. 146, that all characteristics of the accused should be taken into account in assessing whether the objective test for provocation (as understood in English law, and as set out in section 3 of the Homicide Act 1957) was satisfied. *Smith* was distinguished on the principal basis that it dealt with a non-exculpatory defence (provocation), where the focus was upon the scale of punishment to be imposed on the offender: see *Cochrane v. H.M. Advocate, supra*, at pp.668G–669C, para. 25. Where particular characteristics of the accused cannot be taken into account for the purposes of the objective test in coercion, such that the defence fails, those characteristics might still, of course, furnish material to be weighed in mitigation of sentence: see *Cochrane v. H.M. Advocate, supra*, at p.671E, para. 30."

n.17: It is emphasised in *Trotter v. H.M. Advocate*, 2001 S.L.T. 296, that the danger of implementation of the threat has to be imminent, such that there is neither time nor opportunity to seek "the shield of the law"; but where such imminence cannot be shown, there may still be room for mitigation of sentence.

R. v. Hudson [1971] 2 Q.B. 202 (C.A.) was disapproved by the House of Lords in *R. v. Z* [2005] 2 W.L.R. 709: see the speech of Lord Bingham (with which Lords Steyn, Rodger of Earlsferry, and Brown of Eaton-under-Heywood agreed) at pp.720H–721F, para. 27. Thus, the laws of England and Scotland are now at one in requiring the threat to be immediately capable of implementation.

n.20: In *Cochrane v. H.M. Advocate*, 2001 S.C.C.R. 655 at 661D, para. 10, the court affirmed that the assault and robbery there charged amounted to an atrocious crime, but considered it unnecessary to deal with the position of coercion in relation to offences which were less than atrocious.

n.21: For the position adopted by the Draft Scottish Criminal Code relative to murder and coercion, see the entry for para. 13.22, n.94, *supra*.

n.25: In *R. v. Z* [2005] 2 W.L.R. 709 at 726D–E, para. 38, Lord Bingham of Cornhill (with whom Lords Steyn, Rodger of Earlsferry, and Brown of Eaton-under-Heywood agreed) concluded that the "policy of the law must be to discourage association with known criminals, and it should be slow to excuse the criminal conduct of those who do so. If a person voluntarily becomes or remains associated with others engaged in criminal activity in a situation where he knows or ought reasonably to know that he may be the subject of compulsion by them or their associates, he cannot rely on the defence of duress to excuse any act which he is thereafter compelled to do by them." Accordingly, the earlier Court of Appeal case of *R. v. Baker and Ward* (1999) 2 Cr.App.R. 335 (which had insisted that for a defendant to be denied duress, he would have had to have been aware that the group he voluntarily joined might try to coerce him into committing crimes of the type for which he was being tried) was disapproved: see *R. v. Z, supra*, Lord Bingham of Cornhill at p.725G–H, para. 37.

In the third text paragraph on p.522 of the 3rd edition, at lines 7–8, the **13.30** words from "or a sheriff officer" to "court order" should be deleted, and the following substituted: "or an officer of court with theft or embezzlement of goods which he attaches and arranges to have auctioned under the provisions of the Debt Arrangement and Attachment (Scotland) Act 2002 (asp 17)".

n.32: See, in particular, the International Criminal Court (Scotland) Act **13.31** 2001 (asp 13) which also creates domestic law offences.

CHAPTER 14

THEFT

14.01 Under clause 77 of the Draft Scottish Criminal Code, theft would consist of stealing another person's property where stealing "is appropriating property, without the owner's consent, with the intention of depriving the owner permanently of it or being reckless as to whether or not the owner is deprived permanently of it." Non-exclusive examples of what is to be meant by "appropriating property", "depriving a person of property", "intending to deprive the owner of property", and "being reckless as to whether the owner is deprived permanently of property" are provided in sub-clause (3), (a)–(d). This reformulation of theft would extend some aspects of the existing crime while restricting others: in particular, theft would cease to be exclusively a crime of intention, and the common law's current emphasis on possessory rights would be lost (as would the present limitation on the type of property which can be stolen—see clause 112(1)(h), which states "'property' means property of any description, whether moveable or not and whether corporeal or not, and includes money and electricity."). Some misconduct with other's property which the common law currently treats as theft could be brought within the terms of clause 83 of the Code which creates the offence of "criminal interference with property".

14.08 n.48: The House of Lords has decided by a majority that under English law a person who fraudulently signed a hire-purchase agreement (by forging the signature of an existent third party whose driving licence he had dishonestly acquired and tendered as his own in the transaction) was not a true hirer at all, could confer by purported resale to a bona fide purchaser no benefit under the terms of section 27 of the Hire Purchase Act 1964, and had probably stolen the car *ab initio* by virtue of the fraudulent transaction: see *Shogun Finance Ltd. v. Hudson* [2003] 3 W.L.R. 1371, and in particular the opinion of Lord Hobhouse of Woodborough at p.1388A–C, para. 52; see also the opinion of Lord Phillips of Worth Matravers at p.1405G, para. 119.

14.12 n.89: *Cf.* also the Draft Scottish Criminal Code, clause 112(1)(h) where "property" means "property of every description, whether moveable or not and whether corporeal or not, and includes money and electricity."

14.13 n.95: See also the Draft Scottish Criminal Code where neither clause 77 (Theft) nor clause 83 (Criminal interference with property) seems apt to criminalise the unauthorised taking, copying and using of such information.

14.17 n.9: The second sentence of footnote 9 should be deleted (since s.42 of the Telecommunications Act 1984 and the whole of the Telecommunications (Fraud) Act 1997 are repealed by the Communications Act 2003,

Sched. 19(1)) and the following substituted: "It is an offence under s.125 of the Communications Act 2003 dishonestly to obtain an electronic communications service (as defined in s.32(2)) with intent to avoid payment of any applicable charge: maximum penalty five years and a fine on indictment, six months and a fine of the statutory maximum on summary conviction."

n.9: The penultimate sentence of this footnote should be amended by deleting the words "television or sound" and adding after the words "the Copyright, Designs and Patents Act 1988" the words: ", as amended by the Copyright and Related Rights Regulations 2003 (S.I. 2003 No. 2498), Sched. 2." Also, the cross reference in this paragraph should read "15.49" and not "15.55".

The final sentence (in round brackets) should be deleted, and the following substituted: "(See also s.126 of the Communications Act 2003.)"

n.30: After "The Theft Act 1607" add the words: "(as amended by the **14.21** Salmon and Freshwater Fisheries etc. (Scotland) Act 2003 (asp 15), Sched. 4, Part 2)"; and, in consequence, delete the words "and fisches in propir stankis and loches" from the given text. This deletion renders the remainder of the Act of uncertain import, and it may be that the whole of the Act should now be repealed.

Section 11 of the 2003 Act (asp 15) creates the following offence:

"(1) Any person who without legal right, or without permission from a person having such right, fishes in a proper stank or loch shall be guilty of an offence, and liable on summary conviction to a fine not exceeding level 1 on the standard scale.

(2) For the purposes of this section—

'proper stank or loch' means a stank or loch the fishing rights in which are owned by one person; and

'stank' means a reservoir or pond with neither inlet nor outlet sufficient to allow access or egress by fish."

Guilt under this provision is predicated on fishing rather than theft—a possible but unlikely interpretation of the relevant wording of the 1607 Act, since Mackenzie (*Observations on the Acts of Parliament*, Edinburgh 1687, p.327, relative to Jac. 6, 19th Parliament, Act 3—as the 1607 Act was then cited), Hume (I, 82) and Macdonald (5th ed., p.17 and n.5) deal with that wording under "Theft".

n.55: In the second paragraph of text, penultimate line, add after "under **14.24** Pt. VIIA" the following: "(as amended by the Proceeds of Crime Act 2002, Sched. 11, para. 12(2))".

n.66: "Parental rights" under s.8 of the Law Reform (Parent and Child) **14.26** (Scotland) Act 1986 included "custody or access, as the case may require". Such rights are, however, redrawn by s.2 of the Children (Scotland) Act 1995, and include the right of a parent "to have the child living with him or otherwise to regulate the child's residence"—hereafter referred to, for convenience, as the "right of residence". The term "custody" is not used by the 1995 Act. Where a child's parents are married to one another at the time of conception of that child, or where they become married to one another subsequently (see s.3(1) of the 1995 Act), they will both have all parental rights in respect of that child including the right of residence "unless any decree ... regulating its exercise otherwise provides" (see s.2(2)). Section 11 of the Act permits a relevant court to make an order in relation (*inter alia*) to parental rights— including "(a) an order depriving a person of some or all of his ... parental rights in relation to a child" or

"(c) an order regulating the arrangements as to—
   (i) with whom, or
   (ii) if with different persons alternately or periodically, with whom during what periods,

a child ... is to live (any such order being known as a 'residence order') ...".

In *Orr v. K.*, 2003 S.L.T. (Sh. Ct.) 70, a mother failed to return her child to its father (he having gained a residence order in terms of s.11 of the 1995 Act, but she not having been deprived of her parental rights and responsibilities in respect of that child) in breach of a non-judicial arrangement for contact. It seems that the father had to make contact with the police in order to find and secure the return of the child. A charge of plagium was brought against the mother; but that charge was held to be incompetent. The sheriff's view was that the 1995 Act altered matters "by making the change from custody to residence orders", and that "by both maintaining the natural mother's responsibilities and rights to the child and creating a civil law framework in section 11 ... the civil rather than the criminal court ha[d] jurisdiction ...". The correctness of the sheriff's decision is, however, open to doubt. The *effect* of the court order in this case was that the mother *was* de facto deprived of the right of residence in respect of the child; and it is submitted that, notwithstanding the shift in terminology from custody to residence, she could in the circumstances competently be charged with plagium from her husband—*i.e.* the person who, in terms of the court order, effectively had the sole right of residence in respect of that child. That this remains the law in such circumstances is given added credence by Lord Justice-General Cullen in *Brouillard v. H.M. Advocate*, 2004 S.L.T. 727 at 731D, para. 19, where the essence of plagium is quoted from the opinion of Lord Justice-General Hope in *Hamilton v. Wilson*, 1993 S.C.C.R. 9 at 13D.

n.68: In line 2 of the text of this note, after "2 Broun 288" (but before the full-stop) insert: ": see also *Brouillard v. H.M. Advocate*, 2004 S.L.T. 727, L.J.-G. Cullen at p.731D, para. 19"; and, at the end of this note, add (before the full-stop): ": cf. *Brouillard v. H.M. Advocate*, cited above, L.J.-G. Cullen at p.731E–I, paras 20–21".

14.33 n.17: See also James P. Chalmers, *Trusts: Cases and Materials* (Edinburgh, 2002), paras 3.10 to 3.16.

14.36 n.32: Relative to the special situation in relation to motor vehicles under ss.27 and 29 of the Hire Purchase Act 1964 (as substituted by the Consumer Credit Act 1974, Sched. 4), *cf.* the majority decision in *Shogun*

Finance Ltd. v. Hudson [2003] 3 W.L.R. 1371 (H.L.), noted at para. 14.08, above.

n.37: The final reference should now read: "W.W. McBryde, *The Law of* **14.37** *Contract in Scotland* (2nd ed., Edinburgh, 2001), Chaps 13 and 15."

In terms of the general rules on consent proposed by the authors of the Draft Scottish Criminal Code (see clause 111(1)(c)), any consent given by a person is to be discounted if at the time when that consent was given it "was induced by fraud as to the nature of what was being consented to or the identity of the person doing what was consented to." It is not clear to what extent this provision would affect the matters discussed in paragraph 14.38 and following paragraphs of the main text.

n.57: The second reference should now read: "W.W. McBryde, *The Law* **14.39** *of Contract in Scotland* (2nd ed., Edinburgh, 2001), Chaps 13 and 14."

n.68: The final reference should now read: "W.W. McBryde, *The Law of* **14.42** *Contract in Scotland* (2nd ed., Edinburgh, 2001), Chaps 13 and 14."

n.75: The second reference should now read: "W.W. McBryde, *The Law* **14.43** *of Contract in Scotland* (2nd ed., Edinburgh, 2001), Chaps 13 and 14."

The Draft Scottish Criminal Code proposes alterations to the present **14.47** common law position on the *mens rea* of theft. In particular, the Code would restore the element of permanent deprivation, in the sense that (see clause 77(2)) "Stealing is appropriating property ... with the intention of depriving the owner permanently of it or being reckless as to whether or not the owner is deprived permanently of it". Two examples are given where the required recklessness will be taken to be satisfied—namely, if the accused "abandons the property in circumstances where the owner will not necessarily recover it", and if he "takes the property with the intention of using its return, or an offer of its return, to the owner as a means of causing the owner to pay a reward or price or yield to a demand" (clause 77(3)(d)).

CHAPTER 15

AGGRAVATED THEFTS AND ALLIED OFFENCES

15.01 Clause 78 of the Draft Scottish Criminal Code proposes that "Breaking into a building" (as defined in that clause) should be an offence *per se*, rather than merely an aggravation of theft (as discussed in paragraph 15.01 and following paragraphs of the main text) or a part of a preventive offence (see paragraph 15.50 and following paragraphs of the main text). Theft could presumably still be aggravated by, *inter alia*, breaking into a building (see clause 7(1) of the Draft Code—"An offence may be aggravated ... by the manner or circumstances in which it is committed").

15.15 Clause 79 of the Draft Scottish Criminal Code proposes that "Breaking open a locked place" (as defined in that clause) should be an offence *per se*, rather than merely an aggravation of theft or a part of a preventive offence (see paragraph 15.52 of the main text). Theft under the Code could presumably still be aggravated by, *inter alia*, breaking open a locked place (see clause 7(1) of the Code, as noted above at **15.01**).

15.35 n.55: The reference to the Road Traffic Offenders Act 1988 should have read "s.23(3)", and not s.3(3).

15.43 The Trespass (Scotland) Act 1865 is further amended by the Land Reform (Scotland) Act 2003 (asp 2), Sched. 2, para. 1, so that the existing text of s.3 of the 1865 Act becomes subsection (1) thereof: a new subsection (2) then narrates that subsection (1) "does not extend to anything done by a person in the exercise of the access rights created by the Land Reform (Scotland) Act 2003 (asp2)."

Under s.1 of the 2003 Act, everyone has the right to be on land and the right to cross land, such rights being known as "access rights". The right to be on land is exercisable only for "recreational purposes" (which are not defined in the Act); for "carrying on a relevant educational activity" (which means an activity carried on by a person for the purposes of furthering that person's understanding, or of enabling or assisting other persons to further their understanding, of natural or cultural heritage); or for the purpose of carrying on, commercially or for profit, an activity which could be carried on otherwise than commercially or for profit. Although in this context the 2003 Act (in s.32) refers to "land" in a most extensive way (so that the term includes, *inter alia*, "structures built on or over land", "inland waters" and canals), access rights are not exercisable over (or under—see s.1(6)) every type of land without restriction. Section 1(7) points to s.6 which narrates:

"(1) The land in respect of which access rights are not exercisable is land—

(a) to the extent that there is on it—

    (i) a building or other structure [as limited by s.6(2)] or works, plant or fixed machinery;

    (ii) a caravan, tent or other place affording a person privacy or shelter;

(b) which—

    (i) forms the curtilage of a building which is not a house or of a group of buildings none of which is a house;

    (ii) forms a compound or other enclosure containing any such structure, works, plant or fixed machinery as is referred to in paragraph (a)(i) above;

    (iii) consists of land contiguous to and used for the purpose of a school [as defined in s.7(4)];

    (iv) comprises, in relation to a house or any of the places mentioned in paragraph (a)(ii) above, sufficient [as determined by criteria including those set out in s.7(5)] adjacent land to enable persons living there to have reasonable measures of privacy in that house or place and to ensure that their enjoyment of that house or place is not unreasonably disturbed;

(c) to which, not being land within paragraph (b)(iv) above, two or more persons have rights in common and which is used by those persons as a private garden;

(d) to which public access is, by or under any enactment other than this Act, prohibited, excluded or restricted;

(e) which has been developed or set out—[subject to what is stated in s.7(7)]

    (i) as a sports or playing field; or

    (ii) for a particular recreational purpose;

(f) to which—

    (i) for not fewer than 90 days in the year ending on 31st January 2001, members of the public were admitted only on payment; and

    (ii) after that date, and for not fewer than 90 days in each year beginning on 1st February 2001, members of the public are, or are to be, so admitted;

(g) on which—

    (i) building, civil engineering or demolition works; or

    (ii) works being carried out by a statutory undertaker [as defined in s.32, and as that definition is amended by the Communications Act 2003 (Consequential Amendments) Order 2003, Sched. 1, para 15(2) (S.I. 2003 No. 2155)] for the purposes of the undertaking,

are being carried out;

(h) which is used for the working of minerals by surface workings (including quarrying);

(i) in which crops have been sown or are growing [subject to what is stated in s.7(10)];

(j) which has been specified in an order under section 11 [*i.e.* an order made by a local authority and confirmed by the Scottish Ministers] or in byelaws made under section 12 ... as land in respect of which access rights are not exercisable."

In addition to restrictions as to "land", under s.2(1) "A person has access rights only if they are exercised responsibly". Whether or not a person has exercised such rights responsibly is a matter to be determined taking into account, *inter alia*, any disregard of guidance in the "Scottish Outdoor Access Code" (as drawn up by Scottish Natural Heritage or the Scottish Ministers under s.10). There is a presumption, however, that access rights are exercised responsibly "if they are exercised so as not to cause unreasonable interference with any of the rights (whether access rights, rights associated with the ownership of land or any others) of any other person" (s.2(2)). Equally, it is to be taken that a person who, at the time he purports to exercise access rights, "(i) engages in any of the conduct within section 9 ... or within any byelaw made under section 12(1)(a)(i) [by a local authority]; or (ii) does anything which undoes anything done by Scottish Natural Heritage under section 29 [*i.e.* for the purposes of protecting the natural heritage of land subject to access rights]" is not exercising those rights responsibly (s.2(2)(a)). Section 9 refers to such conduct as being on land or crossing land in breach of an interdict or other court order, or for the purpose of doing anything which is an offence, or while responsible for a dog or other animal which is not under proper control. Further, it is stated generally in s.2(3) that "references to the responsible exercise of access rights are references to the exercise of these rights in a way which is lawful and reasonable and takes proper account of the interests of others and of the features of the land in respect of which the rights are exercised."

Given, therefore, the complexities of the legislative provisions relating to "access rights", and the fact that in the final analysis a summary application to the sheriff (see s.28 of the 2003 Act) may be necessary to determine whether land is subject to such rights or whether the purported exercise of such rights has been done responsibly, the effective ambit of s.3 of the Trespass (Scotland) Act 1865 is now difficult to state in any straightforward way. Prosecutors considering the use of the 1865 Act in future charges will have to first satisfy themselves, so far as is possible, that the land or premises in question are not "land" subject to access rights, or, if they are, that the purported exercise of access rights by the accused was not done responsibly.

15.47 Regulation 26(1) of the Copyright and Related Rights Regulations 2003 (S.I. 2003 No. 2498) inserts new subsections (2A) and (4A), following existing subsections (2) and (4) respectively, in s.107 of the Copyright, Designs and Patents Act 1988, *viz*:

"(2A) A person who infringes copyright in a work by communicating to the public—

(a) in the course of a business, or
(b) otherwise than in the course of a business to such an extent as to affect prejudicially the owner of the copyright,

commits an offence if he knows or has reason to believe that, by doing so, he is infringing copyright in the work."

"(4A) A person guilty of an offence under subsection (2A) is liable—

    (a) on summary conviction to imprisonment for a term not exceeding three months or a fine not exceeding the statutory maximum, or both;

    (b) on conviction on indictment to a fine or imprisonment for a term not exceeding two years, or both."

Section 107(3) of the 1988 Act is amended by Sched. 1, para. 9(2) of S.I. 2003 No. 2498 (see above), such that the words "broadcast or cable programme" are replaced by the words "communication to the public".

Section 107(4)(b) of the 1988 Act is amended by s.1(2) of the Copyright, etc. and Trade Marks Act (Offences and Enforcement) Act 2002, such that the maximum prison sentence following conviction on indictment for the stated offences is raised from two year to ten years.

n.6: Regulation 16 of S.I. 1996 No. 2967 is now amended by the above mentioned S.I. 2003 No. 2498, Sched. 1, para. 27.

n.7: Section 27 of the Copyright, Designs and Patents Act 1988 is most recently amended by the above mentioned S.I. 2003 No. 2498: see reg. 20(3) and Sched. 2.

In the paragraph of text (see p.83) which immediately follows the narration of s.107(6) of the 1988 Act, amendments to s.1 of the 1988 Act (see the above mentioned S.I. 2003 No. 2498, reg. 5(2)) necessitate that the comma after "films" should be deleted, the word "or" should be inserted between "films" and "broadcasts", and the words "or cable programmes" should be deleted.

n.10: For the most recent amendments to s.1, see S.I. 2003 No. 2498 (as mentioned above) regs 4 and 5 and Sched. 2, which, *inter alia*, repeal s.7.

Regulation 26(3) of the Copyright and Related Rights Regulations 2003 **15.48** (S.I. 2003 No. 2498) inserts new subsections (1A) and (5A), following existing subsections (1) and (5) respectively, in s.198 of the Copyright, Designs and Patents Act 1988, *viz*:

"(1A) A person who infringes a performer's making available right—

    (a) in the course of a business, or

    (b) otherwise than in the course of a business to such an extent as to affect prejudicially the owner of the making available right,

commits an offence if he knows or has reason to believe that, by doing so, he is infringing the making available right in the recording."

"(5A) A person guilty of an offence under subsection (1A) is liable—

    (a) on summary conviction to imprisonment for a term not exceeding three months or a fine not exceeding the statutory maximum or both;

    (b) on conviction on indictment to a fine or imprisonment for a term not exceeding two years or both."

For the meaning of a performer's "making available right", see s.182CA of the 1988 Act, as inserted by the above mentioned S.I. 2003 No. 2498, reg. 7(1): see also S.I. 2003 No. 2498, reg. 35.

Section 198(2)(b) of the 1988 Act is replaced (by the above mentioned S.I. 2003 No. 2498, reg. 26(3) and Sched. 1, para. 4(5)) such that it now reads: "(b) communicated to the public."

Section 198(5)(b) of the 1988 Act is amended by s.1(3) of the Copyright, etc. and Trade Marks (Offences and Enforcement) Act 2002, such that the maximum period of imprisonment following conviction on indictment for the stated offences is raised from two years to ten years.

n.11: Section 197 of the 1988 Act is amended by the above mentioned S.I. 2003 No. 2498, reg. 20(4) and Sched. 2.

n.12: Section 180 of the 1988 Act is amended by the above mentioned S.I. 2003 No. 2498, Sched. 2.

15.49 Section 297 has been amended by the Copyright and Related Rights Regulations 2003 (S.I. 2003 No. 2498), Sched. 2, such that, in the text of this paragraph the word "programme" (in the second place where it occurs) should be replaced by "broadcasting", and the phrase "(as defined in the Broadcasting Act 1990)" should be deleted.

15.50 In *Cochrane v. H.M. Advocate*, 2002 S.L.T. 1424, the Appeal Court confirmed that housebreaking is not *per se* a crime, and held in consequence that an indictment which charged the appellant with conspiring with others to break into a house was irrelevant: it was also held that the narration of what was allegedly done in furtherance of the conspiracy (breaking into premises and committing robbery there) could not transform the charge by implication into one of conspiracy to commit robbery. As Lord Justice-Clerk Gill, in giving the opinion of the Court, stated at p.426K, para.15: "The nature of the conspiracy cannot be widened by the occurrence of subsequent events." (The procedural point taken by the court—that since the matter of relevancy had not been raised at the trial, the conviction could not be set aside—was overruled in *Jones v. Carnegie*, 2004 S.L.T. 609: see the opinion of the court at para.43.)

CHAPTER 16

ROBBERY

Section 1 of the Aviation Security Act 1982 is extended (and modified) by **16.19**
the Aviation Security and Piracy (Overseas Territories) Order 2000 (S.I.
2000 No. 3059), Sched. 2.

n.78: Section 38(1) of the 1982 Act is also amended by the British
Overseas Territories Act 2002, s.2(3). In consequence, the reference to
"British Dependent Territories Citizen" should now read: "British
overseas territories citizen".

CHAPTER 17

EMBEZZLEMENT

17.08 n.57: S.I. 1983 No. 1568 (The Consumer Credit (Realisation of Pawn) Regulations 1983) is itself amended, in so far as relevant to this note, by art. 11 of the Consumer Credit Act 1974 (Electronic Communications) Order 2004 (S.I. 2004 No. 3236).

17.16 n.5: Poindings and warrant sales have been replaced by the procedure of "attachment" under Part II of the Debt Arrangement and Attachment (Scotland) Act 2002 (asp 17). Under s.31(1) of that Act, following the auction of attached articles, the obligation of the officer (subject to s.37 of the Bankruptcy (Scotland) Act 1985) is to dispose of the proceeds of sale by (a) retaining such amount as necessary to meet his fee and outlays (as these will eventually be taxed under s.33), (b) paying to the creditor the remainder of the proceeds of auction so far as necessary to meet the sum recoverable, and (c) paying to the debtor any surplus remaining. The text of footnote 5 must, therefore, now be read subject to the provisions of the 2002 Act.

17.25 In the text paragraph which begins "Again, if A continues ...", at line 4, for "gods" read: "goods".

17.27 n.49: In the English case of *R. v. Wacker* [2003] 1 Cr.App.R. 329, which involved 58 charges of manslaughter by gross negligence, it was argued that the accused truck driver shared the same illegal purpose as his deceased passengers (who had been illegal immigrants) and thus owed no duty of care towards them. It was held, however, that the civil law concept of *ex turpi causa non oritur actio* had no application to the case, Kay L.J. (who delivered the opinion of the court), at p.338 para. 33, basing the decision on broad policy grounds as follows: "The criminal law has as its function the protection of citizens and gives effect to the state's duty to try those who have deprived citizens of their rights of life, limb and property. It may very well step in at the precise moment when civil courts withdraw because of their very different function. The withdrawal of a civil remedy has nothing to do with whether as a matter of public policy the criminal law applies. The criminal law should not be disapplied just because the civil law is disapplied. It has its own public policy aim which may require a different approach to the involvement of the law."

17.33 n.62: The opinion referred to from "Smith and Hogan" is now to be found at p.549 of the 10th edition.

n.64: A round bracket should be inserted at the end of the text in this note, just before the final full-stop.

In the Draft Scottish Criminal Code, dishonesty is made an essential element of the offence: thus, clause 87 reads—

"A person who—

(a) holds property under an obligation to use it for a specified purpose or in relation to which the person is under an obligation to account to another person; and

(b) dishonestly uses the property for another purpose or dishonestly fails to account,

is guilty of the offence of embezzlement."

It is a matter for debate whether, as the authors state in their Commentary, "[t]his provision reflects the common law."

CHAPTER 18

COMMON LAW FRAUD

18.01 n.7: The page references to "Smith and Hogan", which appear at 659 and 660–661, should now be entered as "678" and "679–681" of the 10th edition.

The English Court of Appeal, in *Attorney-General's Reference (No. 1 of 2000)* [2001] 1 W.L.R. 331, took the view that *R. v. Donnelly* (1984) 79 Cr.App.R. 76 was a decision binding on them, although they somewhat restricted the ambit of that decision.

18.06 n.43: The page references to "Smith and Hogan" at 553–556 should now be entered as "587–589" of the 10th ed.

18.17 The Draft Scottish Criminal Code, in clause 86, makes prejudice an unequivocally essential element of the offence: "A person who, by deception, causes another person to act to the prejudice of that person or a third person is guilty of the offence of fraud." The authors do not, however, require the prejudice to be significant—legally or factually.

18.19 n.17: Section 42 of the Telecommunications Act 1984 is repealed by the Communications Act 2003; the equivalent offence is now contained in s.125 of the 2003 Act, which should be read as amended by the Copyright and Related Rights Regulations (S.I. 2003 No. 2498), Sched. 2. Section 31 of the Fire Services Act 1947 is repealed by the Fire (Scotland) Act 2005 (asp 5), Sched. 4. See now s.85 (set out in the entry for para. 41.14, *infra*) of the 2005 Act. See also the Anti-terrorism, Crime and Security Act 2001, ss.114 and 115 (hoaxes involving noxious substances or things).

18.22 n.27: The page reference to "Smith and Hogan", which appears as 552 should now be entered as "585" of the 10th ed.

18.31 n.69: The book reference which follows "*cf.*" should now read as follows: "W.W. McBryde, *The Law of Contract in Scotland* (2nd ed., 2001), paras 14–15 and 14–16."

18.36 n.93: Section 5 of the Forgery and Counterfeiting Act 1981 has been amended by the Crime (International Co-operation) Act 2003, s.88, the Asylum and Immigration (Treatment of Claimants, etc.) Act 2004, s.3, and the Civil Partnership Act 2004, Sched. 27, para. 67.

18.38 n.4 and **n.8:** Section 1 of the Requirements of Writing (Scotland) Act 1995 has been amended by the Abolition of Feudal Tenures (Scotland) Act 2000 (asp 5), Sched. 12, para. 58.

n.17: Section 15(1)(a) of the Electronic Communications Act 2000 has been amended by the Communications Act 2003, Sched. 17, para. 158, such that it now reads: "(a) by means of an electronic communications network;" such a network is defined in s.32(1) of the 2003 Act.

The portion of text, beginning (8 lines up from the bottom of page 158) **18.42** with the words: "the certificate a" and ending (5 lines up from the bottom of that page) with the words: "to sign his name to a", should be deleted, since it amounts to an erroneous repetition of words immediately above that portion.

CHAPTER 19

STATUTORY FRAUDS

19.06 This paragraph should now read: "The Companies Act 1985, the Insolvency Act 1986 and the Financial Services and Markets Act 2000 provide a number of offences in connection with the liquidation and operation of companies, which are analogous to fraud."

19.07 Certain provisions of the Insolvency Act 1986 (in particular ss.206, 207, 208, 210 and 211, which are quoted in this paragraph) have been applied (some with modifications) to limited liability partnerships: see the Limited Liability Partnerships (Scotland) Regulations 2001 (S.S.I. 2001 No. 128), reg. 4, Sched. 3.

19.10 n.28: After "maximum penalty" the following should be inserted: "(see Sched. 24)".

19.12 The heading to this paragraph should be amended to read: "*Fraudulent use of 'limited', 'public limited company', 'community interest company*[33a]*, or 'community interest public limited company'.*"

Section 33(1) of the Companies Act 1985 is now amended, by para. 5 of Sched. 6 to the Companies (Audit, Investigations etc.) Act 2004 so that at the end of that subsection, prior to the full stop, there is inserted: "; and a community interest company which is not a public company is guilty of an offence if it does so under a name which includes, as its last part [certain Welsh words which are the equivalent of 'community interest public limited company']".

After the text of this paragraph—*i.e.* after the quotation of s.34—the following new text should be added:

"Section 34A[38a] provides:

'(1) A company which is not a community interest company is guilty of an offence if it carries on any trade, profession or business under a name which includes any of the expressions specified in subsection (3).

(2) A person other than a company is guilty of an offence if it carries on any trade, profession or business under a name which includes any of those expressions (or any contraction of them) as its last part.

(3) The expressions are—

(a) "community interest company" or its Welsh equivalent ..., and

(b) "community interest public limited company" or its Welsh equivalent ...

(4) Subsections (1) and (2) do not apply—

(a) to a person who was carrying on a trade, profession or business under the name in question at any time during the period beginning with 1st September 2003 and ending with 4th December 2003, or

(b) if the name in question was on 4th December 2003 a registered trade mark or Community trade mark (within the meaning of the Trade Marks Act 1994 (c.26)), to a person who was on that date a proprietor or licensee of that trade mark.

(5) A person guilty of an offence under subsection (1) or (2) and, if that person is a company, any officer of the company who is in default, is liable to a fine and, for continued contravention, to a daily default fine.'[38b]"

After **n.33**, there should be inserted new footnote **33a**, as follows:

"[33a] 'Community interest' companies are created by the Companies (Audit, Investigations etc) Act 2004: see Part II (s.26 *et seq.*) of that Act."

n.34: Section 26 is amended by para. 2 of Sched. 6 to the Companies (Audit, Investigations etc) Act 2004.

n.36: Add at the end of this note, but before the full-stop: ", and n.34 above".

After **n.38**, there should be inserted new footnotes **38a** and **38b**, as follows:

"[38a] Inserted by para. 6 of Sched. 6 to the Companies (Audit, Investigations etc) Act 2004."

"[38b] Maximum penalty (see Sched. 24, as amended by para. 9(3) of Sched. 6 to the Companies (Audit, Investigations etc) Act 2004) on summary conviction is a fine of level 3 on the Standard Scale and a daily default fine of one-tenth of that level."

In lines 4–5 of the text of this paragraph, on p.180 of the 3rd ed., delete **19.14** the words: "balance sheets and profit and loss accounts to comply with the provisions of the Act"; and substitute: "any accounts required to be prepared under the relevant Part to comply with the provisions of the Act and, where applicable, with Article 4 of the IAS Regulation".

n.41: Add at the end of the text of this note, but before the full-stop: "and amended by the Companies Act 1985 (International Accounting Standards and Other Accounting Amendments) Regulations 2004 (S.I. 2004 No. 2947), Sched.1, para. 4. For "IAS Regulation", see s.262(1) of the Companies Act 1985, as amended by S.I. 2004, No. 2947, Sched. 1, para. 20(2)(c)".

19.15 The existing text of this paragraph should be replaced by the following:

"Investors are principally protected against fraud by the Financial Services and Markets Act 2000."

n.44: This footnote should be deleted. (See **19.16**, below.)

19.16 The Insurance Companies Act 1982 and the Financial Services Act 1986 were repealed by article 3 of the Financial Services and Markets Act 2000 (Consequential Amendments and Repeals) Order 2001 (S.I. 2001 No. 3649) made under s.426 of the Financial Services and Markets Act 2000.

Consequently, for the existing text of **19.16**, substitute the following:

"*Misleading statements and practices.* Section 397 of the Financial Services and Markets Act 2000 provides:

'(1) This subsection applies to a person who—

    (a) makes a statement, promise or forecast which he knows to be misleading, false or deceptive in a material particular;

    (b) dishonestly conceals any material facts whether in connection with a statement, promise or forecast made by him or otherwise; or

    (c) recklessly makes (dishonestly or otherwise) a statement, promise or forecast which is misleading, false or deceptive in a material particular.

(2) A person to whom subsection (1) applies is guilty of an offence if he makes the statement, promise or forecast or conceals the facts for the purpose of inducing, or is reckless as to whether it may induce, another person (whether or not the person to whom the statement, promise or forecast is made)—

    (a) to enter or offer to enter into, or to refrain from entering or offering to enter into, a relevant agreement; or

    (b) to exercise, or refrain from exercising, any rights conferred by a relevant investment.

(3) Any person who does any act or engages in any course of conduct which creates a false or misleading impression as to the market in or the price or value of any relevant investments is guilty of an offence if he does so for the purpose of creating that impression and of thereby inducing another person to acquire, dispose of, subscribe for or underwrite those investments or to refrain from doing so or to exercise, or refrain from exercising, any rights conferred by those investments.

(4) In proceedings for an offence under subsection (2) brought against a person to whom subsection (1) applies as a result of paragraph (a) of that subsection, it is a defence for him to show that the statement, promise or forecast was made in conformity with price stabilising rules or control of information rules.

(5) In proceedings brought against any person for an offence under subsection (3) it is a defence for him to show—

(a) that he reasonably believed that his act or conduct would not create an impression that was false or misleading as to the matters mentioned in that subsection;

(b) that he acted or engaged in conduct—

(i) for the purpose of stabilising the price of investments; and

(ii) in conformity with price stabilising rules; or

(c) that he acted or engaged in the conduct in conformity with control of information rules.

(6) Subsections (1) and (2) do not apply unless—

(a) the statement, promise or forecast is made in or from, or the facts are concealed in or from, the United Kingdom or arrangements are made in or from the United Kingdom for the statement, promise or forecast to be made or the facts to be concealed;

(b) the person on whom the inducement is intended to or may have effect is in the United Kingdom; or

(c) the agreement is or would be entered into or the rights are or would be exercised in the United Kingdom.

(7) Subsection (3) does not apply unless—

(a) the act is done, or the course of conduct is engaged in, in the United Kingdom; or

(b) the false or misleading impression is created there.

(8) A person guilty of an offence under this section is liable—

(a) on summary conviction, to imprisonment for a term not exceeding six months or a fine not exceeding the statutory maximum, or both;

(b) on conviction on indictment, to imprisonment for a term not exceeding seven years or a fine, or both.

(9) 'Relevant agreement' means an agreement—

(a) the entering into or performance of which by either party constitutes an activity of a specified kind or one which falls within a specified class of activity; and

(b) which relates to a relevant investment.

(10) 'Relevant investment' means an investment of a specified kind or one which falls within a prescribed class of investment.

(11) Schedule 2 (except paragraphs 25 and 26) applies for the purposes of subsections (9) and (10) with references to section 22 being read as references to each of these subsections.

(12) Nothing in Schedule 2, as applied by subsection (11), limits the power conferred by subsection (9) or (10).

(13) 'Investment' includes any asset, right or interest.

(14) 'Specified' means specified in an order made by the Treasury.'

Schedule 2 (mentioned in subsection (11) above) provides details of the investment activities and types of investment regulated by the 2000 Act."

19.17 This paragraph falls to be deleted since the Financial Services Act 1986 is repealed by article 3 of the Financial Services and Markets Act 2000 (Consequential Amendments and Repeals) Order 2001 (S.I. 2001 No. 3649) made under s.426 of the Financial Services and Markets Act 2000. Section 397 (see para. **19.16** above) of the 2000 Act now applies to contracts of insurance: see s.397(10) and (11); Sched. 2, Part II, para. 20.

19.18 This paragraph, and paragraph **19.19** as also **nn. 45–49**, fall to be deleted since the Banking Act 1987 is repealed by article 3 of the Financial Services and Markets Act 2000 (Consequential Amendments and Repeals) Order 2001 (S.I. 2001 No. 3649) made under s.426 of the Financial Services and Markets Act 2000.

Under s.19 of the 2000 Act, no person may carry on a regulated activity in the United Kingdom unless he is an authorised or exempt person: for "authorised person", see s.31 of the Act; and for "exempt person", see the provisions referred to in s.417 ("Definitions") there. Under s.22 and Sched. 2 (para. 4), "regulated activities" include the accepting of deposits. Fraudulent inducements relating to deposits are now subsumed by the offences set out in s.397 of the 2000 Act: see para. **19.16**, above.

19.19 See paragraph **19.18**, above.

19.23 For "incoporates" in s.4(1)(a) of the Trade Descriptions Act 1968, read: "incorporates".

19.30 Article 309 of the Financial Services and Markets Act 2000 (Consequential Amendments and Repeals) Order 2001 (S.I. 2001 No. 3649), made under s.426 of the Financial Services and Markets Act 2000, amends s.20 of the Consumer Protection Act 1987 by inserting the following provision after subsection (5)—

> "(5A) A person is not guilty of an offence under subsections (1) or (2) above if, in giving the misleading indication which would otherwise constitute an offence under either of these subsections, he is guilty of an offence under section 397 of the Financial Services and Markets Act 2000 (misleading statements and practices)." [For s.397 of the 2000 Act, see para. **19.16**, above.]

Article 310 of the above mentioned Order amends s.22 of the 1987 Act by repealing subsection (3), as also the "definitions" of "appointed representative", "authorised person" and "investment business" in subsection (5): see art. 310(2) and (3).

n.87: Both of the statutory instruments referred to in this footnote have been revoked by article 3(2) of the Financial Services and Markets Act 2000 (Consequential Amendments and Repeals) Order 2001 (S.I. 2001 No. 3649) made under s.426 of the Financial Services and Markets Act 2000.

In s.24(2) of the Consumer Protection Act 1987, "programme service" has the meaning it has in the Broadcasting Act 1990. Section 210 of the 1990 Act provides the required definition, but that definition has now been amended by the Communications Act 2003, s.360(1) and (2). In s.24(5) of the 1987 Act, the reference to "section 39" is a reference to the defence of "due diligence".

Section 35 of the Registered Designs Act 1949 was, in error, printed as if **19.42** subsection (1) had been set out completely in this paragraph. Some material was in fact omitted, *brevitatis causa*, and should have been represented by the addition of three dots after the words "standard scale". As this error makes it difficult to follow the most recent amendments, and for the avoidance of doubt, both subsections of the section are reproduced below—as altered by the Copyright, Designs and Patents Act 1988, Sched. 3, para. 24, and now by the Registered Designs Regulations 2001 (S.I. 2001 No. 3949), Sched. 1, para. 10.

> "**35.**—(1) If any person falsely represents that a design applied to, or incorporated in, any product sold by him is registered, he shall be liable on summary conviction to a fine not exceeding level 3 on the standard scale; and for the purposes of this provision a person who sells a product having stamped, engraved or impressed thereon or otherwise applied thereto the word 'registered', or any other word expressing or implying that the design applied to, or incorporated in, the product is registered, shall be deemed to represent that the design applied to, or incorporated in, the product, is registered.
>
> (2) If any person, after the right in a registered design has expired, marks any product to which the design has been applied or in which it has been incorporated with the word 'registered', or any word or words implying that there is a subsisting right in the design under this Act, or causes any such product to be so marked, he shall be liable on summary conviction to a fine not exceeding level 1 on the standard scale."

The existing text of, and sub-heading to, this paragraph should be **19.45** replaced by the following:

"*Food.* 'Food' under this Act means any substance or product, whether processed, partially processed or unprocessed, intended to be, or reasonably expected to be ingested by humans, and includes drink, chewing gum and any substance (including water) intentionally incorporated into food during its manufacture, preparation or treatment.[55] It does not include, *inter alia*, live animals (unless they are prepared for placing on the market for human consumption), feed or feeding-stuff intended for oral feeding to animals, plants prior to harvesting, medicinal products, cosmetics, tobacco and tobacco products, and narcotics.[56]"

n.55: Delete the text of this note, and substitute: "Section 1(1), (2) of the Food Safety Act 1990, as substituted by reg. 3 of the Food Safety Act 1990 (Amendment) Regulations 2004 (S.I. 2004 No. 2990) which incorporates the meaning of 'food' set out in Regulation (EC) No. 178/2002 of the European Parliament and of the Council (28th January 2002; see OJ No. L31, 1st February 2002), Articles 2 and 3."

n.56: Delete the text of this note, and substitute: "See Regulation (EC) No. 178/2002 (cited at n.55, above), Articles 2 and 3."

19.47 **n.59:** Add at the end of this note: "See also *Nottingham City Council v. Wolverhampton & Dudley Breweries* [2004] 1 All E.R. 1372 (QBD)—s.14 not restricted to an employee licensee where alcoholic drink (not of the substance demanded by the purchaser) was sold in licensed premises, but applicable also to the owner (prior to the sale) of the drink in question."

n.60: The amendment by the Food Standards Act 1999 is contained in para. 8 (and not para. 2) of Schedule 5.

19.51 In s.21(2) of the Food Safety Act 1990, following amendment by reg. 13 of the General Food Regulations 2004 (S.I. 2004 No. 3279), the phrase "section ... 14 or 15" should be read as: "section 14 or 15".

19.70 On p.214 of the main work, in the eleventh line down from the top of that page, inverted commas to close the quotation should be inserted after the words "particular quantity" but prior to the comma.

19.83 After this paragraph, new paragraph 19.83A should be inserted as follows:

"False monetary instruments

19.83A Section 89 of the Crime (International Co-operation) Act 2003 adds the following provision to the Criminal Law (Consolidation) (Scotland) Act 1995:

'False monetary instruments
46A.—(1) A person who counterfeits or falsifies a specified monetary instrument with the intention that it be uttered as genuine is guilty of an offence.
(2) A person who has in his custody or under his control, without lawful authority or excuse—

  (a) anything which is, and which he knows or believes to be, a counterfeited or falsified specified monetary instrument; or
  (b) any machine, implement or computer programme, or any paper or other material, which to his knowledge is specially designed or adapted for the making of a specified monetary instrument,

is guilty of an offence.
(3) For the purposes of subsections (1) and (2)(a) above, it is immaterial that the specified monetary instrument (or purported specified monetary instrument) is not in a fit state to be uttered or that the counterfeiting or falsifying of it has not been finished or perfected.
(4) A person guilty of an offence under this section is liable on summary conviction—

  (a) to a fine not exceeding the statutory maximum;
  (b) to imprisonment for a term not exceeding six months; or
  (c) both to a fine and to such imprisonment.

(5) A person guilty of an offence—

    (a) under subsection (1) above is liable on conviction on indictment—

        (i) to a fine;

        (ii) to imprisonment for a term not exceeding ten years; or

        (iii) both to a fine and to such imprisonment;

    (b) under subsection (2) above is liable on conviction on indictment—

        (i) to a fine;

        (ii) if it is proved that the offence was committed with the intention that the specified monetary instrument in question be uttered (or as the case may be that a specified monetary instrument be uttered), to imprisonment for a term not exceeding ten years and if it is not so proved, to imprisonment for a term not exceeding two years; or

        (iii) both to a fine and to imprisonment for a term not exceeding ten years, if it is proved as mentioned in subparagraph (ii) above, or both to a fine and to imprisonment for a term not exceeding two years if it is not so proved.

(6) Where an offence under this section which has been committed—

    (a) by a body corporate is proved to have been committed with the consent or connivance of, or to be attributable to any neglect on the part of, a director, manager, secretary or other similar officer of that body; or

    (b) by a Scottish partnership is proved to have been committed with the consent or connivance of, or to be attributable to any neglect on the part of, a member of that partnership,

or by any person who was purporting to act in any such capacity, he as well as the body corporate, or as the case may be the partnership, is guilty of that offence and is liable to be proceeded against and punished accordingly.

(7) Where the affairs of a body corporate are managed by its members, subsection (6) above applies in relation to the actings and defaults of a member in connection with his functions of management as if he were a director of the body corporate.

(8) In subsections (1) to (5) above, "specified" means for the time being specified for the purposes of this section, by order made by the Scottish Ministers.

(9) The power to make an order under subsection (8) above—

    (a) includes power to make such incidental, supplemental, transitional or transitory provision as the Scottish Ministers think necessary or expedient; and

    (b) is exercisable by statutory instrument.

(10) A statutory instrument containing such an order is subject to annulment in pursuance of a resolution of the Scottish Parliament.' "

19.84 Section 173 of the Road Traffic Act 1988 has been amended by the Crime (International Co-operation) Act 2003 (Sched. 5, para.29) such that subsection (2)(aa) now reads as follows:

"the counterpart of a Northern Ireland licence or Community licence;".

19.86 n.64: The penalties have been altered by s.286(1) of the Criminal Justice Act 2003 (s.286 being made applicable to Scotland by virtue of s.337(3)) so that on summary conviction, the maximum is a fine of the statutory maximum and six months imprisonment; and on conviction on indictment, the maximum is a fine and two years imprisonment.

19.98 As a result of amendments by (a) s.76(6)(a) and (b) of the Criminal Justice (Scotland) Act 2003, (b) Sched. 7, para. 6(2)–(4) of the Anti-terrorism, Crime and Security Act 2001, and (c) s.68(5) and (6) of the Energy Act 2004, s.43 (as set out for the purposes of this paragraph) of the Police (Scotland) Act 1967 now reads as follows:

"(1) Subject to the provisions of this section, any person who—

    (a) takes the name, designation or character of a constable or police custody and security officer for the purpose of obtaining admission into any house or other place or of doing or procuring to be done any act which such person would not be entitled to do or procure to be done on his own authority, or for any other unlawful purpose, or

    (b) wears any article of police uniform without being a member of the Civil Nuclear Constabulary or having the permission of the police authority for the police area in which he is, or

    (c) has in his possession any article of police uniform without being able to account satisfactorily for his possession thereof,

shall be guilty of an offence[96] ...

(2) Nothing in [the preceding subsection] shall make it an offence to wear any article of police uniform in the course of taking part in a stage play, or music hall or circus performance, or of performing in or producing a cinematograph film or television broadcast.

(2A) For the purposes of this section—

    (a) 'constable' includes a member of the British Transport Police Force, and

    (b) any reference to 'police' includes a reference to that force.

(3) In this section 'article of police uniform' means any article of uniform or any distinctive badge or mark usually issued by any police authority or by the Civil Nuclear Police Authority or by the British Transport Police Committee to constables or police custody and security officers, or any article having the appearance of such article, badge or mark.

(3A) In its application to articles of the uniform of the Civil Nuclear Constabulary, subsection (1)(b) has effect as if for the words 'or having the permission of the police authority for the police area in which he is' there were substituted the words 'and in circumstances where it gives him an appearance so nearly resembling that of a constable as to be calculated to deceive'.

(3B) For the purposes of this section—

(a) 'constable' includes a member of the Civil Nuclear Constabulary; and

(b) any reference to 'police' includes a reference to that Constabulary.

(4) In its application to articles of British Transport Police Force uniform, subsection (1)(b) has effect as if for the words 'without the permission of the police authority for the police area in which he is' there were substituted the words 'in circumstances where it gives him an appearance so nearly resembling that of a constable as to be calculated to deceive'."

Police custody and security officers are persons certified and appointed by chief constables to assist constables and who have the powers and duties specified or referred to in s.9(1B), (1C) and (1E) of the 1967 Act (as added thereto by the 2003 Act, s.76(2)): see also s.9A of the 1967 Act (as inserted by s.76(3) of the 2003 Act) which relates to the certification of such officers. For "Civil Nuclear Constabulary" and "Civil Nuclear Police Authority", see Part 1, Chapter 3 of the Energy Act 2004.

After paragraph 19.98, the following new paragraph should be added.

"CERTIFICATION   **19.98A**

Under section 9B of the Police (Scotland) Act 1967 (as inserted by section 76(3) of the Criminal Justice (Scotland) Act 2003 (asp 7)), it is an offence for a person, for the purpose of obtaining for himself or another person a certificate of approval for performance of custody and security functions (see 'Police custody and security officers' as noted in the entry for para. 19.98, above), to make a statement which he knows to be false, or recklessly to make a statement which is false, in a material particular: maximum penalty on summary conviction is a fine of level 4 on the standard scale."

n.98: See also s.49A ("Penalty for pretending to hold a licence to prac- **19.100** tice") of the Medical Act 1983, as inserted by the Medical Act 1983 (Amendment) Order 2002 (S.I. 2002 No. 3135), art. 12(7): the maximum penalty is the same as for section 49.

In the text of this paragraph, at line 4, after the words "European lawyer" **19.106** there should be inserted: "or a registered foreign lawyer".

n.7: In line 4 of this note, after "Sched. 1, para. 1(8)", but before the full-stop, there should be inserted: ", and by reg. 6 of the Solicitors (Scotland) Act 1980 (Foreign Lawyers and Multi-national Practices) Regulations 2004 (S.S.I. 2004 No. 383)"; and in line 5, after "2000 No. 121", but again before the full-stop, there should be inserted: "; and for 'registered foreign lawyer' see s.60A (as originally inserted by the Law Reform (Miscellaneous Provisions) (Scotland) Act 1990, s.32, and amended (most recently) by S.S.I. 2004 No. 383, reg.11)".

19.107 The Mental Health (Scotland) Act 1984 has been repealed by the Mental Health (Care and Treatment) (Scotland) Act 2003 (asp 13), Sched. 5, Part 1. Consequently, the heading prior to this paragraph should be replaced by a reference to the Act of 2003, and the text of the paragraph should be replaced by the following:

"Section 318 of the Mental Health (Care and Treatment) (Scotland) Act 2003 (asp 13) provides:

'(1) A person who—

    (a) knowingly makes, in a relevant document, an entry or statement which is false in a material particular; or

    (b) with intent to deceive, makes use of any such entry or statement knowing it to be false,

shall be guilty of an offence.

(2) For the purposes of subsection (1) above, a "relevant document"—

    (a) is—

        (i) an application under this Act;

        (ii) a document accompanying any such application; or

        (iii) any other document required or authorised to be granted, prepared, sent or given for any of the purposes of this Act; but

    (b) does not include—

        (i) a nomination of a named person in accordance with section 250(2) of this Act;

        (ii) a declaration made in accordance with section 253(2) of this Act; and

        (iii) an advance statement.

(3) A person guilty of an offence under this section shall be liable—

    (a) on summary conviction, to imprisonment for a term not exceeding 6 months or to a fine not exceeding the statutory maximum or to both;

    (b) on conviction on indictment, to imprisonment for a term not exceeding 2 years or to a fine or to both.' "

n.9: This footnote should be deleted.

19.108 In the second text paragraph, in line 4, as a result of amendment by para. 50 of Sched. 27 to the Civil Partnership Act 2004, the words "the giver or his spouse[12]" should be read as: "the giver, his spouse or civil partner.[12]".

n.10: Section 43 of the Consumer Credit Act 1974 has been amended by the Financial Services and Markets Act 2000 (Regulated Activities) Order 2001 (S.I. 2001 No. 544), art. 90(3), which adds new subsections (3A) and (3B) to it.

19.110 Between subsections (1) and (2) of s.112 of the Social Security Administration Act 1992 are inserted new subsections (1A) to (1F) by s.16(3) of the Social Security Fraud Act 2001: these new subsections are concerned with offences of failing to notify changes of circumstances affecting entitlement to benefits, payments or advantages under the relevant social security legislation. The Act of 2001, by virtue of s.16(1) and (2), also removes paragraphs (c) and (d) from s.111A(1) of the 1992 Act, inserts the word "or" after paragraph (a), and inserts new subsections (1A) to (1G): these new subsections are likewise concerned with offences of failing to notify changes of circumstances.

After paragraph 19.110, the following should be inserted:

"Regulation of Care (Scotland) Act 2001 (asp 8)

The Regulation of Care (Scotland) Act 2001 includes the following **19.110A** offences:

'21.—(1) Any person who—

(a) provides a care service [see ss.2 and 77] while it is not registered under this Part; or

(b) with intent to deceive, pretends that a care service is registered under this Part,

shall be guilty of an offence and liable on summary conviction to a fine not exceeding level 5 on the standard scale or to imprisonment for a term not exceeding three months or to both. . . .

22. Any person who, in an application—

(a) for registration under this Part; or

(b) for variation or removal of a condition in force in relation to a registration under this Part,

knowingly makes a statement which is false or misleading in a material respect shall be guilty of an offence and liable on summary conviction to a fine not exceeding level 4 on the standard scale. . . .

52.—(1) Any person who, with intent to deceive, while not registered in any relevant register as—

(a) a social worker, takes or uses the title of social worker, or purports in any other way to be a social worker; or

(b) a social service worker of such other description as may be prescribed, takes or uses the title of that description of social service worker, or purports in any other way to be a social service worker of that description,

shall be guilty of an offence and liable on summary conviction to a fine not exceeding level 5 on the standard scale.

(2) For the purposes of subsection (1) above, a register is a relevant register if it is—

(a) the register maintained by the Council under this Part; or

(b) such register as may be prescribed, being a register maintained under a provision of the law of England and Wales or of Northern Ireland which appears to the Scottish Ministers to correspond to section 44(1) of this Act.' "

19.111 n.22: The reference to the Gas Act 1986, Sched. 2B should have more specifically referred to para. 10 of that Schedule.

19.116 n.28: Section 7 of the Consumer Credit Act 1974 has been amended by the Enterprise Act 2002, Sched. 25, para. 6(6), such that for "Director", in each place where it occurs, there is to be substituted "OFT".

19.117 The Telecommunications Act 1984 has been repealed by the Communications Act 2003, Sched. 19(1). Consequently, the italicised sub-heading for, and text of, this paragraph (along with nn. 29 and 30) should be deleted and replaced by the following:

"*Electronic communication services.* Section 125 of the Communications Act 2003 (as amended by the Copyright and Related Rights Regulations 2003 (S.I. 2003 No. 2498), Sched. 2) provides:

'(1) A person who—

    (a) dishonestly obtains an electronic communications service [see s.32(2)], and

    (b) does so with intent to avoid payment of a charge applicable to the provision of that service,

is guilty of an offence.

(2) It is not an offence under this section to obtain a service mentioned in section 297(1) of the Copyright, Designs and Patents Act 1988 (c.48) (dishonestly obtaining a broadcasting service provided from a place in the UK).

(3) A person guilty of an offence under this section shall be liable—

    (a) on summary conviction, to imprisonment for a term not exceeding six months or to a fine not exceeding the statutory maximum, or to both;

    (b) on conviction on indictment, to imprisonment for a term not exceeding five years or to a fine, or to both.' "

[For s. 297 of the Copyright, Designs and Patents Act 1988, see paragraph 15.49 of the main work; s.297 has also been amended by Sched. 2 of S.I. 2003 No. 2498, referred to above.]

19.118 n.33: For an example of a case under the Property Misdescriptions Act 1991 involving both employer and employee as accused (but where an appeal against conviction was successful on the basis of an insufficiency of evidence as to the falsity), see *George Wimpey U.K. Ltd. v. Brown*, 2003 S.L.T. 659.

After para. 19.118, the following new headings and paragraphs should be added:

"*Fraudulent Evasion of Income Tax*

19.119 Under section 144 of the Finance Act 2000, it is an offence for a person to be knowingly concerned in the fraudulent evasion of income tax by him or by another person. The maximum penalties are, on summary conviction six months in prison and a fine of the statutory maximum, and, on conviction on indictment, seven years in prison and a fine.

Fireworks Act 2003

Under section 11(3) of the Fireworks Act 2003, it is an offence for a **19.120** person in giving information (where such information is required under fireworks regulations made under sections 2 and 8) to make a statement which he knows to be, or recklessly to make a statement which is, false in a material particular. The maximum penalty on summary conviction is six months in prison and a fine of level 5 on the standard scale (see s.11(4)).

Crime International Co-operation Act 2003

Section 39 of the Crime (International Co-operation) Act 2003 provides: **19.121**

'(3) A financial institution is guilty of an offence if, in purported compliance with a customer information order, it—

(a) makes a statement which it knows to be false or misleading in a material particular, or
(b) recklessly makes a statement which is false or misleading in a material particular.'

A customer information order is one made by a sheriff on application by a procurator fiscal following a request by a foreign authority to the Lord Advocate. Such an order requires specified financial institutions to provide details relative to particular persons who hold or have held accounts with those institutions (see s.37 of the 2003 Act) and who are being investigated in a foreign country relative to serious criminal charges. The maximum penalties for a contravention of s.39(3) are a fine of the statutory maximum on summary conviction, and a fine on conviction on indictment (see s.34(4)).

Cheating at Gambling

Section 42 of the Gambling Act 2005 provides: **19.122**

'(1) A person commits an offence if he—

(a) cheats at gambling, or
(b) does anything for the purpose of enabling or assisting another person to cheat at gambling.

(2) For the purposes of subsection (1) it is immaterial whether a person who cheats—

(a) improves his chances of winning anything, or
(b) wins anything.

(3) Without prejudice to the generality of subsection (1) cheating at gambling may, in particular, consist of actual or attempted deception or interference in connection with—

(a) the process by which gambling is conducted, or
(b) a real or virtual game, race or other event or process to which gambling relates.

(4) A person guilty of an offence under this section shall be liable—

(a) on conviction on indictment, to imprisonment for a term not exceeding two years, to a fine or to both, or

(b) on summary conviction, to imprisonment for a term not exceeding six months [in Scotland: see subsection (5)], to a fine not exceeding the statutory maximum or to both.'

'Gambling' is defined in s.3 of the 2005 Act as 'gaming', 'betting' or 'participating in a lottery'—these three further terms being explained in ss.6, 9 and 15."

CHAPTER 20

RESET

Clause 89(1) of the Draft Scottish Criminal Code would add property **20.01** obtained by extortion to the definition of reset: thus the clause reads—"A person who receives or retains property which has been acquired by another person by robbery, theft, extortion, fraud or embezzlement and who—(a) knows that the property has been so acquired; and (b) does not have the intention of securing the return of the property to its owner or lawful custodian, is guilty of the offence of reset." (*Cf.* the terms of s.51 of the Criminal Law (Consolidation) (Scotland) Act 1995.) This clause also describes part of the *mens rea* requirement negatively: in practice, however, this description is probably no different from the common law position; see, for example, *Mearns v. McFadyen*, 2001 S.C.C.R. 25, where at p.27B–D, the Appeal Court apparently approved the submission of the advocate-depute that the essentials of reset were "the retention of goods knowing them to be stolen [as was the contention in the case, since the original charge had been one of theft] with the intention of detaining them from the true owner."

n.6: The Salmon Fisheries (Scotland) Act 1868 was repealed in its entirety **20.02** by the Salmon and Freshwater Fisheries (Consolidation) (Scotland) Act 2003 (asp 15), Sched. 4, Part 2. For the modern equivalent of the offence under s.21 of the former enactment, see the 2003 Act, s.16 (buying and selling salmon in close time).

The subject matter of this paragraph should be compared with clause **20.08** 89(2) of the Draft Scottish Criminal Code which reads: "Property ceases to be within subsection (1) [see **20.01**, above] once it has been returned to its owner or other lawful custodian." This would appear to resolve the problems discussed here.

n.36: The page references to "Smith and Hogan" at 632–634 should now be entered as "651–653" of the 10th ed.

n.44: The page references to "Smith and Hogan" at 645–656 should now **20.09** be entered as "664–665" of the 10th ed.

CHAPTER 21

EXTORTION AND CORRUPTION

21.01 n.2: The page references to "Smith and Hogan" at 605–611 should now be entered as "623–629" (*i.e.* chapter 20) of the 10th ed.

21.09 n.32: The citation for the case of *James Miller* should read: "(1862) 4 Irv. 238" (and not 328).

21.21 n.73: The page references to "Smith and Hogan" at 86–87 should now be entered as "103–104" of the 10th ed.

With respect to the third text paragraph and n.73, it should be noted that the approach of English law to "honesty of belief" in rape has been altered by recent statutory provision: see the Sexual Offences Act 2003, s.1, where any relevant belief on the part of the defendant must be reasonable.

21.22 Section 2(1) of the Unsolicited Goods and Services Act 1971 is amended for the purposes of "distance contracts" (see reg. 4), other than excepted contracts (see reg. 5) and subject to the qualifications set out in reg. 6, by the Consumer Protection (Distance Selling) Regulations 2000 (S.I. 2000 No. 2334), reg. 22(3), such that after the word "them" there is inserted the words "for the purposes of his trade or business". Under reg. 3(1), a "distance contract" means "any contract concerning goods or services concluded between a supplier and a consumer under an organised distance sales or service provision scheme run by the supplier who, for the purposes of the contract, makes exclusive use of one or more means of distance communication up to and including the moment at which the contract is concluded"; "consumer" means "any natural person who, in contracts to which these Regulations apply, is acting for purposes which are outside his business"; "means of distance communication" means "any means which, without the simultaneous physical presence of the supplier and the consumer, may be used for the conclusion of a contract between those parties" (an indicative list of such means being set out in Schedule 1); and, "supplier" means "any person who, in contracts to which these regulations apply, is acting in his commercial or professional capacity".

As s.2(1) is thus restricted to the supply of unsolicited goods to businesses, the above mentioned Regulations, in reg. 24, cater separately for non-business recipients of such goods as follows:

"(4) A person who, not having reasonable cause to believe there is a right to payment, in the course of a business makes a demand for payment, or asserts a present or prospective right to payment, for what he knows are—

94

(a) unsolicited goods sent to another person with a view to his acquiring them for purposes other than those of his business, or

(b) unsolicited services supplied to another person for purposes other than those of his business,

is guilty of an offence and liable, on summary conviction, to a fine not exceeding level 4 on the standard scale.

(5) A person who, not having reasonable cause to believe there is a right to payment, in the course of any business and with a view to obtaining payment for what he knows are unsolicited goods sent or services supplied as mentioned in paragraph (4)—

(a) threatens to bring any legal proceedings, or

(b) places or causes to be placed the name of any person on a list of defaulters or debtors or threatens to do so, or

(c) invokes or causes to be invoked any other collection procedure or threatens to do so,

is guilty of an offence and liable, on summary conviction, to a fine not exceeding level 5 on the standard scale.

(6) In this regulation—

'acquire' includes hire;

'send' includes deliver;

'sender', in relation to any goods, includes—

(a) any person on whose behalf or with whose consent the goods are sent;

(b) any other person claiming through or under the sender or any person mentioned in paragraph (a); and

(c) any person who delivers the goods; and

'unsolicited' means, in relation to goods sent or services supplied to any person, that they are sent or supplied without any prior request made by or on behalf of the recipient.

(7) For the purposes of this regulation, an invoice or similar document which—

(a) states the amount of a payment, and

(b) fails to comply with the requirements of regulations made under section 3A of the Unsolicited Goods and Services Act 1971 or, as the case may be, Article 6 of the Unsolicited Goods and Services (Northern Ireland) Order 1976 applicable to it,

is to be regarded as asserting a right to the payment.
..."

[Note: s.3A of the 1971 Act was inserted by s.1 of the Unsolicited Goods and Services (Amendment) Act 1975.]

Section 3 of the Unsolicited Goods and Services Act 1971 is significantly amended by the Unsolicited Goods and Services Act 1971 (Electronic Communications) Order 2001 (S.I. 2001 No. 2778), regs 2–6, so that that section now reads as follows:

"(1) A person ('the purchaser') shall not be liable to make any payment, and shall be entitled to recover any payment made by him, by way of charge for including or arranging for the inclusion in a directory of an entry relating to that person or his trade or business, unless—

    (a) there has been signed by the purchaser or on his behalf an order complying with this section,

    (b) there has been signed by the purchaser or on his behalf a note complying with this section of his agreement to the charge and before the note was signed, a copy of it was supplied, for retention by him, to him or a person acting on his behalf, or

    (c) there has been transmitted by the purchaser or a person acting on his behalf an electronic communication which includes a statement that the purchaser agrees to the charge and the relevant condition is satisfied in relation to that communication.

(2) A person shall be guilty of an offence punishable on summary conviction with a fine not exceeding the prescribed sum [or an unlimited fine on indictment: Unsolicited Goods and Services (Amendment) Act 1975, s.3(1)] if, in a case where a payment in respect of a charge would, in the absence of an order or note of agreement to the charge complying with this section and in the absence of an electronic communication in relation to which the relevant condition is satisfied [see subs.(3A), below], be recoverable from him in accordance with the terms of subsection (1) above, he demands payment, or asserts a present or prospective right to payment, of the charge or any part of it, without knowing or having reasonable cause to believe that—

    (a) the entry to which the charge relates was ordered in accordance with this section,

    (b) a proper note of the agreement has been duly signed, or

    (c) the requirements set out in subsection (1)(c) above have been met.

. . .

(3A) In relation to an electronic communication which includes a statement that the purchaser agrees to a charge for including or arranging the inclusion in a directory of any entry, the relevant condition is that—

    (a) before the electronic communication was transmitted the information referred to in subsection (3B) below was communicated to the purchaser, and

    (b) the electronic communication can readily be produced and retained in a visible and legible form.

(3B) That information is—

    (a) the following particulars—

        (i) the amount of the charge;

        (ii) the name of the directory or proposed directory;

        (iii) the name of the person producing the directory;

    (iv) the geographic address at which that person is established;

    (v) if the directory is or is to be available in printed form, the proposed date of publication of the directory or of the issue in which the entry is to be included;

    (vi) if the directory or the issue in which the entry is to be included is to be put on sale, the price at which it is to be offered for sale and the minimum number of copies which are to be available for sale;

    (vii) if the directory or the issue in which the entry is to be included is to be distributed free of charge (whether or not it is also to be put on sale), the minimum number of copies which are to be so distributed;

    (viii) if the directory is or is to be available in a form other than in printed form, adequate details of how it may be accessed; and

  (b) reasonable particulars of the entry in respect of which the charge would be payable.

(3C) In this section 'electronic communication' has the same meaning as in the Electronic Communication Act 2000 [see s.15(1) of that Act, as amended by the Communications Act 2003, Sched. 17, para. 158]."

21.23 Section 1 of the Prevention of Corruption Act 1906 is amended by s.108(2) of the Anti-terrorism, Crime and Security Act 2001 (as extended to Scotland by the Criminal Justice (Scotland) Act 2003 (asp 7), s.68(2)) in that following subsection (3) of the said s.1, the undernoted new subsection is added:

"(4) For the purposes of this Act it is immaterial if—

  (a) the principal's affairs or business have no connection with the United Kingdom and are conducted in a country or territory outside the United Kingdom;

  (b) the agent's functions have no connection with the United Kingdom and are carried out in a country or territory outside the United Kingdom."

Under s.69 of the Criminal Justice (Scotland) Act 2003 (asp 7), the jurisdiction of the Scottish courts in respect of anything done outside the United Kingdom by a United Kingdom national, Scottish partnership or incorporated body is extended if what was done would constitute, *inter alia*, an offence under "the first two offences under section 1 of the Prevention of Corruption Act 1906" if it had been done in Scotland: in such cases, s.11(3) of the 1995 Act applies.

DAMAGE TO PROPERTY

22.01 Where malicious mischief involves damage to crops, it may sometimes be a defence that the accused was at the material time exercising "access rights" responsibly under Part 1 of the Land Reform (Scotland) Act 2003 (asp 2). Although, under s.6(1)(i), the land over which such rights are exercisable does not include land "in which crops have been sown or are growing", this is modified by s.7(10) which reads:

> "For the purposes of section 6(1)(i) ... land on which crops are growing—
>
> (a) includes land on which grass is being grown for hay and silage which is at such a late stage of growth that it is likely to be damaged by the exercise of access rights in respect of the land in which it is growing, but otherwise does not include grassland;
> (b) does not include headrigs, endrigs or other margins of fields in which crops are growing
>
> and 'crops' means plants which are cultivated for agricultural, forestry or commercial purposes."

It follows that the factual situation in *Ward v. Robertson*, 1938 J.C. 32 (referred to in **n.7**) could not now result in a conviction even if the accused had known, or been indifferent to the fact that, his conduct would cause damage. There was no evidence in *Ward v. Robertson* that the grass which had been walked over by the appellant was being grown for "hay and silage"; even if it had been so grown, there would (in terms of the 2003 Act) have had to have been evidence that the crop was at a suitably late stage of growth for a conviction to be sustained. Nor is it now maintainable, *quantum valuit*, in such a case that the accused was a trespasser (see opinion of Lord Justice-Clerk Aitchison at pp.35–36): under s.5(1) of the Land Reform (Scotland) Act 2003 (asp 2) "The exercise of access rights does not of itself constitute trespass".

The case of *Rigg v. Trotter* (1714) Hume i, 123, mentioned in **n.7**, is unaffected by the 2003 Act referred to above, since "access rights" are not exercisable over, *inter alia*, a bowling green "on which grass is grown": 2003 Act (asp 2), s.7(7)(b).

22.12 In line 4 of the second text paragraph, the first word should read "contend" rather than "content".

22.14 After this paragraph, the following new paragraph should be inserted:

"A preventative offence, associated with a particular aspect of vandalism, **22.14A** is now to be found in the Antisocial Behaviour etc. (Scotland) Act 2004 (asp 8). Section 122 of that Act provides:

'(1) A person who sells to a person under the age of 16 a spray paint device shall be guilty of an offence.
(2) In subsection (1), "spray paint device" means a device which—

(a) contains paint stored under pressure; and
(b) is designed to permit the release of the paint as a spray.

(3) A person guilty of an offence under subsection (1) shall be liable on summary conviction to a fine not exceeding level 3 on the standard scale.
(4) It shall be a defence for a person charged with an offence under subsection (1) to show that the person took all reasonable precautions and exercised all due diligence to avoid the commission of the offence.'

Under section 123 of the 2004 Act, an appropriate notice, conforming to regulations and intimating the illegality of selling a spray paint device (as defined in section 122) to anyone under the age of 16, must be displayed prominently at all premises (as defined in subsection (10)) where such devices are sold by retail; any person carrying on a relevant business where no such notice is displayed is guilty of an offence with a maximum penalty (on summary conviction) of a fine of level 2 on the standard scale: it is a defence, however, for such a person to show that he took all reasonable precautions and exercised all due diligence to avoid committing the offence."

In the text of s.3(1) of the Submarine Telegraph Act 1885 as reproduced **22.15** here, in line 4 thereof, after the words "United Kingdom" but before footnote number 62, the following should be inserted: "or under waters in any area designated under section 1(7) of the Continental Shelf Act 1964".

n.62: The existing text of this note should be deleted and the following substituted: "See the Continental Shelf Act 1964, s.8(1), (1A) (subsection (1A) having been added by the Petroleum Act 1998, Sched. 4, para. 2(4)) as amended by s.103(1) of the Energy Act 2004; damage to power cables and pipelines is criminal whether or not it affects communications."

n.66: The Merchant Shipping (Dangerous Goods and Marine Pollutants) Regulations 1997 (S.I. 1997 No. 2367) are amended by the Merchant Shipping (Vessel Traffic Monitoring and Reporting Requirements) Regulations 2004 (S.I. 2004 No. 2110), Sched. 2.

n.72: Section 24 of the Merchant Shipping and Maritime Security Act **22.18** 1997 is amended (as is every enactment which uses such title descriptions directly or by reference to the British Nationality Act 1981) by s.2 of the British Overseas Territories Act 2002 (which substitutes "British overseas territories citizen [or citizenship]" for "British Dependent Territories citizen [or citizenship]".

In the last line of the text of this paragraph, the date of the Protection of Military Remains Act should read "1986" and not "1985".

22.19   After this paragraph, the following new paragraph should be inserted:

22.19A   "*Ploughing of core paths or rights of way.* Under section 23 of the Land Reform (Scotland) Act 2003 (asp 2), the owner (as defined in s.32) of land which is a core path (as explained in s.17) or right of way, which has been ploughed or has had its surface disturbed in accordance with good husbandry, must reinstate that path or right of way within 14 days (or such longer period as a local authority may allow) of the ploughing or disturbance, otherwise he is guilty of an offence carrying a maximum penalty on summary conviction of a fine of level 3 on the standard scale."

22.25   After this paragraph, the following new paragraphs should be inserted:

22.25A   "*Fireworks.* Under section 11(1) of the Fireworks Act 2003, it is an offence for any person to contravene a prohibition imposed by fireworks regulations made under section 2. Regulations under section 2(1) may be made to secure that "there is no risk that the use of fireworks [as defined in s.1(1) or (2); see also s.14] will have the consequences specified in subsection (2), or ... that the risk that the use of fireworks will have those consequences is the minimum that is compatible with their being used." The specified consequences under subsection (2) include "(e) destruction of, or damage to property"; and the prohibitions which such regulations may include are specified in sections 3–7 and 9: in particular, section 6 permits the prohibition of operating public fireworks displays (as defined in subsection (5)) unless certain preconditions are met. The maximum penalty for an offence under section 11 is, on summary conviction, imprisonment for 6 months and a fine of level 5 on the standard scale: s.11(4). Defences are set out in section 11(7) and (8).

22.25B   "*Sites of special scientific interest.* Section 19 of the Nature Conservation (Scotland) Act 2004 (asp 6) provides:

> '(1) Any person who intentionally or recklessly damages any natural feature [including causing it to deteriorate, or, where the feature consists of fauna, disturbing it or harassing it to the specified extent: s.58(1),(2),(3)] specified in an SSSI notification [see below] is, subject to subsection (2), guilty of an offence.
>
> (2) Any person who does anything which would, but for this subsection, amount to an offence under subsection (1) is not guilty of the offence if it is shown that—
>
> (a) the act was the incidental result of a lawful operation,
> (b) the person who carried out the lawful operation—
>
>> (i) took reasonable precautions for the purpose of avoiding carrying out the act, or
>> (ii) did not foresee, and could not reasonably have foreseen, that the act would be an incidental result of the carrying out of the lawful operation, and
>
> (c) that person took such steps as were reasonably practicable in all the circumstances to minimise the damage caused.
>
> (3) Any person who, without reasonable excuse—

(a) contravenes section 13(1) [see below]...

is guilty of an offence.

(4) Any person guilty of an offence under subsection (1) or (3) is liable—

(a) on summary conviction, to a fine not exceeding £40,000,

(b) on conviction on indictment, to a fine.

(5) It is not a defence in proceedings for an offence under subsection (3) of contravening section 13(1) ... that the carrying out of the operation did not damage any natural feature specified in an SSSI notification.'

Scottish Natural Heritage (SNH) has a duty under section 3 of the 2004 Act to notify interested parties (see s.48(2) of the Act) where it considers land to be a site of special scientific interest: such notification is known as 'SSSI notification' (see s.3(5)). A 'natural feature', by reason of which such notification is considered necessary, must be specified by SNH in a document accompanying the notification (see s.3(4)(a)) whereupon that feature becomes a 'protected natural feature' (see s.58(1)); there must also be specified such acts or omissions which appear to SNH to be likely to damage that feature. Under section 13(1) 'A public body or office-holder [as defined in s.58(1)] must not carry out any operation which is likely to damage any natural feature specified in an SSSI notification except—(a) with the written consent of SNH given on an application under subsection (3), (b) where subsection (1) of section 14 applies [*i.e.* where such an operation is, for example, permitted or authorised, as specified there], or (c) in accordance with subsection (2) of that section [*i.e.* where certain conditions are fulfilled].' "

In *McCue v. Currie*, 2004 S.C.C.R. 200, where a thief accidentally **22.28** dropped a lit cigarette lighter thus causing the destruction by fire of the caravan he was ransacking, it was held that the thief's subsequent failure to make any attempt to extinguish the fire he had accidentally started, or to summon assistance for that purpose (although "plainly reprehensible to a high degree": opinion of the court at p.207E, para. 26), was not sufficient to make him liable for culpable and reckless fire-raising, since "fire raising which is merely accidental does not demonstrate the necessary mens rea and is not a crime, and cannot become so by subsequent behaviour", and "mens rea has always been determined by reference to the act of starting the fire and not by reference to something which took place thereafter" (opinion of the court at p.207D, para. 25, and p.207A, para. 23). For a critique of the decision in that case, see James Chalmers, "Fireraising by Omission", 2004 S.L.T. (News) 59, and the Commentary at 2004 S.C.C.R., pp.207–208.

There is now authority against the correctness of Lord Young's view in **22.29** *Robert Smillie* (1883) 5 Couper 287 at 291, that setting fire "while engaged in some illegal act" amounts to culpable and reckless fire-raising: see *McCue v. Currie*, 2004 S.C.C.R. 200, opinion of the court at p.206E–F, para. 22, where the appellant set fire to a caravan from which he was stealing goods.

CHAPTER 23

MURDER

23.02 **n.7:** The page reference to "Smith and Hogan" at 338, which should correctly have referred to p.330 of the 9th ed., should now be entered as "354" of the 10th ed.

23.03 The exception referred to here (relating to a doctor who prescribes pain-killing drugs in the knowledge that these will shorten the patient's life) would be given a statutory basis in the Draft Scottish Criminal Code: see clause 37(2) thereof. This is achieved by creating an exception to the extended definition of intention given by the Code in clause 9(1)(a).

23.10 (And following paragraphs) Where no issue of provocation, diminished responsibility or self-defence arises, the Appeal Court seems content to refer to the two possibilities for the *mens rea* of murder as "intention to kill" and "utter and wicked disregard for the consequences to the victim": see *Arthur v. H.M. Advocate*, 2002 S.C.C.R. 796, opinion of the court at p.800E–F, para. 12.

23.19 In *Arthur v. H.M. Advocate*, 2002 S.C.C.R. 796, it was affirmed that proof of the use of life-threatening violence or life-endangering means by an accused person against his victim is not sufficient for conviction of murder unless the *mens rea* of involuntary murder (*i.e.* utter and wicked disregard for the consequences to the victim) can also be inferred from such violence or means: opinion of the court at p.800D–F, para.12.

23.20 **n.3:** See also *Arthur v. H.M. Advocate*, 2002 S.C.C.R. 796, opinion of the court at p.800D–E, para. 12.

23.21 The opinion of the court in *Arthur v. H.M. Advocate*, 2002 S.C.C.R. 796, may also be thought to support the view that wicked recklessness is essentially a jury question.

23.22 **n.15:** Section 208 of the Criminal Procedure (Scotland) Act 1995 (the "1995 Act") is amended and extended by the Criminal Justice Act 2003, s.290(3)—which refers to the Firearms Act 1968, s.51A; s.51A is inserted into the 1968 Act by the 2003 Act, s.287.

n.17: That "intent to do serious bodily harm" could be sufficient intent for murder seems incompatible with the reasoning of the Appeal Court in *Arthur v. H.M. Advocate*, 2002 S.C.C.R. 796.

23.23 **n.20:** In the quotation from Lord Justice-General Hope in *Brown v. H.M. Advocate*, 1993 S.C.C.R. 382 at 391F, the quotation marks should begin after (and not before) the word "with".

In the art and part case of *McKinnon v. H.M. Advocate*, 2003 S.C.C.R. 224, Lord Justice-General Hope's observations in *Brown v. H.M. Advocate*, 1993 S.C.C.R. 382 at 391D–392B were disapproved by a court of five judges: see the opinion of that court at p.237C, para. 24, *viz*: "... we are of the view that the observations ... did not adequately address the issue of antecedent conduct in that case or the well recognised approach to guilt on the basis of antecedent concert, and should not be regarded as authoritative in regard to that subject." It is difficult to see, therefore, that Lord Justice-General Hope's remarks can now have any significant bearing on the *mens rea* of murder generally.

In the case of *McKinnon v. H.M. Advocate*, 2003 S.C.C.R. 224, a decision **23.28** by a court of five judges involving, *inter alia*, the issue of homicide in the course of robbery, it was stated (at p.238F, para. 31) that "... it is not a rule of law that homicide in pursuance of the commission of a crime involving the use of violence is necessarily murder". This was stated in the context of the law of antecedent concert, and without reference to the earlier cases—particularly *Miller and Denovan*. It is unlikely, however, that the interpretation of *Miller and Denovan* given in the text of paragraph 23.28 of the Third Edition will be applied today; and it may be taken that what is stated in *McKinnon* represents the modern law.

In the second line of the first text paragraph, in the quotation from **23.31** Macdonald, the word "is" should be inserted between "crime" and "murder".

CHAPTER 24

SELF-DEFENCE

24.01 **n.1:** The page reference to "Smith and Hogan" at 259 *et seq.* should now be entered as "275 *et seq.*" of the 10th ed.

The Draft Scottish Criminal Code, at clause 23, uses the traditional term "self-defence", but seeks to extend or clarify the ambit of the common law by (for example) allowing that self-defence should apply to the protection of property as also to the prevention or ending of unlawful intrusion or presence on property.

24.04 **n.13:** The definition of rape in Scots law no longer requires that the woman should resist her attacker: see *Lord Advocate's Reference (No. 1 of 2001)*, 2002 S.L.T. 466, and Chapter 33, below.

24.11 **n.73:** In the 10th edition of "Smith and Hogan", the statement narrated in the text appears at p.281.

24.13 **n.79:** *Drury v. H.M. Advocate* is now reported at 2001 S.L.T. 1013.

24.16 For an account of the law of self-defence in English law, particularly with respect to the defence of property, see *R. v. Martin (Anthony)* [2002] 1 Cr. App.R. 27 (C.A.), where the appellant's conviction for murder was eventually quashed and manslaughter substituted on the grounds of diminished responsibility.

24.17 "Resistance to the utmost by the victim" is no longer a requirement of rape in Scots law: *Lord Advocate's Reference (No. 1 of 2001)*, 2002 S.L.T. 466: see Chapter 33, below. If the ratio of *McCluskey v. H.M. Advocate*, 1959 J.C. 39, as set out by Lord Justice-General Clyde, at pp.42–43, is correct, then killing in resistance to sodomy is not justifiable unless the man in question was compelled to take life in order to save his own: but there is no authority for that ratio, which was followed without discussion in *Elliott v. H.M. Advocate*, 1987 S.C.C.R. 278. Further, Hume's view (at i, 218) is simply this: "In like manner as a man may kill in resistance of an attempt on his life, so may a woman in resistance of an attempt to commit a rape on her person, an attempt at which she is entitled to feel the highest indignation and resentment." And Alison (at i, 135) narrates that "[a] woman may lawfully kill to defend herself from a rape, if her honour cannot otherwise be preserved". Considering, therefore, the undoubted rule that a woman may kill (subject probably to proportionality) "in hindrance of rape" (as the side-note at Hume, i, 218, states) and the way in which the Institutional writers present the matter, as also the modern trend to treat as rape (at least in jurisdictions other than Scotland) non-consensual vaginal and anal penetration (see, for example, the Sexual Offences Act 2003, s.1), it may be that the ratio of *McCluskey* is open to doubt.

n.97: The reference for *McCann and Ors. v. United Kingdom* should read: **24.18** 1996 21 [and not 221] E.H.R.R. 97".

VOLUNTARY CULPABLE HOMICIDE

25.01 n.9: Section 205 of the 1995 Act should be read as amended by the Convention Rights (Compliance) (Scotland) Act 2001 (asp 7), s.2. See also s.205D—inserted into the 1995 Act by the said s.2.

n.12: The analysis criticised in *Drury v. H.M. Advocate*, 2001 S.L.T. 1013, also underlies the account of English law given in the Law Commission's Consultation Paper (No. 173, October 31, 2003): "Partial Defences to Murder". (*Cf.* The Scottish Law Commission's "Report on Insanity and Diminished Responsibility", Scot. Law Com. No. 195, July 2004, especially para. 3.16 and the Draft "Criminal Responsibility and Unfitness for Trial (Scotland) Bill" at section 3, where the view is taken that diminished responsibility reduces what would otherwise be murder to culpable homicide, following the decision of the court in *Galbraith v. H.M. Advocate*, 2001 S.L.T. 953: the Scottish Law Commission, however, was not concerned with provocation (or its analysis) in that Report. *Cf.* also, the Draft Scottish Criminal Code at clause 38.)

25.19 In the penultimate line of text on p.341, "in equivalence" should be read as: "inequivalence".

25.23 n.83: See the entry for n.9, above.

25.23– Under clause 38 of the Draft Scottish Criminal Code, the existing law of
25.37 provocation would be clarified and extended such that—

> "(3) A person who, but for this sub[clause], would be guilty of murder is not guilty of murder, but is guilty of culpable homicide, if—
>
> > (a) the person, at the time of the killing, had lost self-control as a result of provocation; and
> > (b) an ordinary person, thus provoked, would have been likely to react in the same way.
>
> (4) For the purposes of sub[clause] (3)—
>
> > (a) the provocation may be by acts or words or both (whether by the deceased or another person); and
> > (b) the ordinary person is assumed—
> >
> > > (i) to have any personal characteristics of the accused that affect the provocative quality of the acts or words giving rise to the loss of self-control; and
> > > (ii) to have a normal ability to exercise a reasonable measure of self-control."

25.37 n.70a: *Cochrane v. H.M. Advocate* is now reported at 2001 S.C.C.R. 655.

CHAPTER 26

INVOLUNTARY CULPABLE HOMICIDE

The expression "involuntary culpable homicide" is employed expressly as **26.01** a descriptive term by Lord Osborne in his opinion in *Transco Plc. v. H.M. Advocate*, 2004 S.L.T. 41: see *e.g.* p.43D, para. 2; p.43K, para. 4.

Lord Osborne, in *Transco* (at p.44B–D and E–F, para. 4), after quoting from Lord Justice-Clerk Aitchison's "classic" definition of involuntary culpable homicide in *Paton v. H.M. Advocate*, 1936 J.C. 19 at 22, opines that use of the word "negligence" in the context of involuntary culpable homicide "introduces a potential for confusion" since the word "may properly be used in two senses"—the first as in the English tort of negligence, and the second "in the more general English parlance, which connotes some degree of carelessness or neglect of duty in a non-legal context". Nevertheless, since the court in *Transco* seems agreed that something akin to reckless (or utter) disregard of the consequences, or recklessness of a degree which involves an indifference to the consequences, is an essential element of involuntary culpable homicide, use (in para. 26.01 of the third edition) of the words "with a degree of negligence which is regarded as sufficient to make the homicide culpable but not murderous" may still perhaps be defended in a general description of the crime.

In line 7 of the first paragraph of text, the semi-colon after the word **26.07** "quiet" should be replaced by a comma.

n.42: See also *Transco Plc. v. H.M. Advocate*, 2004 S.L.T. 41, although **26.09** the charge of culpable homicide was eventually dismissed as irrelevant in the context of the requirements for corporate criminal liability.

n.44: The maximum penalty for causing death by dangerous driving is now 14 years in prison: Criminal Justice Act 2003, s.285(2), (3) (which is made applicable to Scotland by s.337(7)(b) of the Act).

n.47: The identification theory also pertains in Scotland: see *Transco Plc. v. H.M. Advocate*, 2004 S.L.T. 41.

n.64: *Cf. Transco Plc. v. H.M. Advocate*, 2004 S.L.T. 41, discussed in **26.12** para. 26.12A, below.

After this paragraph, the following new paragraph should be added:

"*Mens rea.* In the modern case of *Transco Plc. v. H.M. Advocate*, 2004 **26.12A** S.L.T. 41, a company (a public gas transporter with certain duties and responsibilities relative to the safe transmission of gas) was charged with culpable homicide in that, knowing of particular (specified) risks associated with the corrosion potential of underground gas pipes, it failed, with complete and utter disregard for the safety of the public (and in particular for the safety of four persons actually killed as a result of an explosion), to have or implement safety measures in relation to such risks. The charge was found to be irrelevant on appeal, since the Crown was unable to demonstrate that the Scottish 'rules' for corporate criminal liability could be satisfied (see Vol. I, Chap. 8); but the Appeal Court took the opportunity to affirm that 'lawful act' culpable homicide requires *mens rea*. Lord Hamilton, in particular, at p.54G, para. 38, emphasised that it was not possible to let guilt or innocence in this form of criminal homicide be 'determined solely on the basis of proof that the conduct in question fell below an objectively set standard'. The court did not, however, make entirely clear what the test for *mens rea* should be. Both Lord Osborne (at pp.44L–45A, para. 4) and Lord Hamilton (at p.54F, para. 37) ultimately quote with approval what was said by Lord Justice-General Rodger (in delivering the opinion of the court) in *McDowall v. H.M. Advocate*, 1998 J.C. 194 at 198G, namely that (in a case of 'motor vehicle' culpable homicide) what the jury had to consider was whether 'the appellant showed complete disregard of potential dangers and of the consequences of his driving for the public'. Lord Osborne (at p.45C–D, para. 4) also cited with approval what was said by Lord Marnoch in delivering the opinion of the court in the non-culpable homicide case of *Cameron v. Maguire*, 1999 J.C. 63 at 66, namely that the test to be applied was whether the Crown had demonstrated a 'recklessness so high as to involve an indifference to the consequences for the public generally'. (*Cameron v. Maguire* involved a charge of reckless discharge of firearms; but Lord Osborne (at p.45C, para. 4) was of the view that the 'necessary criminal intent' expressed in that case was 'equally applicable in a case where death results and the issue is one of culpable homicide'.) 'Complete disregard of potential dangers' or 'indifference to the consequences' can readily be accepted as a mental state; and the court in *Transco* accepts that such a mental state can be proved 'by evidence of external factors, including inferences from a comparison of what the accused did or failed to do against standards of conduct to be expected of persons carrying on operations of the relevant kind': Lord Hamilton at p.55J, para. 44; see also the passages from Hume and Macdonald quoted by Lord Osborne at p.43E–F, para. 3. But what (actual or inferred) knowledge of the potential dangers or risks an accused should be demonstrated to have is unclear from the opinions. Lord Hamilton (at p.55L, para. 45) stated that '[i]n a case such as the present the state of knowledge of the accused is clearly critical. That is of importance in considering whether, and if so how, a body corporate can commit this common law crime.' But to what extent is the accused's state of knowledge of importance where corporate criminal liability is not involved? If it is correct that *mens rea* in Scots law is a subjective matter proved objectively, then any necessary knowledge of the relevant risk will surely be attributed to an accused who can be shown from his conduct (actions or omissions) to have demonstrated complete disregard for the safety (and indeed the lives) of others—or, at least, this will be so save in very special situations such as were conceded by the Crown in *Transco* (namely, hypoglycaemic attack or coercion: see the opinion of Lord Hamilton at p.55C–D, para. 41). The approach to *mens rea* in statutory driving offences involving death is, of course, quite different (see paras 26.13 and 26.14 of the 3rd edition)."

The test for "driving dangerously" offences is wholly objective—the **26.13** critical question being the nature and quality of the driving (see *Young v. Barbour*, 2002 S.C.C.R. 84; *Attorney General's Reference (No. 4 of 2000)* [2001] R.T.R. 415); but the issue of whether the manner of driving was deliberate or not was considered to have some relevance to that critical question in *Young v. Barbour (supra)*.

n.65: (and text just before n.72 on p.371) The maximum penalty for a contravention of s.1 of the Road Traffic Act 1988 is now 14 years in prison: see the Criminal Justice Act 2003, s.285(2), (3)—which is applied to Scotland by s.337(7)(b).

Text from foot of p.371 to top of p.372: The *Paton* test was criticised by the Appeal Court in *Transco Plc. v. H.M. Advocate*, 2004 S.L.T. 41 (see opinions of Lord Osborne at p.44C–F, para. 4, and Lord Hamilton at p.54B–D, paras 36 and 37) but not overruled.

n.78: The maximum penalty for a contravention of s.3A of the Road **26.14** Traffic Act 1988 is now 14 years in prison: see the Criminal Justice Act 2003, s.285(2), (4)—which is applied to Scotland by s.337(7)(b).

n.3: Lord Cooper's statements in *H.M. Advocate v. Rutherford*, 1947 J.C. **26.19** 1 at 6, *viz.* "Where violence is used ... and it results in fatal consequences, that is not by the law of Scotland assault. It is culpable homicide" were quoted with approval by the Appeal Court in the recent case of *McDonald v. H.M. Advocate*, 2004 S.C.C.R. 161 at 167F, para. 17. *McDonald* was not, however, a case where the injuries inflicted were slight; indeed the accused had originally been charged with murder.

In *McDonald v. H.M. Advocate*, 2004 S.C.C.R. 161, the accused caused **26.21** fatal injuries to his wife by the use of a whip handle in the course of a sexual encounter. On the assumption that the victim had consented throughout to the use of such an instrument (since any suggestion of consent relied heavily on the accused's evidence), counsel at the appeal seems to have agreed that if the appellant had intended to cause physical injury to her, then "the consent of the deceased would not provide him with a defence": opinion of the court at p.168B, para. 18. The physical injuries inflicted were, however, severe.

n.63: *Cf.* the Draft Scottish Criminal Code, clause 38 (which must be read **26.27** with clause 10, since the meaning of "recklessly" is given there).

With respect to the last paragraph of text on p.385 of the 3rd edition, the reference there to the "*Paton* standard" should now be read subject to the criticism of that standard offered by Lords Osborne and Hamilton in *Transco Plc. v. H.M. Advocate*, 2004 S.L.T. 41 at 44B–F, para. 4 and 54B–D, paras 36–37, respectively.

CHAPTER 28

ABORTION

28.01 n.3: The page references to "Smith and Hogan" at 396–397 should now be entered as "407–408" of the 10th ed.

28.05 n.17: The latest relevant case to reach the European Court of Human Rights is that of *Vo v. France*, Grand Chamber decision of July 8, 2004 (application no. 53924/00), where what was at stake was summarised by the Court (at para. 81) as follows: "The Court is faced with a woman who intended to carry her pregnancy to term and whose unborn child was expected to be viable, at the very least in good health. Her pregnancy had to be terminated as a result of an error by a doctor and she therefore had to have a therapeutic abortion on account of negligence by a third party. The issue is consequently whether, apart from cases where the mother has requested an abortion, harming a foetus should be treated as a criminal offence in the light of Article 2 of the Convention, with a view to protecting the foetus under that article. This requires a preliminary examination of whether it is advisable for the Court to intervene in the debate as to who is a person and when life begins, in so far as Article 2 provides that the law must protect 'everyone's right to life'." The result of that examination was that the Court, in view of the diversity of views at national level on the point that life begins, decided to leave the State "with considerable discretion on the matter" (para. 82) such that "the issue when the right to life begins comes within the margin of appreciation which the Court generally considers that States should enjoy in this sphere ...". In addition, the Court concluded (at para. 85) that "it is neither desirable, nor even possible as matters stand, to answer in the abstract the question whether the unborn child is a person for the purposes of Article 2 of the Convention ...". In any event, even if the Court were persuaded that the foetus "might have rights protected by Article 2", it did not follow that "only a criminal remedy would have been capable of satisfying the requirements of Article 2 of the Convention" (para. 87): in particular and according to the Court's own jurisprudence, where "the infringement of the right to life or to physical integrity is not caused intentionally, the positive obligation imposed by Article 2 to set up an effective judicial system does not necessarily require the provision of a criminal-law remedy in every case" (para. 90). In short, such obligation may be satisfied by remedy in the civil courts—a remedy which would have been available to the applicant in the instant case had she acted timeously.

Section 1(3) of the Abortion Act 1967 is amended by the Health and Social Care Etc. Act 2003, Sched. 4, paras 9 and 10, such that after the words "National Health Service Trust" there are inserted the words: "or a National Health Service foundation trust".

CHAPTER 29

ASSAULT AND REAL INJURY

n.3: To have intercourse with a sleeping woman might now be charged as **29.01** rape: to the extent that it had required force as an essential element of rape, *Chas. Sweenie* (1858) 3 Irv. 109, was overruled by a court of seven judges in *Lord Advocate's Reference (No. 1 of 2001)*, 2002 S.L.T. 466. Consequently, in so far as *Wm. Thomson* (1872) 2 Cooper 346 and *H.M. Advocate v. Logan*, 1936 J.C. 100 follow, approve or rely upon that aspect of *Chas. Sweenie*, they no longer represent the law. But, in *Spendiff v. H.M. Advocate*, 2005 S.C.C.R. 522 at 525F–526A, paras 5 and 6, the Appeal Court made plain that the "Lord Advocate remains master of the instance, and may, if he thinks fit, libel the clandestine penetration of an unconscious female as indecent assault", and that "[i]n circumstances such as the present case discloses [penetration begun when the woman was asleep but continued once she awoke and made clear her lack of consent], the single continuing act of intercourse might now be libelled as a single charge of rape, without attracting criticism as amalgamating in a single charge the disparate elements of clandestine injury and rape. But the essential characteristics of the assault have not changed, and it remains a matter within the Lord Advocate's discretion how the allegations are libelled, and in particular how clandestine penetration of an unconscious woman is libelled." *Spendiff* was a case in which the appellant had been convicted on an indictment raised prior to, but where his appeal was lodged and disposed of after, the decision in *Lord Advocate's Reference (No. 1 of 2001)*.

Subsections (1) and (2) of s.41 of the Police (Scotland) Act 1967 are **29.12** amended by the Criminal Justice (Scotland) Act 2003 (asp 7), s.76(5)(a),(b), so that the offences there now extend to a "police custody and security officer" as well as to a constable. (For "police custody and security officer" see s.76(2) of the 2003 Act, which amends and extends s.9 of the 1967 Act.) In addition, references to "a constable in the execution of his duty" in s.41(1) and (2) of the 1967 Act now include references to a member of the Civil Nuclear Constabulary who "(a) is exercising any of the powers or privileges conferred on him by section 56 [of the Energy Act 2004]; or (b) is otherwise performing his duties under the direction and control of the chief constable or as an employee of the Police Authority." (For the 'Civil Nuclear Constabulary', see Part 1, Chapter 3 (ss.51–71) of the Energy Act 2004.)

Section 104(2) of the Police Reform Act 2002 also adds the following new subsections to s.41:

"(4) In this section references to a person assisting a constable in the execution of his duty include references to any person who is neither a constable nor in the company of a constable but who—

(a) is a member of an international joint investigation team that is led by a constable of a police force or by a member of the National Criminal Intelligence Service or of the National Crime Squad; and

(b) is carrying out his functions as a member of that team.

(5) In this section 'international joint investigation team' means any investigation team formed in accordance with—

(a) any framework decision on joint investigation teams adopted under Article 34 of the Treaty on European Union;

(b) the Convention on Mutual Assistance in Criminal Matters between the Member States of the European Union, and the Protocol to that Convention, established in accordance with that Article of that Treaty; or

(c) any international agreement to which the United Kingdom is a party and which is specified for the purposes of this section in an order made by the Secretary of State with the consent of the Scottish Ministers.

(6) A statutory instrument containing an order under subsection (5) shall be subject to annulment in pursuance of a resolution of either House of Parliament."

n.58: The opinion of the court in *Walsh v. McFadyen*, 2002 J.C. 93 at 96E–I, para.8, emphasises that "A person who deliberately performs some action with his body so as to place some difficulty in the way of police constables who are trying to take a section 14(1) [of the 1995 Act] detainee to a police station, and especially if he does so in a way calculated to cause the constables to resort to the use of force to effect their purpose, is clearly hindering them in the execution of their duty. If it be the case that the word 'hinders' requires a physical aspect or physical element then, in our opinion, that physical element was provided in the present case by the deliberate decision of the appellant to sit on the couch and remain inert, thus rendering it necessary for the police constables to use force, as permitted by section 14(8) of the 1995 Act." The interpretation of "hinders" as "placing a difficulty in the way of the police who are in the execution of their duty" was drawn from *Skeen v. Shaw and Anr.*, 1979 S.L.T. (Notes) 58 at 58.

29.13 After this paragraph, the following should be added:

29.13A "(3) Emergency Workers (Scotland) Act 2005 (asp 2). This enactment provides:

'**1.**—(1) A person who assaults, obstructs or hinders another person acting in a capacity mentioned in subsection (3) [*i.e.* the capacity of a constable, a person employed by a relevant authority as defined in s.6 of the Fire (Scotland) Act 2005 (asp 5) or providing assistance under arrangements made by virtue of ss.35 or 36 of that Act relative to certain functions, or a person acting for the Scottish Ambulance Service Board (in relation to a particular function of that Board)] ... commits an offence.

(2) No offence is committed under subsection (1) above unless the person who assaults, obstructs or hinders knows or ought to know that the person being assaulted, obstructed or hindered is acting in that capacity.

(3) [summarised, as amended by s.38 of the Fire (Scotland) Act 2005 (asp 5), as part of (1), above].

2.—(1) A person who assaults, obstructs or hinders another while that other person is, in a capacity mentioned in subsection (3) [*i.e.* the capacity of a prison officer (as defined), a member of H.M. Coastguard, a member of the crew of a vessel—operated as defined—or "a person who musters the crew of such a vessel or attends to its launch", a registered medical practitioner, a registered nurse, a registered midwife, a social worker (as defined and acting in particular circumstances), or, a mental health officer (as defined)] ... responding to emergency circumstances, commits an offence.

(2) No offence is committed under subsection (1) above unless the person who assaults, obstructs or hinders knows or ought to know that the person being assaulted, obstructed or hindered—

    (a) is acting in that capacity; and
    (b) is or might be responding—

        (i) to emergency circumstances; or
        (ii) as if there were emergency circumstances.

(3) [summarised above, as part of (1)].

(4) For the purposes of this section and section 3 [see below] of this Act, a person is responding to emergency circumstances if the person—

    (a) is going anywhere for the purpose of dealing with emergency circumstances occurring there; or
    (b) is dealing with emergency circumstances or preparing to do so.

(5) For the purposes of this Act, circumstances are "emergency" circumstances if they are present or imminent and—

    (a) are causing or are likely to cause—

        (i) serious injury to or the serious illness (including mental illness) of a person;
        (ii) serious harm to the environment (including the life and health of plants and animals and the fabric of buildings); or
        (iii) a worsening of any such injury, illness or harm; or

    (b) are likely to cause the death of a person.

3.—(1) A person who assaults, obstructs or hinders another in the circumstances described in subsection (2) below commits an offence.

(2) Those circumstances are where the person being assaulted, obstructed or hindered is assisting another while that other person is, in a capacity mentioned in section 1(3) or 2(3) of this Act, responding to emergency circumstances.

(3) No offence is committed under subsection (1) above unless the person who assaults, obstructs or hinders knows or ought to know—

(a) that the person being assisted is acting in that capacity;

(b) that the person being assisted is or might be responding—

(i) to emergency circumstances; or

(ii) as if there were emergency circumstances; and

(c) that the person being assaulted, obstructed or hindered is assisting the person acting in that capacity.

4.—(1) A person may be convicted of the offence under section 1, 2 or 3 of this Act of obstructing or hindering notwithstanding that it is—

(a) effected by means other than physical means; or

(b) effected by action directed only at any vehicle, apparatus, equipment or other thing or any animal used or to be used by a person referred to in that section.

(2) A person who gives false information with the intention that a person acting in a capacity mentioned in subsection (3) of section 2 of this Act will act upon that information is to be regarded, for the purposes of that section, as hindering the person acting in that capacity.

(3) A person who gives false information with the intention that a person acting in a capacity mentioned in subsection (3) of section 2 of this Act will, while responding to emergency circumstances or instead of doing so, act upon that information is to be regarded, for the purposes of that section, as hindering the person acting in that capacity.

(4) Subsections (2) and (3) above do not prejudice the generality of subsection (1)(a) above.

(5) For the purposes of sections 2 and 3 of this Act, circumstances to which a person is responding are to be taken to be emergency circumstances if the person believes and has reasonable grounds for believing they are or may be emergency circumstances.

. . .

5.—(1) A person who, in a hospital or on land adjacent to and used wholly or mainly for the purposes of a hospital, assaults, obstructs or hinders a person acting in a capacity mentioned in subsection (3) [*i.e.* the capacity of a registered medical practitioner, a registered nurse, a registered midwife, or a person acting for the Scottish Ambulance Service Board (as defined)] ... or a person assisting such a person commits an offence.

(2) No offence is committed under subsection (1) above unless the person who assaults, obstructs or hinders knows or ought to know that the person being assaulted, obstructed or hindered is acting in that capacity or, as the case may be, that the person being assisted is acting in that capacity and that the person being assaulted, obstructed or hindered is assisting the person acting in that capacity.

(3) [summarised above, as part of (1)].

(4) A person may be convicted of the offence under subsection (1) above of obstructing or hindering notwithstanding that it is—

  (a) effected by means other than physical means;
  (b) effected by action directed only at any vehicle, apparatus, equipment or other thing used or to be used by a person referred to in that subsection.'

The maximum penalty for a person guilty of any of the above offences is, on summary conviction, imprisonment for nine months and a fine of level 5 on the standard scale (s.6); and it is expressly stated that nothing in the Act is to affect section 41(1) of the Police (Scotland) Act 1967 (s.7, as amended by the Fire (Scotland) Act 2005 (asp 5), Sched.3, para.25)."

and n.68: As a result of amendments introduced by s.51(5) of the **29.17** Criminal Justice (Scotland) Act 2003 (asp 7), s.12 of the Children and Young Persons (Scotland) Act 1937 no longer applies to assaults. Assaults against children are now, therefore, solely a matter of common law, save where statute has intervened—*e.g.* to regulate the physical punishment of a child under 16 years of age by a person exercising a parental right or a right derived from having charge or care of such a child: see s.51(1)–(2) of the above Act of 2003.

n.89: Obtaining sexual intercourse with a woman without her consent is **29.24** now chargeable as rape or as indecent assault, depending upon the circumstances and the discretion of the Lord Advocate: see *Lord Advocate's Reference (No. 1 of 2001)*, 2002 S.L.T. 466 (court of seven judges), *Spendiff v. H.M. Advocate*, 2005 S.C.C.R. 522, the entry for para. 29.01, above, and Chapter 33, below.

In the text of s.241(1)(a) of the Trade Union and Labour Relations **29.28** (Consolidation) Act 1992, the word "wife" should be replaced by the words "spouse or civil partner" following amendment by the Civil Partnership Act 2004, Sched. 27, para. 145.

In the recent case of *McDonald v. H.M. Advocate*, 2004 S.C.C.R. 161, **29.30** where the appellant had been convicted of culpable homicide on the basis of an assault on his wife as part of a sexual encounter (which the Crown accepted as being at least initially consensual), the Appeal Court (at p.170D, para. 23) quoted with evident approval Macdonald's statement (at p.115) that "evil intention is of the essence of assault" as also what was observed in *Smart v. H.M. Advocate*, 1975 J.C. 30 at 33—which seemed to suggest that *evil intent* might be conflated with "intent to injure and do bodily harm". In the course of argument as to whether an intent to inflict pain would suffice for conviction of assault, the Advocate Depute (as précised by the Court at p.167D, para. 15) conceded, at least for the purposes of the instant case, that "if the appellant had only intended to cause pain, as opposed to actual significant injury, then that would not constitute evil intent and the convictions could not be maintained". Although their Lordships were prepared to proceed on the basis of the Advocate Depute's concession, they also observed: "we wish to reserve our opinion as to whether, in an appropriate case, notwithstanding consent to the infliction of pain in a sexual context, an intention to cause pain could justify a conviction for assault in the absence of an intention to cause actual physical injury".

29.38 The common law toleration of moderate, non-vindictive chastisement of children has been further significantly modified by s.51 of the Criminal Justice (Scotland) Act 2003 (asp 7). A child for the purposes of that section (see subsection (4)) is a person who was under 16 years of age at the time when something was done to him by a person claiming that what was done was physical punishment in exercise of a parental right or "of a right derived from having charge or care of the child". When such a claim is advanced before a court, that court, in determining whether or not a finding of justifiable assault can be made, must (under s.51(1)) have regard to a series of particular factors, namely—

"(a) the nature of what was done, the reason for it and the circumstances in which it took place;

(b) its duration and frequency;

(c) any effect (whether physical or mental) which it has been shown to have had on the child;

(d) the child's age; and

(e) the child's personal characteristics (including without prejudice to the generality of this paragraph, sex and state of health) at the time the thing was done."

Factors such as these may well have been considered by courts in cases under the common law; but they are now considerations of express prescription in every case. A court may also, under s.51(2), have regard to such other factors as it thinks appropriate in the circumstances of the case before it. If, however, what was done involved or included a blow to the head, shaking or the use of an implement, a court cannot determine that there was a justified assault by virtue of the exercise of a parental right or of a right derived as stated above.

Additionally, reg. 4(3) of the Regulation of Care (Requirements as to Care Services) (Scotland) Regulations 2002 (S.S.I. 2002 No. 114), as amended by the Regulation of Care (Requirements as to Care Services) (Scotland) Amendment Regulations 2003 (S.S.I. 2003 No. 149), reg. 2(2), (3), provides:

"A provider of day care or child minding or a child care agency shall not administer, or permit any person employed [which includes, in the case of a child care agency, a person introduced to a service user by the provider] in the provision of the service to administer, physical chastisement or punishment to any child who is looked after or cared for by the service."

Under regulation 26, a contravention of or failure to comply with, *inter alia*, regulation 4(3) is an offence: the maximum penalty on summary conviction is a fine of level 5 on the standard scale (see the parent Act— the Regulation of Care (Scotland) Act 2001 (asp 8), s.29(10), (11)). The definitions of "day care of children", "child minding" and "child care agency" are to be found in s.2 of the 2001 Act; a "child" for these purposes is a person under the age of 16 years (see s.77(1) of the 2001 Act); and, the meanings of "provider" and "service user" are contained in S.S.I. 2002 No. 114, reg. 2 (as amended by S.S.I. 2003 No. 149, reg. 2(2)).

n.43: The Mental Health (Scotland) Act 1984 is repealed by the Mental Health (Care and Treatment) (Scotland) Act 2003 (asp 13), Sched. 5, Part 1. Consequently, s.122 of the 1984 Act ("Protection for acts done in pursuance of this Act") has been repealed, and there is no equivalent provision in the 2003 Act.

n.47: Section 14 (and indeed most other provisions) of the Sexual **29.39** Offences Act 1956 is (and are) repealed by the Sexual Offences Act 2003, Sched. 7. The approach of the 2003 Act is quite different to prior relevant enactments, and no direct comparison between its provisions and those of relevant Scottish enactments is possible.

With respect to the second and third text paragraphs of 29.39 (on p.414 of the 3rd edition), and following what was said by the court in *McDonald v. H.M. Advocate*, 2004 S.C.C.R. 161 at 170E–F, para. 23, it may be that consent is a good defence to a charge of assault (where no other crime is involved) provided that the accused did not act with intent to cause any bodily harm or with intent, in a sexual context, to cause pain: but the court reserved its opinion on this issue.

The last text paragraph on p. 416 of the 3rd edition should be deleted, **29.41** and the following substituted:

"Under the statutory law, ritual or customary female genital mutilation is prohibited by the Prohibition of Female Genital Mutilation (Scotland) Act 2005 (asp 8) even when performed by a recognised medical practitioner, and thus qualifies as an 'illegal operation.'[61]"

n.61: Delete the existing text of this note and substitute:

"See s.1(1), (2) and (6) of the 2005 Act. Maximum penalty: on indictment, 14 years and a fine; on summary conviction, six months and a fine of the statutory maximum (s.5). It is also an offence (see s.3), carrying the same maximum penalty, to aid, abet, counsel, procure or incite the commission of such mutilation, even outside the United Kingdom by a non United Kingdom national or non permanent United Kingdom resident (as defined in s.6). Exceptions are created by s.1(3)–(5) for surgery which is necessary for the physical or mental health of the woman, provided it is performed by a registered medical practitioner or, in connection with labour or the giving of birth, by such a practitioner or a registered midwife or a person who is in training with a view to qualifying as such a practitioner or midwife."

n.68: Section 47(2) of the Adults with Incapacity (Scotland) Act 2000 (asp **29.43** 4) is amended by the Mental Health (Care and Treatment) (Scotland) Act 2003 (asp 13), Sched. 4, para. 9(3) and Sched. 5, Part 1; and s.48(1) of the 2000 Act is repealed by the 2003 Act, Sched. 5, Part 1.

n.92: See also *Borwick v. Urquhart*, 2003 S.C.C.R. 243. **29.48**

n.93: In *Borwick v. Urquhart*, 2003 S.C.C.R. 243, it was held on appeal that where B (a male aged 28 years) had invited SB (a female aged 13 years) to a party, suggested to SB that she should give him money (which she did) so that he might buy her some alcohol, and bought her a half-bottle of vodka (which she consumed), he was guilty of an offence "very directly within the decision in *Khaliq*" (p.247C–D, para. 7). The court took the view that such a quantity of alcohol, which SB consumed in a very short period of time, was a substantial amount for an adult to consume over an evening "and plainly was likely to be damaging to a young girl" (p.247C, para. 7). According to the facts found, SB vomited and urinated over herself, and became comatose as a result of ingestion of the alcohol. The court found it unnecessary here to refer in any detail to discussion of the crime of "culpable and reckless conduct" in *Khaliq* or other cases: see p.247C, para. 7.

29.50 Section 105 (and indeed the remaining provisions) of the Mental Health (Scotland) Act 1984 is (and are) repealed by the Mental Health (Care and Treatment) (Scotland) Act 2003 (asp 13), Sched. 5, Part 1. Under the 2003 Act, however, s.315 provides:

> "(1) This section applies to a person (a 'relevant person') who—
>
>> (a) is an individual employed in, or contracted to provide services in or to, a hospital;
>> (b) not being the Scottish Ministers, is a manager of a hospital;
>> (c) provides care services; or
>> (d) is an individual who, otherwise than—
>>
>>> (i) by virtue of a contract of employment or other contract with any person; or
>>> (ii) as a volunteer for a voluntary organisation,
>>
>> provides care or treatment.
>
> (2) A relevant person who—
>
>> (a) whether under this Act or otherwise—
>>
>>> (i) is providing care or treatment; or
>>> (ii) purports to provide care or treatment,
>>
>> to a patient; and
>> (b) ill-treats, or wilfully neglects, that patient,
>
> shall be guilty of an offence."

The maximum penalties are six months imprisonment and a fine of the statutory maximum on summary conviction, and two years imprisonment and a fine on indictment: s.315(3). Under s.315(4) of the 2003 Act, provision of care services is to be construed in accordance with s.313(5)—which in turn refers to certain provisions of s.2 of the Regulation of Care (Scotland) Act 2001 (asp 8); for the meaning of "managers" in relation to a hospital, "hospital", and "voluntary organisation" see s.329(1) of the 2003 Act. "Patient" (under s.329(1) of that Act) means "a person who has, or appears to have, a mental disorder" ("mental disorder" being defined in s.328).

n.5: In line 6 of this footnote, after "mental disorder", the text in round **29.51** brackets should be deleted, and the following substituted: "which has the meaning assigned by s.328 of the Mental Health (Care and Treatment) (Scotland) Act 2003 (asp 13)". Section 47(2) of the Adults with Incapacity (Scotland) Act 2000 is amended by the 2003 Act, Sched. 4, para 9(3) and Sched. 5, Part 1; and s.87(1) of the 2000 Act is amended by the 2003 Act, Sched. 4, para. 9(5).

n.7: At the end of this footnote, after the words "against a police officer", **29.52** there should be added: ", and *Brouillard v. H.M. Advocate*, 2004 S.L.T. 727, opinion of the court at p.731C, para. 18".

The Genocide Act 1969 was repealed by s.1(3) of the International **29.53** Criminal Court (Scotland) Act 2001 (asp 13). The following, therefore, should be substituted for the text of para. 29.53, and accompanying footnote 15, of the 3rd edition.

"Genocide, crimes against humanity and war crimes. Section 1(1), which **29.53** must be read with section 8 (mental element), of the International Criminal Court (Scotland) Act 2001 (asp 13) makes it an offence for a person to commit genocide, a crime against humanity or a war crime where the acts involved are committed in Scotland or outwith the United Kingdom by a United Kingdom national or a United Kingdom resident (s.1(2): and see s.28(1) for the definitions of United Kingdom national (as amended by the British Overseas Territories Act 2002, s.2) and United Kingdom resident). (For such acts committed in other parts of the United Kingdom, see the International Criminal Court Act 2001, Part 5.) Acts which amount to genocide, a crime against humanity or a war crime are detailed in Schedule 1, under the titles 'Article 6', 'Article 7' and 'Article 8' respectively, these Articles being part of the 'Statute of the International Criminal Court, done at Rome on 17th July 1998' (see s.28(2)). Under section 2, it is an offence for, *inter alia*, a person to engage in conduct ancillary to an offence under section 1(1). Such offences can be tried only on indictment (s.3(2)); and under section 3(4), if a person is convicted of an offence under section 1 or section 2 and that offence involves murder (as understood in Scots law) or an offence ancillary (see s.7, for the meaning of this word under Scots law) to an offence involving murder, that person will be dealt with as for murder or the corresponding ancillary offence; a person convicted of any other offence under section 1(1) or section 2 will face a maximum penalty of 30 years in prison (s.3(5))."

The Geneva Conventions Act 1957 is further amended by the Interna- **29.54** tional Criminal Court Act 2001, s.70, such that, *inter alia*, grave breaches of the Schedule Conventions will be offences triable only on indictment; and a person convicted of such an offence involving murder will be dealt with as for the offence of murder, and a person convicted of any other such offence will be liable to a maximum prison sentence of 30 years. (**N.17** should accordingly be deleted.)

The view expressed judicially and otherwise in these paragraphs that the **29.57** required degree of negligence is that stated by Lord Justice-Clerk **29.58** Aitchison in *Paton v. H.M. Advocate*, 1936 J.C. 19 at 22, requires **29.61** qualification on account of the criticisms of Lord Aitchison's formulation expressed by Lords Osborne and Hamilton in *Transco Plc. v. H.M. Advocate*, 2004 S.C.C.R. 1 at 32F–33C, para. 4 and 48F–49C, para. 36 respectively. The Scottish courts today seem satisfied that the standard of negligence for involuntary culpable homicide and for a common law offence of the nature discussed in these paragraphs is the same—namely, recklessness or complete indifference to the consequences for a particular individual or, as appropriate, for individuals more generally.

29.58 **n.41:** *Cf. Mallin v. Clark*, 2002 S.C.C.R. 901, where a person detained under s.14 of the 1995 Act was held to have no duty (relative to a charge of 'culpable and reckless conduct') to disclose to police officers about to search him that he had an unprotected used syringe in his shirt pocket: the fact that he had not delivered himself of any active denial as to the existence of the syringe about his person, and the terms of s.14(9) of the 1995 Act were considered to be material issues by the court.

29.61 **n.57:** See also *Borwick v. Urquhart*, 2003 S.C.C.R. 243, which dealt with the supply of alcohol to a 13-year-old girl.

29.66 **n.83:** After "s.1(1)(a)" there should be inserted: "and (1A),"—to which s.1(1)(a) now refers—"as amended/inserted by the Sexual Offences Act 2003, Sched. 6, para. 22(a), (b)".

CHAPTER 30

STATUTORY OFFENCES CONCERNED WITH PERSONAL INJURY

n.23: The English test set out here was recently applied to "wheel spin- **30.04**
ning" (*i.e.* causing the driving wheels of a motor vehicle to spin by
operation of the engine and controls—but without causing actual
movement of the vehicle itself). The defendant was considered, on appeal
by the Crown, to have been "driving": see *D.P.P. v. Alderton* [2004]
R.T.R. 367. The court derived some support for its conclusion from the
Scottish case of *Hoy v. McFadyen*, 2000 S.C.C.R. 875 (see n.17 to para.
30.04).

In *Clark v. Higson*, 2004 S.L.T. 336, the test set out in the English case of **30.06**
Burns v. Currell [1963] 2 Q.B. 433, was applied as the correct one for
assessing whether what the appellant had been driving on a road was a
motor vehicle for the purposes of s.103(1)(b), driving it whilst disqualified, and s.143(1)(a) and (2), using it without insurance. Under
s.185(1), a motor vehicle means "a mechanically propelled vehicle
intended or adapted for use on roads". There was no doubt that the
vehicle in question was mechanically propelled and that it had not been
adapted for use on roads: indeed, it was described as an "off road" trail
bike. In particular, it had no lights, indicators or stop-lights. What the
appellant himself intended to do with the bike, and the use he might
normally have put it to, were not considered relevant considerations.
"The test is whether a reasonable person looking at [it] would say that
one of its uses would be use on the roads, in the sense that some general
use on the roads must be contemplated" (opinion of the court at p.340B,
para. 19), the application of the test depending upon the facts and cir-
cumstance of each case (see p.339L, para. 19). The court's conclusion was
that, in this case, the "trail bike" was indeed a motor vehicle: see also
D.P.P. v. Saddington [2001] R.T.R. 227 (status of a "go-ped").

In the text of this paragraph, at p.443, for "the Road Traffic Act 1998" **30.07**
read: "the Road Traffic Act 1988".

n.56: For the effect of the Land Reform (Scotland) Act 2003 (asp 2) on
s.30 of the Countryside (Scotland) Act 1967, see the 2003 Act (asp 2),
Sched. 2, paras 4, 6 and 7.

nn.75 and 76: See also *Planton v. D.P.P.* [2002] R.T.R. 107, where a
causeway linking an island to the mainland was in the circumstances held
not to be a public place.

For a case in which the high standard required under s.2A of the Road **30.08**
Traffic Act 1988 was not met on the evidence, see *R. v. Conteh* [2004]

R.T.R. 1 (C.A.). See also *R. v. Marchant; R. v. Muntz* [2004] R.T.R. 231 (C.A.), where it was held that a vehicle was not driven dangerously (relative to s.2A(2), (3)) if the only criticism of the driving of that vehicle related to the fact that the vehicle's inherent (and officially approved) design presented a danger of personal injury whenever it was driven on a road.

Mens rea, at least in the sense of the deliberateness of the driving in question, is not necessarily a completely irrelevant consideration in assessing whether the two-part test in s.2A has been satisfied: the primary consideration remains, however, the nature and quality of the driving. See *Young v. Barbour*, 2002 S.C.C.R. 84, where deliberate and protracted close-following of the complainer's car by an enraged driver was considered sufficient, since such driving (which distracted and alarmed the complainer, and might have led to the complainer's losing control of his vehicle with possibly fatal consequences) was considered to fall far below what would have been expected of a competent and careful driver, and to be obviously dangerous (in the estimation of such a driver).

30.09 **n.1:** Use (or causing or permitting the use) of a hand-held mobile telephone by a person when that person is driving (or such use by a person who is supervising the holder of a provisional licence who is driving) a motor vehicle is now a "construction and use" offence by virtue of the Road Vehicles (Construction and Use) (Amendment) (No. 4) Regulations 2003 (S.I. 2003 No. 2695), which inserts reg. 110 into the Road Vehicles (Construction and Use) Regulations 1986 (S.I. 1986 No. 1078).

30.13 With respect to burdens of proof on the accused, *cf.* now *Sheldrake v. D.P.P.* [2005] 1 A.C. 264 (H.L.).

30.15 The English common law defence of duress of circumstances seems to be available, in a suitable case, as a defence to a charge under s.5(1)(a) of the Road Traffic Act 1988: see *D.P.P. v. Tomkinson* [2001] R.T.R. 583.

n.37: It should be noted that s.6 of the Road Traffic Act 1988 has been replaced by new ss.6 and 6A–6E, and that ss.7, 9, 10 and 11 of that 1988 Act have been amended: see the Railways and Transport Safety Act 2003, Sched. 7, para. 1.

30.16 **n.46:** The Traffic Signs Regulations and General Directions 1994 (S.I. 1994 No. 1519) are revoked, and replaced, by the Traffic Signs Regulations and General Directions 2002 (S.I. 2002 No. 3113).

30.19 After 30.19, the following new paragraph should be inserted.

30.19A "*Shipping generally.* The Railways and Transport Safety Act 2003 creates the following offences based to some extent on "Road Traffic" models. (These offences do not apply to members of the armed forces acting in the course of their duties: see s.90(1).)

'**78.**—(1) This section applies to—

(a) a professional master of a ship,

    (b) a professional pilot of a ship, and

    (c) a professional seaman in a ship while on duty.

(2) A person to whom this section applies commits an offence if his ability to carry out his duties is impaired because of drink or drugs.

(3) A person to whom this section applies commits an offence if the proportion of alcohol in his breath, blood or urine exceeds the prescribed limit. [Under s.81(1), the "prescribed limit" is the same as presently pertains under the Road Traffic Act 1988.]

(4) For the purposes of this section a master, pilot or seaman is professional if (and only if) he acts as master, pilot or seaman in the course of a business or employment.

(5) Where a person is charged with an offence under this section in respect of the effect of a drug on his ability to carry out duties on a fishing vessel, it is a defence for him to show that—

    (a) he took the drug for a medicinal purpose on, and in accordance with, medical advice, or

    (b) he took the drug for a medicinal purpose and had no reason to believe that it would impair his ability to carry out his duties.

    79.—(1) This section applies to a professional seaman in a ship at a time when—

    (a) he is not on duty, but

    (b) in the event of an emergency he would or might be required by the nature or terms of his engagement or employment to take action to protect the safety of passengers.

(2) A person to whom this section applies commits an offence if his ability to take the action mentioned in subsection (1)(b) is impaired because of drink or drugs.

(3) A person to whom this subsection applies commits an offence if the proportion of alcohol in his breath, blood or urine exceeds the prescribed limit.

(4) For the purposes of this section a seaman is professional if (and only if) he acts as a seaman in the course of a business or employment.

(5) Where a person is charged with an offence under this section in respect of the effect of a drug on his ability to take action it is a defence for him to show that—

    (a) he took the drug for a medicinal purpose on, and in accordance with, medical advice, or

    (b) he took the drug for a medicinal purpose and had no reason to believe that it would impair his ability to take the action.

    80.—(1) This section applies to a person who—

    (a) is on board a ship which is under way,

    (b) is exercising, or purporting or attempting to exercise, a function in connection with the navigation of the ship, and

    (c) is not a person to whom section 78 or 79 applies.

(2) A person to whom this section applies commits an offence if his ability to exercise the functions mentioned in subsection (1)(b) is impaired because of drink or drugs.

(3) A person to whom this section applies commits an offence if the proportion of alcohol in his breath, blood or urine exceeds the prescribed limit.

(4) The Secretary of State may make regulations providing for subsection (3) not to apply in specified circumstances.

(5) Regulations under subsection (4) may make provision by reference, in particular—

(a) to the power of a motor;
(b) to the size of a ship;
(c) to location.'

The maximum penalty for an offence under these sections is, on conviction on indictment, two years imprisonment and a fine; and on summary conviction a fine of the statutory maximum: s.82. The provision of specimens relative to these offences is governed by s.83 (which adapts relevant provisions of the Road Traffic Act 1988). The statutory offence of "drunkenness on duty" under s.117 of the Merchant Shipping Act 1995 is replaced by these new offences: see s.87 of the 2003 Act. Definitions of various terms (such as "ship" [see also s.91], "navigation of a vessel", "pilot" and "drug" [which includes any intoxicant other than alcohol]) used in these new offences will be found in s.89."

30.23 After 30.23, the following new paragraph should be inserted.

30.23A "RAILWAYS AND TRANSPORT SAFETY ACT 2003. This act creates the following offences which are in general based on "Road Traffic" models. (These offences do not apply to members of the armed forces acting in the course of their duties: see s.101).

'**92.**—(1) A person commits an offence if—

(a) he performs an aviation function at a time when his ability to perform the function is impaired because of drink or drugs, or
(b) he carries out an activity which is ancillary to an aviation function at a time when his ability to perform the function is impaired because of drink or drugs.

(2) In this section "drug" includes any intoxicant other than alcohol.

(3) Section 94 defines "aviation function" and "ancillary activity" for the purposes of this Part.

93.—(1) A person commits an offence if—

(a) he performs an aviation function at a time when the proportion of alcohol in his breath, blood or urine exceeds the prescribed limit, or
(b) he carries out an activity which is ancillary to an aviation function at a time when the proportion of alcohol in his breath, blood or urine exceeds the prescribed limit.

(2) The prescribed limit of alcohol is (subject to subsection (3))—

    (a) in the case of breath, 9 microgrammes of alcohol in 100 millilitres,

    (b) in the case of blood, 20 milligrammes of alcohol in 100 millilitres, and

    (c) in the case of urine, 27 milligrammes of alcohol in 100 millilitres.

(3) In relation to the aviation function specified in section 94(1)(h) the prescribed limit is—

    (a) in the case of breath, 35 microgrammes of alcohol in 100 millilitres,

    (b) in the case of blood, 80 milligrammes of alcohol in 100 millilitres, and

    (c) in the case of urine, 107 milligrammes of alcohol in 100 millilitres.

(4) The Secretary of State may make regulations amending subsection (2) or (3).

(5) Section 94 defines "aviation function" and "ancillary activity" for the purposes of this Part.

94.—(1) For the purposes of this Part the following (and only the following) are aviation functions—

    (a) acting as a pilot of an aircraft during flight,

    (b) acting as flight navigator of an aircraft during flight,

    (c) acting as flight engineer of an aircraft during flight,

    (d) acting as flight radio-telephony operator of an aircraft during flight,

    (e) acting as a member of the cabin crew of an aircraft during flight,

    (f) attending the flight deck of an aircraft during flight to give or supervise training, to administer a test, to observe a period of practice or to monitor or record the gaining of experience,

    (g) acting as an air traffic controller in pursuance of a licence granted under or by virtue of any enactment (other than a licence granted to a student), and

    (h) acting as a licensed aircraft maintenance engineer.

(2) For the purposes of subsection (1)(h) a person acts as a licensed aircraft maintenance engineer if—

    (a) he issues a document relating to the maintenance, condition or use of an aircraft or equipment in reliance on a licence granted under or by virtue of an enactment relating to aviation, or

    (b) he carries out or supervises work on an aircraft or equipment with a view to, or in connection with, the issue by him of a document of the kind specified in paragraph (a).

(3) For the purposes of this Part a reference to an activity which is ancillary to an aviation function is a reference to anything which falls to be treated as such by virtue of subsections (4) to (6).

125

(4) An activity shall be treated as ancillary to an aviation function it if is undertaken—

    (a) by a person who has reported for a period of duty in respect of the function, and

    (b) as a requirement of, for the purpose of or in connection with the performance of the function during that period of duty.

(5) A person who in accordance with the terms of an employment or undertaking holds himself ready to perform an aviation function if called upon shall be treated as carrying out an activity ancillary to the function.

(6) Where a person sets out to perform an aviation function, anything which he does by way of preparing to perform the function shall be treated as an activity ancillary to it.

(7) For the purposes of this Part it is immaterial whether a person performs a function or carries out an activity in the course of an employment or trade or otherwise. . . .'

See also s.102 for territorial considerations. The maximum penalty for an offence under s.92 or 93 is, on conviction on indictment, two years imprisonment and a fine; and on summary conviction, a fine of the statutory maximum: s.95. The provision of specimens relative to these offences is governed by s.96 (which adapts relevant provisions of the Road Traffic Act 1988."

30.26 Section 1(3)(b) of the Firearms Act 1968 is amended by s.39(2) of the Anti-social Behaviour Act 2003, such that after the words "air pistol" there is added the phrase: "which does not fall within section 5(1) and which is".

30.30 After s.5(1)(ae), the following new paragraph must be added, by virtue of s.39(3) of the Anti-social Behaviour Act 2003:

"(af) any air rifle, air gun or air pistol which uses, or is designed or adapted for use with, a self-contained gas cartridge system;".

It should be noted, however, that the addition of paragraph (af) is qualified by the following subsections of s.39 of the 2003 Act:

"(4) If at the time when subsection (3) comes into force a person has in his possession an air rifle, air gun or air pistol of the kind described in section 5(1)(af) of the Firearms Act 1968 (inserted by subsection (3) above)—

    (a) section 5(1) of that Act shall not prevent the person's continued possession of that air rifle, air gun or air pistol.

    (b) section 1 of that Act shall apply, and

    (c) a chief officer of police may not refuse to grant or renew, and may not revoke or partially revoke, a firearm certificate under Part II of that Act on the ground that the person does not have a good reason for having the air rifle, air gun or air pistol in his possession.

(5) But subsection (4)(a) to (c) shall not apply to the possession in any circumstances described in section 8 of that Act (authorised dealing).

n.35 and n.39: The penalties referred to in these notes have changed as a result of ss.287 and 288 of the Criminal Justice Act 2003. In particular, offences under s.5(1)(a), (ab), (aba), (ac), (ad), (ae), (af) and (c), and under s.5(1A)(a) of the Firearms Act 1968 are now triable only on indictment with a maximum penalty of 10 years in prison and a fine: in addition, persons, who were aged at least 16 at the time of the commission of the offence and who have been convicted of any of these offences must be sentenced to a minimum period of imprisonment or detention unless the sentencing court is of opinion that there are exceptional circumstances relating to the offence or the offender which justify its not imposing that minimum. In Scotland, the minimum period required is, in the case of an offender aged at least 21 when he committed the offence, five years, and, in the case of an offender aged under 21 at that time, three years. (The Secretary of State has power under s.291 of the 2003 Act to amend these minimum sentence provisions, such that they would apply only to those aged at least 18 at the time of commission of the offence.) Offences under s.5(1)(b) and 5(1A)(b) carry maximum penalties, on summary conviction, of six months and a fine of the statutory maximum, and, on conviction on indictment, 10 years and a fine.

[Text on p.467] Section 1(4) of the Firearms (Amendment) Act 1988 has been extended by the Anti-social Behaviour Act 2003, s.39(6), such that the Secretary of State now has power to apply the provisions of the Firearms Act 1968 relating to prohibited weapons and ammunition to "any air rifle, air gun or air pistol which is not for the time being specified in that subsection [*i.e.* s.5(1) of the 1968 Act] but appears to him to be specially dangerous".

n.49: The reference for the European directive here should read: "No. 91/ **30.33** 477 EEC (O.J., L, vol. 34, No. 256, 12.09.91, p.51)".

As a result of amendment by s.37(1) of the Anti-social Behaviour Act **30.35** 2003, s.19 of the Firearms Act 1968 now reads as follows:

"A person commits an offence if without lawful authority or reasonable excuse (the proof whereof lies on him) he has with him in a public place—

    (a) a loaded shotgun,
    (b) an air weapon (whether loaded or not),
    (c) any other firearm (whether loaded or not) together with ammunition suitable for use in that firearm, or
    (d) an imitation firearm."

Section 22 of the Firearms Act 1968 has been amended by s.38(2) of the **30.41** Anti-social Behaviour Act 2003, such that in subsection (4) of s.22 "seventeen" is substituted for "fourteen", and subsection (5) is to be omitted. Consequently, in the text paragraph beginning "Section 22(4) does not apply", the number "14" should be replaced by "17", and the words "under either subsection" should be read as: "under that subsection".

n.83: Section 23(2) is also amended by the Anti-social Behaviour Act 2003, s.38(3)(a): and s.38(3)(b) of the 2003 Act adds the following subsections after s.23(2):

> "(3) It is not an offence under section 22(4) of this Act for a person of or over the age of fourteen to have with him an air weapon or ammunition on private premises with the consent of the occupier.
>
> (4) But where a person has with him an air weapon on premises in circumstances where he would be prohibited from having it with him but for subsection (3), it is an offence for him to use it for firing any missile beyond these premises."

The maximum penalty for an offence under s.23(4) is, on summary conviction, a fine of level 3 on the standard scale: see Sched. 6, Part I of the Firearms Act 1968, entry for s.23(4), as inserted by s.38(5)(d) of the 2003 Act.

In the text paragraph beginning "Section 24(4) makes it an offence", as a result of amendment made by s.38(4) of the Anti-social Behaviour Act 2003, for the number "14", in both places where it appears, the number "17" should be substituted.

30.48 **n.59:** In *McAuley v. Mulholland*, 2003 S.C.C.R. 326, the observation (quoted in n.59) of Lord Justice-General Hope in *Stewart v. Friel*, 1995 S.C.C.R. 492 at 495D, was qualified to the extent that a knife (the blade of which was about two inches in length), which had a non-operational device to lock the blade in the open position when the blade was extended, was considered to be a folding pocket knife, since it met the criteria proffered by the English Court of Appeal (in *Harris v. D.P.P.* [1993] 1 W.L.R. 82 at 87F), namely that the blade should be readily and immediately foldable at all times, simply by the folding process, and that the knife could be carried in a pocket. (In *Stewart v. Friel*, by way of contrast, the blade of the knife in question had been of such construction that it automatically locked in the extended position when the blade was opened.) It is, therefore, not so much a question of whether the knife at issue has a locking device relative to the blade, but rather of whether that device is in working order at the material time: the ease with which such a non-operational device may be restored to working order was not considered in the case.

n.60: A person who purchases an article to which s.49 of the Criminal Law (Consolidation) (Scotland) Act 1995 would apply, and is in the course of taking his purchase home, has "good reason" for having it with him in a public place, since otherwise "the Act [would be] being interpreted in a manner which would render illegal the purchase of items to which it applied, which plainly it does not do": *McGuire v. Higson*, 2003 S.C.C.R. 440, opinion of the court at p.443D.

n.61: "For use at work" covers the person who has a relevant article with him in a public place only if he necessarily requires to take that article to and from his place of work. Where, therefore, an appellant was required to leave craft knives at his place of work but claimed that they were discovered by the police in his pocket (in a public place) because he had forgotten they were there, it was held that the statutory defence under s.49(5)(a) was not available to him: *Robertson v. Higson*, 2003 S.C.C.R. 685 (in which *Douglas v. McFadyen*, 1999 S.C.C.R. 884, was distinguished). Lord Marnoch, in his opinion (at p.687A–B, para. 5), observed that the specific cases mentioned in s.49(5) may be intended "more as examples of the 'good reason' defence referred to in subsection (4) rather than as anything essentially different from that defence". (*Cf.* what is stated in n.60 to para. 30.48 of the 3rd edition; see also *L. v. D.P.P.* [2002] 1 Cr.App.R. 420 at 423, para. 5.)

n.76: The Criminal Justice Act 1988 (Offensive Weapons) Order 1988 **30.52** (S.I. 1988 No. 2019) has been amended by the Criminal Justice Act 1988 (Offensive Weapons) Amendment (Scotland) Order 2002 (S.S.I. 2002 No. 323), art. 2.

CHAPTER 31

OFFENCES AGAINST CHILDREN

31.02 The words "assaults," and "assaulted," must now be deleted from s.12(1) of the Children and Young Persons (Scotland) Act 1937: see the Criminal Justice (Scotland) Act 2003 (asp 7), s.51(5)(a)".

31.07 The words "an assault on a child, or" and "An assault, or other", and the comma following "ill-treatment", must now be removed from the text of this paragraph (on p.493 of the 3rd edition) in view of amendments to s.12 of the Children and Young Persons (Scotland) Act 1937 made by s.51(5) of the Criminal Justice (Scotland) Act 2003 (asp 7): see entry for para. 31.02, above.

31.08 Section 12(7) of the Children and Young Persons (Scotland) Act 1937 has been repealed by s.51(5)(b) of the Criminal Justice (Scotland) Act 2003 (asp 7): on chastisement of children, see the entry for para. 29.38, above.

31.10 **n.54:** With respect to s.18 of the Children and Young Persons (Scotland) Act 1937, for the present reference there to "under sixteen" the Scottish Ministers may substitute (by Statutory Instrument) "such other higher age or ages as they consider appropriate": Smoking, Health and Social Care (Scotland) Act 2005 (asp 13), s.9.

31.12 and As the formatting of these two paragraphs (in the 3rd edition) had gone
31.13 wrong leading to the apparent reproduction of spurious provisions of the Criminal Law (Consolidation) (Scotland) Act 1995, the paragraphs are set out below as they should have appeared. (The relative footnotes will be found on pp.495–496 of the 3rd edition.)

31.12 *"Criminal Law (Consolidation) (Scotland) Act 1995.* This Act contains a number of sexual offences in connection with persons under 16 years of age. These include the following which replace sections 13 and 14 of the 1937 Act:

4. It is an offence for any person having parental responsibilities (within the meaning of the Children (Scotland) Act 1995) in relation to, or having charge or care of, a girl under 16 to cause or encourage her seduction, or unlawful sexual intercourse with or prostitution of her, or the commission upon her of an indecent assault or an offence against section 6 of the Criminal Law (Consolidation) (Scotland) Act 1995.[56] As the latter section deals with lewd practices committed upon consenting girls aged between 12 and 16, 'indecent assault' in relation to girls under 12 is probably meant to include lewd practices whether or not any actual assault is involved.

A person is deemed to have caused or encouraged the seduction, etc. of a girl 'if he has knowingly allowed her to consort with, or to enter or continue in the employment of, any prostitute or person of known immoral character.'[57] 'Knowingly allows' refers to 'such a permission as can be deemed to be causing or encouraging', and mere negligence in controlling the child's activities is not sufficient.[58]

5. It is an offence for any person having parental responsibilities **31.13** (within the meaning of the Children (Scotland) Act 1995) in relation to or having charge or care of a child or young person between four and 16 to allow him or her 'to reside in or frequent a brothel.'[59]"

After this paragraph, the following new paragraph should be inserted: **31.14**

"*Protection of Children (Scotland) Act 2003 (asp 5)*. Under section 10 **31.15** (which receives minor amendment by virtue of section 24(1) of the Criminal Procedure (Amendment) (Scotland) Act 2004 (asp 5)) of this Act, if an individual is convicted of an offence against a 'child' (*i.e.* a person under the age of 18 years: see s.18(1)), the court in question must, if that offence is a relevant one (as defined in Schedule 1), or may, where the offence is not a relevant one, 'propose to refer' the case of that individual to the Scottish Ministers. A court's ability to so refer such a case is qualified, however, in that if the individual was under 18 at the time of commission of the offence, the court may propose to refer the case only if satisfied that he is likely to commit a further offence against a child; if that individual was over 18 at that time, the court must not refer the case if satisfied that the individual is unlikely to commit a further such offence: see s.10(3), (4). If the Scottish Ministers receive such a reference, they must (under s.10(7)) include the individual in the list they maintain (under s.1(1) of the Act) of persons considered unsuitable to work with children. The effect of inclusion in that list is that the individual in question is disqualified from working with children (see ss.17 and 18(1)). It is an offence (see s.11(1), (3) which are subject to s.11(6)) for a person to apply for, offer to do, accept or do any work in a 'child care position' (as interpreted in Schedule 2) if he is disqualified from working with children, or for an organisation to offer him (or fail to remove him from) such work if he is so disqualified—maximum penalty, on summary conviction, six months in prison and a fine of the statutory maximum, or, on conviction on indictment, five years in prison and a fine. Specific defences are set out in subsections (2) and (4) of section 11."

"*Protection of Children and Prevention of Sexual Offences (Scotland) Act* **31.16** *2005 (asp 9)*. This Act contains a number of provisions intended to protect children of various ages from sexual harm. These include the following:

'**1.**—(1) A person ("A") commits an offence if—

    (a) having met or communicated with another person ("B") on at least one earlier occasion, A—

        (i) intentionally meets B;
        (ii) travels, in any part of the world, with the intention of meeting B in any part of the world; or

(iii) makes arrangements, in any part of the world, with the intention of meeting B in any part of the world, for B to travel in any part of the world;

(b) at the time, A intends to engage in unlawful sexual activity involving B or in the presence of B—

(i) during or after the meeting; and
(ii) in any part of the world;

(c) B is—

(i) aged under 16; or
(ii) a constable;

(d) A does not reasonably believe that B is 16 or over; and
(e) at least one of the following is the case—

(i) the meeting or communication on an earlier occasion referred to in paragraph (a) (or, if there is more than one, one of them) has a relevant Scottish connection;
(ii) the meeting referred to in sub-paragraph (i) of that paragraph or, as the case may be, the travelling referred to in sub-paragraph (ii) of that paragraph or the making of arrangements referred to in sub-paragraph (iii) of that paragraph, has a relevant Scottish connection;
(iii) A is British citizen or resident in the United Kingdom.

(2) In subsection (1) above—

(a) the reference to A's having met or communicated with B is a reference to A's having met B in any part of the world or having communicated with B by any means from or in any part of the world (and irrespective of where B is in the world); and
(b) a meeting or travelling or making of arrangements has a relevant Scottish connection if it, or any part of it, takes place in Scotland; and a communication has such a connection if it is made from or to or takes place in Scotland.

(3) For the purposes of subsection (1)(b) above, it is not necessary to allege or prove that A intended to engage in a specific activity.
(4) A person guilty of an offence under this section is liable—

(a) on summary conviction, to imprisonment for a term not exceeding 6 months or a fine not exceeding the statutory maximum or both;
(b) on conviction on indictment, to imprisonment for a term not exceeding 10 years or a fine or both.

(5) ...

9.—(1) A person ("A") commits an offence if—

(a) A intentionally obtains for himself or herself the sexual services of another person ("B");
(b) before obtaining those services, A—

(i) makes or promises payment for those services to B or to a third person; or

(ii) knows that another person has made or promised such a payment; and

(c) either—

(i) B is aged under 18, and A does not reasonably believe that B is aged 18 or over; or

(ii) B is aged under 13.

(2) In subsection (1)(b) above, "payment" means any financial advantage, including the discharge of an obligation to pay or the provision of goods or services (including sexual services) gratuitously or at a discount.

(3) For the purposes of subsections (1) and (2) above, "sexual services" are—

(a) the performance of sexual activity; or

(b) the performance of any other activity that a reasonable person would, in all the circumstances, consider to be for the purpose of providing sexual gratification,

and a person's sexual services are obtained where what is obtained is the performance of such an activity by the person.

(4) A person guilty of an offence under this section in respect of a person aged 16 or over is liable—

(a) on summary conviction, to imprisonment for a term not exceeding 6 months or a fine not exceeding the statutory maximum or both;

(b) on conviction on indictment, to imprisonment for a term not exceeding 7 years.

(5) A person guilty of an offence under this section in respect of a person aged under 16 is liable—

(a) on summary conviction, to imprisonment for a term not exceeding 6 months or a fine not exceeding the statutory maximum or both;

(b) on conviction on indictment, to imprisonment for a term not exceeding 14 years.

10.—(1) A person ("A") commits an offence if—

(a) A intentionally causes or incites another person ("B") to become a provider of sexual services, or to be involved in pornography, in any part of the world; and

(b) either—

(i) B is aged under 18, and A does not reasonably believe that B is aged 18 or over; or

(ii) B is aged under 13.

(2) A person guilty of an offence under this section is liable—

(a) on summary conviction, to imprisonment for a term not exceeding 6 months or a fine not exceeding the statutory maximum or both;

(b) on conviction on indictment, to imprisonment for a term not exceeding 14 years.

11.—(1) A person ("A") commits an offence if—

    (a) A intentionally controls any of the activities of another person ("B") relating to B's provision of sexual services or involvement in pornography in any part of the world; and

    (b) either—

        (i) B is aged under 18, and A does not reasonably believe that B is aged 18 or over; or

        (ii) B is aged under 13.

(2) A person guilty of an offence under this section is liable—

    (a) on summary conviction, to imprisonment for a term not exceeding 6 months or a fine not exceeding the statutory maximum or both;

    (b) on conviction on indictment, to imprisonment for a term not exceeding 14 years.

12.—(1) A person ("A") commits an offence if—

    (a) A intentionally arranges or facilitates the—

        (i) provision of sexual services in any part of the world by; or

        (ii) involvement in pornography in any part of the world of,

    another person ("B"); and

    (b) either—

        (i) B is aged under 18, and A does not reasonably believe that B is aged 18 or over; or

        (ii) B is aged under 13.

(2) A person guilty of an offence under this section is liable—

    (a) on summary conviction, to imprisonment for a term not exceeding 6 months or a fine not exceeding the statutory maximum or both;

    (b) on conviction on indictment, to imprisonment for a term not exceeding 14 years.'

Under section 13 of the 2005 Act, definitions are given of various expressions used in the above provisions: in particular, 'a person is involved in pornography if an indecent image of that person is recorded; and similar expressions, and "pornography" are to be construed accordingly' (see s.13(1)); and, 'provider of sexual services' means 'a person ("B") who, on at least one occasion and whether or not compelled to do so, offers or provides B's sexual services to another person in return for payment or a promise of payment to B or a third party; and "provision of sexual services" is to be construed accordingly' (see s.13(2), 'payment' and 'sexual services' being construed as they are (*mutatis mutandis*) for the purposes of section 9(2) and (3) above (see s.13(3) and (4)). 'Sexual activity' is defined in section 19 of the 2005 Act as: 'an activity that a reasonable person would, in all the circumstances, consider to be sexual; and a reference to engaging in sexual activity includes ... (a) a reference to an attempt or conspiracy to engage in such activity; and (b) a reference to aiding, abetting, counselling, procuring or inciting another person to engage in such activity.' With respect to proceedings for other common law or statutory charges which might be brought in circumstances similar to those in the 2005 Act, section 14 of that Act provides that sections 9 to 12 (above) do not exempt any person from such proceedings; but section 13(5) provides: 'A person does not commit an offence under section 10, 11 or 12 by reason only of doing something within section 52(1) or 52A(1) of the Civic Government (Scotland) Act 1982 (c.45).' (For sections 52 and 52A of the 1982 Act, see paragraphs 41.21 and 41.22, below.)"

CHAPTER 32

CRUELTY TO ANIMALS

32.04 The words "or, under certain circumstances, to coursing or hunting" at the end of the text of this paragraph should be omitted (whilst retaining n.23), since they refer to the exceptions stated in s.1(3)(b) of the Protection of Animals (Scotland) Act 1912, s.1(3)(b) having been repealed by the Protection of Wild Mammals (Scotland) Act 2002 (asp 6), Sched., para. 3.

n.23: The text of this note should be amended to read: "Section 1(3)(a)".

32.09 n.33: It should be noted that certain parts of ss.1, 3, 5 and 8 of the Wildlife and Countryside Act 1981 are repealed by the Criminal Justice (Scotland) Act 2003 (asp 7), Sched. 5; that s.21 (maximum penalties) of the 1981 Act is amended by Sched. 3, para. 6, to the Criminal Justice (Scotland) Act 2003 (asp 7); and that ss.1, 2, 3, 5, 9, 10, 11 and 21 of the 1981 Act are significantly amended, or further amended, by Sched. 6 to the Nature Conservation (Scotland) Act 2004 (asp 6).

n.34: The Wild Mammals (Protection) Act 1996 is amended by the Protection of Wild Mammals (Scotland) Act 2002 (asp 6), Sched., para. 6, such that s.2(b) of the 1996 Act now reads:

"A person shall not be guilty of an offence under this Act by reason of—

. . .

    (b) the killing in a reasonably swift and humane manner of any such wild mammal [as defined in s.3] if he shows that the wild mammal had been injured or taken in the course of either lawful shooting, hunting, coursing or lawful pest control activity;".

n.36: Subsections (4) to (9) of s.8 of the Protection of Badgers Act 1992 (which relate to exceptions—relative to the hunting of foxes with hounds—to the offence under s.3 of interfering with badger setts) are repealed by the Protection of Wild Mammals (Scotland) Act 2002 (asp 6), Sched., para. 5, in view of the terms of that 2002 Act (see para. 32.10, below). Sections 3, 6 and 8 of the 1992 Act are also amended by the Nature Conservation (Scotland) Act 2004 (asp 6), Sched., para. 26.

The penalties for the offences mentioned in the text, *i.e.* s.2(1)(a) (cruelly ill-treating a badger), (b) (use of badger tongs), and (c) (digging for a badger), have been altered by the Nature Conservation (Scotland) Act 2004 (asp 6), Sched., para. 26, which adds a new subsection (1b) to s.12, under which on conviction on indictment for any such offence, the maximum penalty is three years in prison and a fine.

Following the text of para. 32.09, the following new paragraph should be added:

"Section 1 of the Protection of Wild Mammals (Scotland) Act 2002 (asp **32.10** 6) creates the following offences:

'(1) A person who deliberately hunts a wild mammal [which includes an escaped wild mammal or one which has been released from captivity, as also any mammal which is living wild, but does not include a rabbit or rodent: s.10(1)] with a dog [or dogs: s.10(1)] commits an offence.

(2) It is an offence for an owner [the term not including a creditor in a heritable security who is not in possession: s.10(1)] or occupier [the term including any person who has control: s10(1)] of land knowingly to permit another person to enter or use it to commit an offence under subsection (1).

(3) It is an offence for an owner of, or person having responsibility for, a dog knowingly to permit another person to use it to commit an offence under subsection (1).'

'Hunting' is stated in the Act as including 'to search for or course' (see s.10(1)), but the term is otherwise undefined. In *Fraser v. Adams*, 2005 S.C.C.R. 54 (Sh.Ct.) at 57D, para. 8, it was held by the sheriff that the activity struck at by the legislation 'is the diligent pursuit of a wild mammal with dogs and in terms of section 10(1) that includes "searching"', and that it did not matter whether that activity was 'carried out on foot, by motor vehicle or on horseback'.

There are, however, a number of complex exceptions to the offence, and these are set out in the Act as follows:

'2.—(1) A person who is, or who has the permission of, the owner or lawful occupier of the land on which the stalking, searching ["searching" is not in fact referred to in this provision] or flushing referred to in this subsection takes place does not commit an offence under section 1(1) by using a dog under control [as defined in s.10(4)] to stalk a wild mammal, or flush it from cover (including an enclosed space within rocks, or other secure cover) above ground for the purpose of—

(a) protecting livestock, ground-nesting birds, timber, fowl (including wild fowl), game birds or crops from attack by wild mammals;
(b) providing food for consumption by a living creature, including a person;
(c) protecting human health;
(d) preventing the spread of disease;
(e) controlling the number of a pest species [which, until modified by the Scottish Ministers, is confined to foxes, hares, mink, stoats and weasels: s.10(1),(2)]; or
(f) controlling the number of a particular species to safeguard the welfare of that species,

but only if that person acts to ensure that, once the target wild mammal is found or emerges from cover, it is shot, or killed by a bird of prey, once it is safe to do so.

(2) Where a person is using a dog in connection with the despatch of a wild mammal, being of a pest species, with the intention of flushing the wild mammal from cover or from below ground in order that it may be shot or killed by lawful means, that person does not commit an offence under section 1(1) by virtue of the dog killing that wild mammal in the course of that activity.

(3) A person does not commit an offence under section 1(1) by using a dog under control to flush a fox or mink from below ground or by using a dog under control to flush a fox from an enclosed space within rocks or other secure cover above ground, but only if that person—

(a) does so for one or more of the purposes specified in paragraphs (a) to (f) of subsection (1);

(b) takes reasonable steps to ensure that the fox or mink is flushed as soon as reasonably possible after it is located and shot as soon as possible after it is flushed;

(c) takes all reasonable steps to prevent injury to the dog including steps to prevent the dog becoming trapped underground and, it if does become trapped underground, steps to ensure it is rescued as soon as is practicable;

(d) is in possession of a firearm for which the person holds a valid firearms or shotgun certificate; and

(e) either—

(i) is the owner or lawful occupier of the land on which the activity takes place; or

(ii) has the permission of the owner or lawful occupier of that land to undertake that activity.

3. Where an occupier of land (or a person acting with the occupier's permission) is using a bird of prey, or a firearm or shotgun, for the purpose of sport, that person does not commit an offence under section 1(1) by using a dog under control to stalk a wild mammal, or flush it from cover above ground, for the purpose of providing quarry for the sport, but only if—

(a) that person acts to ensure that, once a wild mammal is found or emerges from cover, it is shot, or killed by a bird of prey, as soon as possible;

(b) where a firearm or shotgun is used, that person holds a valid firearms or shotgun certificate or a valid visitor's firearm or shot gun permit; and

(c) where a wild mammal is shot and injured, that person takes all reasonable steps to retrieve it and, once retrieved, to kill it as humanely as possible.

4.—(1) An authorised person does not commit an offence under section 1(1) by using a dog to search for, or catch, a wild mammal if that person does so with no intention of harming the wild mammal.
(2) In subsection (1) "authorised person" means—

(a) an officer of a local authority acting in pursuance of any function of the local authority;
(b) any person authorised by such an officer to search for, or catch, a wild mammal; and
(c) a constable.

5.—(1) A person does not commit an offence under section 1(1) by using a dog under control in order to—

(a) retrieve a hare which has been shot;
(b) locate a wild mammal which has escaped, or been released, from captivity (but only if that person acts to ensure that the mammal is captured or shot once it is located); or
(c) retrieve or locate a wild mammal which that person reasonably believes is seriously injured or orphaned (but only if that person acts to ensure that the mammal, once located, is captured, treated or killed as humanely as possible in order to relieve its suffering).

(2) Subsection (1)(b) does not apply if the mammal—

(a) is a fox or hare;
(b) is a deer, boar or mink, unless it has escaped from a farm or zoo; or
(c) has been raised or released for the purpose of being hunted.

(3) A person who is an occupier of land (or is acting with the occupier's permission) does not commit an offence under section 1(1) by using a dog under control below ground on that land in order to locate a fox which that person reasonably believes is orphaned [*i.e.* a fox which is too young to survive on its own, its mother being dead: s.10(1)], but only if that person takes reasonable steps to ensure that the fox, once located, is despatched by a single dog or otherwise killed as humanely as possible.

6.—(1) A person does not commit an offence under section 1(1) by participating in an excepted activity.
(2) For the purposes of subsection (1), an "excepted activity" is an activity excepted under any provision of this Act, and such other activity as the Scottish Ministers may, by order made by statutory instrument, specify.'

Under section 10(4), a dog is 'under control' if the person responsible for it is able to direct its activity by 'physical contact or verbal or audible command', or 'the dog is carrying out a series of actions appropriate to the activity undertaken, having been trained to do so'. The maximum penalty for an offence under section 1 is, on summary conviction, six months in prison and a fine of level 5 on the standard scale (s.8(1)): in addition, a court may make an order for the care or disposal of a dog which was in the custody of the offender at the time when the offence was committed or which has been in his custody at any time since then, or it may make an order disqualifying the offender from having custody of any dog for such period as it thinks fit, or it may make both such orders (s.9(1)).

In *Fraser v. Adams*, 2005 S.C.C.R. 54 (Sh.Ct.), the accused was acquitted of a charge under section 1(1) of the 2002 Act, in that the sheriff found on the facts that although the accused had deliberately searched for foxes with dogs, those dogs were under his control, he had permission to be on the land where the searching took place, and all other requisite conditions of section 2(1) relative to the exception allowed by the Act had been met. It appears that a fox had been flushed from cover by the dogs; but the sheriff rejected the submission of the prosecutor that, since that fox had not been shot (indeed it had escaped), this showed that the accused had not acted to ensure that it was shot once it had emerged from cover—the submission having ignored the statutory caveat that it was to be shot in those circumstances 'once it [was] safe to do so'. The sheriff did, however, emphasise (at p.65B–C, paras 52 and 53) that stalking, searching, and flushing with dogs—to fall within an excepted activity under the relevant provisions of the Act—would require to be accompanied by 'realistic, and one would expect, effective arrangements for the shooting of pest species', given that the main intent of the legislation was the humane despatch of target or pest species by shooting."

CHAPTER 33

RAPE

[The following is to be substituted for the text of chapter 33 in the 3rd edition.]

Rape is committed when a male person has sexual intercourse with a **33.01** female person without her consent.[1] Prior case law[2] and text writings,[3] which required that the intercourse be obtained by force (or threats of force) and (correlatively) in the face of such physical resistance as the complainer could muster, have been set aside in a recent restatement of the crime.[4] Physical force and resistance may, of course, be present in a particular case[5]; but such factors are simply evidence of lack of consent on the part of the complainer: they are not essential elements of the

---

[1] *Lord Advocate's Reference (No. 1 of 2001)* 2002 S.L.T. 466, court of seven judges, the majority (Lords Marnoch and McCluskey dissenting) preferring the account of rape given (*obiter*) by the judges in *Wm Fraser* (1847) Ark. 280, to that accepted by the majority in *Chas. Sweenie* (1858) 3 Irv. 109.

[2] In particular, *Chas. Sweenie* (1858) 3 Irv. 109, which is overruled by *Lord Advocate's Reference (No. 1 of 2001)*, 2002 S.L.T. 466.

[3] Hume, i, 301–303; Burnett, p.101; Alison, i, 209; Macdonald, p.119.

[4] *Lord Advocate's Reference (No. 1 of 2001)*, 2002 S.L.T. 466. The rationale and implications of the "correction" of the law in this case (by a majority of five of the seven judges present at the appeal) have not been received without criticism: see, *e.g.* P.W. Ferguson, "The Definition of Rape", 2002 S.L.T. (News) 163; James Chalmers, "How (Not) to Reform the Law of Rape" (2002) 6 Edin.L.R. 388; Christopher Gane, "In the courts: redefining rape" (2002) 7 S.L.P.Q. 204; but the decision itself accords well with the conclusions of the European Court of Human Rights in *M.C. v. Bulgaria*, 15 B.H.R.C. 627 (Applic. No. 39272/98; December 4, 2003), where it was held that *de facto* insistence (since art. 152(1) of the Bulgarian Criminal Code did not so require) upon acceptance of resistance on the part of the victim as a prerequisite of prosecution of an alleged rape constituted a violation of Arts 3 and 8 of the European Convention on Human Rights (see the Human Rights Act 1998, Sched. 1). The Court based its conclusions on trends evident in the criminal law and practice of many different countries, and, *inter alia*, stated at paras 158–159: "In common law jurisdictions, in Europe and elsewhere, any reference to physical force has been removed from legislation and/or case law (see paras 98, 100 and 138–147, above in relation to the United Kingdom [which did not include any account of Scots law], Ireland, the United States of America and other jurisdictions). Irish law explicitly states that consent cannot be inferred from lack of resistance ... In most European countries influenced by the continental legal tradition the definition of rape contains references to the use of violence or threats of violence by the perpetrator. It is significant, however, that in case law and legal theory lack of consent, not force, is seen as the constituent element of the offence of rape ...". The restatement or correction of the law in *Lord Advocate's Reference (No. 1 of 2001)*, *supra*, has been considered to comply with Art. 7 of the European Convention on Human Rights, and with the jurisprudence of the European Court of Human Rights, in respect of what is allowable by way of gradual clarification of the law: see *H.M. Advocate v. H.*, 2002 S.L.T. 1380, *per* Lord Maclean at p.1381E–I, paras 4–5.

[5] See, *e.g. H.M. Advocate v. Hercus*, 2004 S.C.C.R. 140.

141

crime.[6] It is an essential element, however, that there be an absence of an honest belief, on the part of the male, that the female consented to the intercourse,[7] the *mens rea* of the crime being knowledge that she did not consent, or recklessness as to whether she consented.[8] In the *Lord Advocate's Reference (No. 1 of 2001)*,[9] the view was advanced (in the absence of legal debate on the matter) that "recklessness" was to be understood in a "subjective" sense—*i.e.* in the sense of the accused's failing to think about, or being indifferent to, whether the complainer was consenting.[10] Mistaken but genuine belief that the complainer was a consenting party, even if not based on reasonable grounds is, therefore, a defence.[11] It is not a defence that at the material time the female person was the male person's wife.[12]

---

[6] *Lord Advocate's Reference (No. 1 of 2001)*, 2002 S.L.T. 466, L.J.-G. Cullen at pp.472I–J, para. 25 (where he quotes with approval from Lord Cockburn's opinion in *Wm Fraser* (1847) Ark. 280, at 308) and 474A, para. 31.

[7] *Meek v. H.M. Advocate*, 1982 S.C.C.R. 613 at 618 *per* L.J.-G. Emslie; *Jamieson v. H.M. Advocate (No. 1)*, 1994 S.C.C.R. 181 at 186A *per* L.J.-G. Hope; *Lord Advocate's Reference (No. 1 of 2001)*, 2002 S.L.T. 466 at 473C-G, para. 28 *per* L.J.-G. Cullen.

[8] *Lord Advocate's Reference (No. 1 of 2001)*, 2002 S.L.T. 466 at 476B, para. 44 *per* L.J.-G. Cullen. The burden of proving *mens rea* rests, of course, on the Crown: *McKearney v. H.M. Advocate*, 2004 S.C.C.R. 251; *Cinci v. H.M. Advocate*, 2004 S.C.C.R. 267. Where physical force is used by the accused against the victim, *mens rea* may be inferred from the use of such force; but where no force is used and the victim, though non-consenting, provides little or nothing to indicate her lack of consent to the accused, the trial judge will have to direct the jury as to the *mens rea* which the Crown must prove and may also have to direct them to consider whether the accused might have had an honest belief in the complainer's consent, even (perhaps) if a proper basis for such a belief has not emerged from the evidence at the trial: *McKearney v. H.M. Advocate*, 2004 S.C.C.R. 251 at 254E-F, para. 12 *per* L.J.-C. Gill; *cf.* Lord McCluskey at p.265D, para. 35. See also *Gordon v. H.M. Advocate*, 2004 S.C.C.R. 641 and *Spendiff v. H.M. Advocate*, 2005 S.C.C.R. 522.

[9] 2002 S.L.T. 466.

[10] *ibid.*, L.J.-G. Cullen at pp.473H, para. 29, and 476B, para. 44.

[11] *Meek v. H.M. Advocate*, 1982 S.C.C.R. 613; *Jamieson v. H.M. Advocate (No. 1)*, 1994 S.C.C.R. 181. Both *Meek* and *Jamieson* apparently apply the law formerly laid down for England in *R. v. Morgan* [1976] A.C. 182, H.L. But the "subjective" approach championed in *Morgan* has been set aside by recent legislation for England and Wales: thus in the Sexual Offences Act 2003, s.1 ("Rape") provides:
"(1) A person (A) commits an offence if
   (a) he intentionally penetrates the vagina, anus or mouth of another person (B) with his penis,
   (b) B does not consent to the penetration; and
   (c) A does not reasonably believe that B consents.
(2) Whether a belief is reasonable is to be determined having regard to all the circumstances, including any steps A has taken to ascertain whether B consents…".
It has been held in New Zealand that if the accused initially believes the woman is consenting, but realises after penetration that this is not the case and carries on nonetheless, he is guilty of rape: *Kaitamaki v. The Queen* [1985] A.C. 147; the basis of the decision in that case (the Privy Council, at p.152A, having agreed with the New Zealand Appeal Court) is that sexual intercourse (though completed by penetration) is a continuing activity from the beginning of penetration by, to the withdrawal of, the male person's penis—which is reflected in current English law (see above) by the definition of "penetration" given in s.79(2) of the Sexual Offences Act 2003, *viz.* "Penetration is a continuing act from entry to withdrawal".
It has been held in both England and Canada that an error as to consent resulting from the defendant's self-induced intoxication is an irrelevant error as far as recklessness is concerned: *R. v. Woods* (1981) 74 Cr.App.R. 312; *Leary v. The Queen* [1978] 1 S.C.R. 29; see also Vol. I, para. 12.25.

[12] *S. v. H.M. Advocate*, 1989 S.L.T. 469. See also *H.M. Advocate v. Duffy*, 1983 S.L.T. 7; *H.M. Advocate v. Paxton*, 1985 S.L.T. 96. This is also the law in England: *R. v. R.* [1992] 1 A.C. 599 (H.L.), where the rejection of the "marital exemption" as a defence to rape

"A male person". It is not rape for a female person to force a man or boy **33.02** to have intercourse with her.[13] Nor is it rape for a female person to force another female to indulge in penetrative sexual relations with her. A female person can, however, be art and part guilty of a rape committed by a male.[14]

"Sexual intercourse". Rape is completed by penetration of the female **33.03** person's private parts: emission of semen into the body is unnecessary. Penetration must be intended to be *per vaginem*. Other forms of intercourse, such as buggery, do not constitute rape even when obtained forcibly, but only indecent assault. It was at one time thought that it was only *proof* of emission which was unnecessary,[15] but it is now settled that rape can be committed even where there is proof that there was no emission.[16] Penetration to any extent is sufficient, even if it is not complete, and Macdonald refers to an unreported case in which a plea of guilty to rape was tendered although the woman's hymen was unbroken.[17] In practice, however, it will be very difficult to obtain a conviction for rape in such a case where the hymen is unbroken.

It follows from the definition of rape in terms of penetration that a eunuch may be guilty of rape.[18] Nor is there any presumption in Scots law that a male person under the age of puberty cannot commit rape[19]; in

---

was subsequently held not to have contravened Art. 7(1) of the European Convention on Human Rights: *S.W. v. U.K.* (1996) 21 E.H.R.R. 363. See also *R. v. C.* [2004] 2 Cr.App.R. 253 (C.A.), where the appellant, who had been convicted in April 2002 for a rape on his wife committed between 1967 and 1971, unsuccessfully argued that his conviction for that rape amounted to an abuse of process, since, at the material time, forcible intercourse with one's spouse was not rape under English law and no lawyer consulted as to the then state of the law could have advised that it was. The court took the view that the supposed immunity of a husband from a rape prosecution where the victim was his wife was always a legal fiction (opinion of the court at p. 259, paras 18–19), and also stated (in para. 19) that to the extent that the European Court of Human Rights in *S.W. v. U.K.* (*supra*) had proceeded on the basis that a husband could rape his wife with complete impunity prior to the decision in *R. v. R.* (*supra*), "its analysis was not fully informed".

[13] Mackenzie suggests that a woman can commit rape: Mackenzie, I. 16.5, but he may be thinking of the crime of *"raptus"* which consisted in forcible abduction: Burnett, 102.

[14] See *Chas. Matthews and Margt. Goldsmith*, Glasgow High Court, Dec. 1910, unreported; *Walker and McPherson*, Dundee High Court, March 1976, unreported. For the position of transsexuals, see n. 22 and para. 33.05, below.

[15] See Alison, i. 209. *Cf. Duncan Macmillan* (1833) Bell's Notes 82.

[16] *Arch. Robertson* (1836) 1 Swin. 93; Macdonald, 120.

[17] *Frank McCann* (1891) Macdonald, 120. There are suggestions in earlier cases that at any rate where the victim is adult penetration must be complete: *Arch. Robertson, supra*, Lord Meadowbank at p. 102; *cf. Richd. Jennings* (1850) Macdonald, 120, a conviction for raping a child without complete penetration. *Robertson Edney* (1833) Bell's Notes 83 was a case where the hymen was unruptured and the labia only slightly irritated and the jury convicted of assault with intent to ravish only, but the case is not of value as an authority and only the verdict is reported. In *Alex. Macrae* (1841) Bell's Notes 83, on the other hand, it was said that so long as there was penetration its extent was unimportant and it was not necessary to prove that the vagina had been entered.

[18] *Arch. Robertson, supra*, Lord Meadowbank at p. 102, Lord Medwyn at pp. 105–106.

[19] Burnett, 102; Macdonald, 121. (The presumption in English law that a boy under the age of 14 was not capable of sexual intercourse and thus not capable of committing rape was abolished under the Sexual Offences Act 1993.)

Robt. Fulton, Jun.[20] a boy aged 13 years and 10 months was convicted of the rape of a girl aged five.

33.04 *"With a female person"*. The crime of rape may be committed upon any female, whatever her age or condition. A prostitute is entitled to the same protection as any other woman.[21]

Under Scots law, a male person cannot be raped.[22]

33.05 THE GENDER RECOGNITION ACT 2004

Since rape under Scots law is (at present) a gender-specific offence ("by a male person on a female person") involving the accused engaging in sexual activity, it is affected by the Gender Recognition Act 2004, section 20 of which provides:

> "(1) Where (apart from this subsection) a relevant gender-specific offence could be committed or attempted only if the gender of the person to whom a full gender recognition certificate has been issued were not the acquired gender, the fact that the person's gender has become the acquired gender does not prevent the offence being committed or attempted.
>
> (2) An offence is a 'relevant gender-specific offence' if—
>
> (a) either or both of the conditions in subsection (3) are satisfied, and
> (b) the commission of the offence involves the accused engaging in sexual activity.
>
> (3) The conditions are—
>
> (a) that the offence may be committed only by a person of a particular gender, and
> (b) that the offence may be committed only on, or in relation to, a person of a particular gender,
>
> and the references to a particular gender include a gender identified by reference to the gender of the other person involved."

---

[20] (1841) 2 Swin. 564.

[21] Hume, i. 304–305; Macdonald, 121; *Ed. Yates and Henry Parkes* (1851) J. Shaw 528. *Dub.* Burnett, 104 and Alison, i. 214–215.

[22] It has been held in England that a person who was born male and remained biologically of that sex was a man for the purpose of criminal charges which required the defendant to be a male, notwithstanding that the actual defendant had had gender reassignment surgery and hormone treatment to alter his physical characteristics so that they approximated to those of a woman; and it was considered to be of no consequence that the defendant had become philosophically, psychologically and socially a female: *R. v. Tan & Ors.* [1983] Q.B. 1053 (C.A.). Other cases also supported this view: see, *e.g. Re. P. & G. (Transsexuals)* [1996] 2 F.L.R. 90; *Cossey v. U.K.* (1990) 13 E.H.R.R. 622; *cf. B. v. France* (1992) 16 E.H.R.R. 1. But the decision by the European Court of Human Rights (Grand Chamber) in *Goodwin v. United Kingdom*, 13 B.H.R.C. 120 (Applic. No. 28957/95, July 11, 2002), not to follow prior decisions of the court, and to hold that refusal by a State to afford full legal recognition to post-operative transsexuals as persons of the gender indicated by their gender re-assignment treatment was a violation of Arts 8 and 12 of the European Convention on Human Rights, undermined any such view in domestic law; and the law in Scotland is now governed by the Gender Recognition Act 2004 (see para. 33.05, below).

Under this Act,[23] a person of either gender and of at least 18 years of age may apply for a gender recognition certificate, which must be granted[24] if that person has lived in the other gender (known as "the acquired gender"[25]) throughout a period of two years prior to the making of the application and intends to continue to live in that acquired gender until death,[26] or has changed gender (also known as "the acquired gender"[27]) under the law of a country or territory outside the United Kingdom and meets the requirements of section 2(2). Such a certificate must be granted as a "full gender recognition certificate" unless the applicant is married, when the certificate will be an interim one—until the grant of a decree of nullity or divorce (or the death of the applicant's spouse) in terms of section 5.[27a] Once a full gender recognition certificate is issued to a person, "the person's gender becomes for all purposes the acquired gender (so that, if the acquired gender is the male gender, the person's sex becomes that of a man and, if it is the female gender, the person's sex becomes that of a woman)"[28]—for all purposes, that is to say, except (in particular) those covered by section 20, above.[29]

Since a full gender recognition certificate under the 2004 Act may be issued to a person who has not had gender re-assignment surgery, it follows that the terms of section 20 are necessary to ensure, for example, that such a person (who has acquired a male gender) may in an appropriate case be considered as a victim of rape or attempted rape, whilst such a person (who has acquired a female gender) may in an appropriate case be charged with rape or attempted rape.

"*Without her consent*". The leading modern case authority[30] makes **33.06** reasonably clear that "without her consent" means "without her active consent".[31] It follows, therefore, that a female person who is

---

[23] See s.1(1) and (3).

[24] Provided the requirements of s.3 are met; s.3 has been amended to take account of civil partnerships: see the Civil Partnership Act 2004, s.250(2).

[25] See s.1(2)(a).

[26] See s.2(1), which also requires the applicant to have (or have had) "gender dysphoria" (which is defined in s.25 as "the disorder variously referred to as gender dysphoria, gender identity disorder and transsexualism") and to be able to meet the requirements of s.3. See also s.27 (for modified requirements relating to applications made within two years of the commencement of the Act).

[27] See s.1(2)(b).

[27a] Section 5 must be read subject to the Civil Partnership Act 2004, s.250(3): see also s.5A, as inserted by the 2004 Act, s.250(4).

[28] s.9.

[29] See also s.12, under which an acquired gender recognised under the 2004 Act "does not affect the status of the person as the father or mother of a child", and s.19 (which deals with prohibitions or restrictions relative to "gender-affected" sports).

[30] *Lord Advocate's Reference (No. 1 of 2001)*, 2002 S.L.T. 466.

[31] *ibid.*, L.J.-G. Cullen at p. 475F, para. 39, where, in turning to examine some "wider considerations", he states that he does so "on the basis that the absence of the woman's 'consent' refers to a lack of active consent, as opposed to mere submission or permission." The Lord Justice-General had also previously quoted with approval (at pp. 470L–471E, para. 19) from Lord Ivory's opinion in *Chas. Sweenie* (1858) 3 Irv. 109 at 140, viz., "If a man finds a woman in such a condition that she can neither consent nor dissent—if he finds an utterly unconscious person ... [t]here is an absence of any active consent ...". See also *H.M. Advocate v. Shearer*, 2003 S.L.T. 1354, opinion of the court at p. 1357E, para. 12.

asleep,[32] intoxicated,[33] or unconscious for some other reason, and who is taken advantage of in that condition by a male person's having sexual intercourse with her, is a victim of rape and the male person who thus took advantage of her is indictable for that crime (at least in so far as the absence of consent is concerned) rather than some different offence, such as indecent assault[34] or "clandestine injury": indeed clandestine injury as a crime distinct from rape[35] has probably ceased to exist following the restatement of rape effected by the majority decision of a court of seven judges in *Lord Advocate's Reference (No. 1 of 2001)*;[36] but recent authority has, *per contra*, emphasised that "[t]he Lord Advocate remains master of the instance, and may, if he thinks fit, libel the clandestine penetration of an unconscious female as indecent assault".[37]

Where violence or threats of imminent violence are used to coerce the victim into submitting to sexual intercourse, that submission would clearly not be regarded as amounting to consent[38]: but if violence is unrelated to the act of intercourse and precedes it by a significant interval of time, whether or not there was consent to that act (or whether there was room for the accused honestly to believe that there was such consent at the material time) is a question of fact for the jury.[39] To obtain intercourse by threats of future action (such as dismissal from employment) is probably extortion and not rape; and it may not be rape to wear a female person's reluctance down by persuasion, or even perhaps by ill-treatment, such as kidnapping and imprisoning her, if in the end she consents to intercourse, provided that that consent was obtained "without any use of threats or violence at the time or recently before".[40] *Stante*

---

[32] *Cf. Chas. Sweenie* (1858) 3 Irv. 109—now overruled by *Lord Advocate's Reference (No. 1 of 2001)*, 2002 S.L.T. 466. Modern cases, where the female was asleep, may now be charged as rape: see, *e.g.* the charges in *H.M. Advocate v. Shearer*, 2003 S.L.T. 1354 and *Allan v. H.M. Advocate*, 2004 S.C.C.R. 278; *cf. Spendiff v. H.M. Advocate*, 2005 S.C.C.R. 522.

[33] *Cf. H.M. Advocate v. Logan*, 1936 J.C. 100; *H.M. Advocate v. Grainger and Rae*, 1932 J.C. 40; *Sweeney and Anr. v. X*, 1982 S.C.C.R. 509—all of which would now be considered as examples of rape, irrespective of whether the accused or some other person or some chance event was the cause of the victim's state of insensibility.

[34] Rape can be regarded, of course, as an aggravated indecent assault, where the aggravation is "constituted by the sexual intercourse having taken place without the consent of the woman": *Lord Advocate's Reference (No. 1 of 2001)*, 2002 S.L.T. 466 at 474J, para. 35, *per* L.J.-G. Cullen; see also the opinions of Lady Cosgrove at p. 480K, para.10, and Lord Nimmo Smith at p. 482K, para. 6.

[35] See, *e.g. Rodgers v. Hamilton*, 1994 S.L.T. 822, opinion of the court at p. 823B-C; and *cf. Paton v. H.M. Advocate*, 2002 S.C.C.R. 57 and *H.M. Advocate v. Shearer*, 2003 S.L.T. 1354, opinion of the court at p. 1357A-C, para. 11.

[36] 2002 S.L.T. 466.

[37] *Spendiff v. H.M. Advocate*, 2005 S.C.C.R. 522 at 525F, opinion of the court at para. 5.

[38] *Cf. Barbour v. H.M. Advocate*, 1982 S.C.C.R. 195, Lord Stewart's charge to the jury at pp. 197–198: in that case, the accused was in fact convicted, *inter alia*, of assault with intent to ravish; and the Appeal Court dismissed his appeal against conviction without delivering an opinion. See also *Lord Advocate's Reference (No. 1 of 2001)*, 2002 S.L.T. 466, where L.J.-G. Cullen states at p. 475F, para. 39: "I turn finally to some wider considerations. I do so on the basis that the absence of the woman's 'consent' refers to a lack of active consent, as opposed to mere submission or permission." *Cf.* the Sexual Offences Act 2003, s.75, which (for England and Wales) sets up a rebuttable presumption under which, in certain specific circumstances, a complainant will be taken not to have consented.

[39] *McKearney v. H.M. Advocate*, 2004 S.C.C.R. 251.

[40] Hume, i, 302.

the decision in *Lord Advocate's Reference (No. 1 of 2001)*,[41] however, and the "wider considerations" referred to by the Lord Justice-General[42] and discussed by Lady Cosgrove,[43] the precise meaning of "consent" in such circumstances is unclear.[44]

Where consent is obtained by fraud, the common law is still governed by the old case of *Wm. Fraser*.[45] F had intercourse with a married woman by pretending to be her husband. He was charged with rape, and also with the innominate crime of "Fraudulently and Deceitfully obtaining Access to and having Carnal Knowledge of a Married Woman, by pretending to be her husband, or otherwise conducting himself, and behaving towards her so as to deceive her into the belief that he was her husband." The court were agreed that the innominate offence constituted a crime, as being a species of fraud,[46] but the majority held that the circumstances did not constitute rape. The ground of decision was that the intercourse had been obtained with the woman's consent, albeit a consent impetrated by fraud. It was argued that the fraud was of such a nature as to vitiate any apparent consent, but this argument was rejected by the majority of the court.

To have intercourse with a married woman by pretending to be her husband was declared to be rape by section 4 of the Criminal Law Amendment Act 1885[47] (now section 7(3) of the Criminal Law (Consolidation) (Scotland) Act 1995, as amended by the Crime and Punishment (Scotland) Act 1997, Schedule 1, paragraph 18(3)), but other forms of "fraudulent intercourse" fall to be dealt with at common law, except that it is an offence under section 7(2)(b) of the 1995 Act to procure a woman to have intercourse with oneself or others by fraud.[48] It is clear from *Fraser*[49] that it is not rape for A to induce B to have intercourse with him by pretending that he is X,[50] but the law regarding other types of fraud is unsettled. In *R. v. Flattery*[51] it was held in England that it was rape for A to have intercourse with B by pretending that he was giving

---

[41] 2002 S.L.T. 466.

[42] *ibid.*, p. 475F–J, paras 39–41, which he did not rely upon in coming to his conclusions (see p. 475L, para. 43).

[43] *ibid.*, p. 481B–D, paras 13–14.

[44] *Cf.* the Sexual Offences Act 2003, s.74 ("Consent"), which states (for England and Wales) that "... a person consents if he agrees by choice, and has the freedom and capacity to make that choice", and ss.75 and 76, which contain rebuttable and conclusive presumptions relative to consent. *Cf.* also the Draft Scottish Criminal Code, clauses 61 ("Rape") and 111 ("Rules on consent").

[45] (1847) Ark. 280. In the *Lord Advocate's Reference (No. 1 of 2001)*, 2002 S.L.T. 466, L.J-G. Cullen at p. 475B, [36], said: "The question whether such a case [*i.e.* one of impersonation] is truly one of rape depends on the difficult question whether the woman's apparent consent to intercourse is or is not vitiated by her error as to the identity of the person with whom she has intercourse. This is not a matter which requires to be resolved in dealing with the present reference."

[46] Lord Cockburn at Ark. 312; *cf. supra*, para. 18.15.

[47] See *infra*, para. 33.12.

[48] See *infra*, para. 36.29.

[49] (1847) Ark. 280.

[50] Lord Cockburn at Ark. 310–311. *Cf. Allan v. H.M. Advocate*, 2004 S.C.C.R. 278, where (apart from the fact that the accused pled guilty) no question of fraud arose for consideration since the victim assumed that the accused was her boyfriend without any pretence on the accused's part; also, there was no suggestion that she actively consented on the basis of that assumption.

[51] (1877) 2 Q.B.D. 410; see also *R. v. Williams* [1923] 1 K.B. 340.

her medical treatment, but there is no Scots reported case of this kind. The error induced in such a case is distinguishable from that in *Fraser* since it is an error as to subject-matter, so to speak, and not as to person. The woman in *Fraser* did consent to have sexual intercourse; the woman in *Flattery* did not. But in each case intercourse is obtained by fraud, and the *Flattery* type case might well be charged as fraud in Scotland, if only because such a charge would be clearly relevant and avoid the difficulties which a rape charge would present. Again, there is much force in the argument that if an error as fundamental as that in *Fraser* does not vitiate consent, no other form of error would be regarded as vitiating it.[52]

Constructive rape

33.07 There are three types of case in which rape can be committed even if the female person apparently consents.

(1) *Where the female person is under 12 years old.* It is rape for a male person to have sexual intercourse with a female person below the age of puberty, that is to say with a girl less than 12 years old. In the older authorities, this is said to be because such a female is incapable of consenting or having a proper will in the matter at all[53]; but in the leading modern case authority on rape, it is stated that this rule is based on the presumption (presumably irrebutable) of lack of consent on the part of such a girl.[54] On principle, it seems problematic to assume lack of consent where consent had been given in fact; and the better view may be that there is a rule of law that intercourse with a girl under 12 years of age is always rape.

---

[52] For England and Wales, the issue is now settled by the Sexual Offences Act 2003, s.76 which applies to rape by virtue of s.1(3), and which provides: "(1) If in proceedings for an offence to which this section applies it is proved that the defendant did the relevant act and that any of the circumstances specified in subsection (2) existed, it is to be conclusively presumed—(a) that the complainant did not consent to the relevant act, and (b) that the defendant did not believe that the complainant consented to the relevant act. (2) The circumstances are that—(a) the defendant intentionally deceived the complainant as to the nature or purpose of the relevant act; (b) the defendant intentionally induced the complainant to consent to the relevant act by impersonating a person known personally to the complainant." (See also s.77, which declares what is meant by "the relevant act" and "the complainant" in relation to, *inter alia*, the crime of rape under s.1.) In *R. v. Linekar* [1995] 2 Cr. App.R. 49 (C.A.), it was held that a prostitute who had allowed the defendant to have sexual intercourse with her following his promise to pay her £25 was not raped by him although he refused to honour that promise and had had no intention of honouring it from the outset: although there had been fraud, it did not deceive her either as to the nature of the act involved or as to the identity of the person with whom the act was to be performed—and this conclusion would still follow under the law set out in the 2003 Act.

In Scotland, error of the *Fraser* type has been held to vitiate consent in the law of contract, *supra*, para. 14.43, and should logically have the same result in rape. Lord Cockburn in *Fraser* did not seem to appreciate that there is a difference between pretending to be Mr B., the victim's husband, and pretending that one has gone through a valid marriage ceremony with her. The latter situation is clearly not rape (see *Gray v. Criminal Injuries Compensation Board*, 1993 S.L.T. 28 (O.H.), Lord Weir at p. 21B; 1999 S.C.L.R. 191 (I.H.), Lord Coulsfield at pp. 197B–198A) but it does not follow that the former is not rape either. Cf. *Papadimitropoulos v The Queen* (1957) 98 C.L.R. 249; *R. v. K.*, 1966 (1) S.A. 366 (S.R.,A.D.); *Bolduc and Bird v. R.* [1967] S.C.R. 678. See "Absence of Consent in Rape," 1958 S.L.T. (News) 181.

[53] Hume, i, 303; Alison, i, 213.

[54] *Lord Advocate's Reference (No. 1 of 2001)*, 2002 S.L.T. 466, L.J.-G. Cullen (with whose conclusions Lady Cosgrove and Lords Nimmo Smith, Wheatley and Menzies agreed) at p. 476A, para. 44, at (ii).

MENS REA. On principle it should be a defence to rape of this kind that A **33.08**
believed the girl to be over the age of 12 since it is a defence to any rape
that A believed the woman was a consenting party.[55] The question has
never been raised in a Scots case, and could be avoided by charging the
accused under section 5(1) of the Criminal Law (Consolidation) (Scotland) Act 1995,[56] either as the sole charge or as an alternative to a charge
of rape.[57] Section 5 (1) does not require *mens rea* for the offence it creates,
that is to say the offence of having sexual intercourse with a girl under the
age of 13. If the question were to arise the court would doubtless have
scant sympathy with the accused and might well hold that *mens rea* as to
age was unnecessary.[58] At best for the accused the court would, it is
thought, hold that only recklessness was required.

(2) *Where the female is mentally disordered.* The fact that the woman was **33.09**
of weak intellect seems at one time to have been regarded mainly as an
adminicle of evidence which entitled the court to hold that there had been
rape although the other evidence in the case did not indicate either the use
of any considerable force by the accused or any considerable resistance
by the woman,[59] force and resistance at that time being regarded as
required elements of the offence. In *Chas. Sweenie*,[60] however, although
the question did not fall to be decided the judges were prepared to accept
that an idiot, and in some cases a lunatic, was probably in the same

---

[55] *Cf. R. v. Z.* 1960 S.A. 739 (A.D.).

[56] Section 5(1) provides: "Any person who has unlawful sexual intercourse with any girl
under the age of 13 years shall be liable on conviction on indictment to imprisonment for
life."

[57] Formerly, under the Sexual Offences (Scotland) Act 1976 s.15 (now repealed by the
Crime and Punishment (Scotland) Act 1997, Sched. 3), it was possible for a person
accused of the rape of a girl under 12 years of age to be convicted of, *inter alia*, a
contravention of s.3(1) of that Act—the then equivalent of s.5(1) of the Criminal Law
(Consolidation) (Scotland) Act 1995: but the terms of s.14 of the 1995 Act mean that an
alternative verdict of guilty of a s.5(1) offence cannot now be returned by the jury unless a
specific charge under that subsection has been inserted as an alternative in the indictment.

[58] *Cf. R. v. Prince* (1875) L.R. 2 C.C.R. 154, which admittedly dealt with a statutory
offence; *cf.* also, *B. (A Minor) v. D.P.P.* [2000] 2 W.L.R. 452 (H.L.), where it was held
that the offence under s.1(1) of the (English) Indecency with Children Act 1960 required
mens rea, i.e. an absence of belief that the victim was aged 14 years or above, and *R. v. K.*
[2001] 3 W.L.R. 471, H.L., where it was held that the offence under s.14(1), as read with
subs.(2), of the Sexual Offences Act 1956 (indecent assault on a girl under the age of 16)
equally required *mens rea, i.e.* an absence of belief that the girl in question was aged 16
years or above. The decision in *R. v. K.* depended, however, upon the 1956 Act not being
a single, coherent legislative scheme but rather a consolidation of provisions from many
different Acts, created at different times (so that its provisions could not necessarily be
read together in order to arrive at a specific conclusion concerning the availability or non-
availability of *mens rea*), and upon the presumption that statutory offences require *mens
rea* unless by express words or necessary implication that presumption is excluded: neither of these criteria can have any bearing on the common law; and it is doubtful whether
s.5(1) of the Criminal Law (Consolidation) (Scotland) Act 1995 is open to such construction (see para. 36.07, below). In any event, *R. v. K.* and *B. (A Minor) v. D.P.P.* have
been overtaken by the Sexual Offences Act 2003—a single coherent legislative scheme
which (a) repeals the statutory provisions considered in these two cases, and (b) creates
new offences which make quite plain, where an offence is age related, whether the absence
of *reasonable* belief that the victim was above the crucial age is an element of the offence:
cf., e.g. s.5 of the 2003 Act (rape of a child of less than 13 years of age) and s.9(1) (sexual
activity with a child greater than 13 but less than 16 years of age).

[59] *Hugh McNamara* (1848) Ark. 521.

[60] (1858) 3 Irv. 109.

position as a child, and their opinions suggest that it is always rape to have intercourse with a person incapable through mental abnormality of giving a proper consent, although no force is used and the woman offers no resistance.[61] *Sweenie* also suggests that idiots, like children, are deemed incapable of consent,[62] while in the case of other mentally abnormal persons their ability to consent is a question of fact in each case.

The leading modern case authority on rape simply opines that if females (for any reason other than that they are under the age of 12 years) "are incapable of giving ... consent [to sexual intercourse], the absence of consent should be presumed ...".[63] It seems, therefore, that the modern common law (which is unlikely to refer to "idiots" or "lunatics", but rather to those who are "mentally disordered") treats the matter as one of capacity in all cases of mentally disordered females: thus, if it is proved to the satisfaction of the jury in a rape case that at the material time the complainer was suffering from a mental disorder which made her incapable of validly consenting to sexual intercourse, then she will be presumed not to have consented. This, if correct, begs the question as to what is meant by a "valid" consent; in addition, it leaves unanswered which mental disorders affect consensual capacity to the required extent, what the common law should understand by "mental disorder",[64] and whether the absence of an honest belief in capacity validly to consent is an element of the offence.[65] Some of these problematic issues could be avoided by charging the accused under section 311 of the Mental Health (Care and Treatment) (Scotland) Act 2003 (asp 13),[66] which includes, but is not confined to, situations which the common law would count as rape in relation to mentally disordered complainers.[67]

33.10 MENTAL HEALTH (CARE AND TREATMENT) (SCOTLAND) ACT 2003 (asp 13). Section 311 ("Non-consensual sexual acts") of this Act provides:

"(1) Subject to subsection (5) below, a person who engages in an act mentioned in subsection (2) below with, or towards, a mentally

---

[61] *ibid.*, Lord Ardmillan at p. 137, Lord Ivory at p. 140, Lord Cowan at p. 144, Lord Deas at p. 147, Lord Neaves at p. 153.

[62] *ibid. Cf.* Anderson, 161; *H.M. Advocate v. Grainger and Rae*, 1932 J.C. 40 at 41, *per* Lord Anderson.

[63] *Lord Advocate's Reference (No. 1 of 2001)*, 2002 S.L.T. 466, L.J.-G. Cullen (with whose conclusions Lady Cosgrove and Lords Nimmo Smith, Wheatley and Menzies agreed) at p. 476A, para. 44 at (ii).

[64] *Cf.* the Mental Health (Care and Treatment) (Scotland) Act 2003 (asp 13), s.328, which provides: "(1) Subject to subsection (2) below, in this Act 'mental disorder' means any— (a) mental illness; (b) personality disorder; or (c) learning disability, however caused or manifested; and cognate expressions shall be construed accordingly. (2) A person is not mentally disordered by reason only of any of the following—(a) sexual orientation; (b) sexual deviancy; (c) transsexualism; (d) transvestism; (e) dependence on, or use of, alcohol or drugs; (f) behaviour that causes, or is likely to cause, harassment, alarm or distress to any other person; (g) acting as no prudent person would act."

[65] *Cf.* s.311 of the Mental Health (Care and Treatment) (Scotland) Act 2003 (asp 13): see para. 33.10, below.

[66] See para. 33.10, below; *cf.* s.313 (of the 2003 Act), the main part of which being set out in para. 33.11, below.

[67] In particular, it will be seen from the text of s.311 that the offence is not confined to female complainers and male accused, nor to vaginal sexual intercourse (nor, indeed, to sexual intercourse). A s.311 offence may also be tried summarily: see para. 33.10, below.

disordered[68] person shall be guilty of an offence if, at the time of the act, the mentally disordered person—

    (a) does not consent to the act; or

    (b) by reason of mental disorder, is incapable of consenting to the act.

(2) The acts referred to in subsection (1) above are—

    (a) sexual intercourse (whether vaginal or anal); and

    (b) any other sexual act.

(3) For the purposes of subsection (1)(a) above, a person shall be regarded as not consenting if the person purports to consent as a result of—

    (a) being placed in such a state of fear; or

    (b) being subjected to any such—

        (i) threat;

        (ii) intimidation;

        (iii) deceit; or

        (iv) persuasion,

as vitiates that person's consent.

(4) For the purposes of subsection (1)(b) above, a person is incapable of consenting to an act if the person is unable to—

    (a) understand what the act is;

    (b) form a decision as to whether to engage in the act (or as to whether the act should take place); or

    (c) communicate any such decision.

(5) Where a person is charged with an offence under subsection (1)(b) above it shall be a defence for such person to prove that, at the time of the sexual intercourse or other sexual act, such person did not know, and could not reasonably have been expected to know, that the other person—

    (a) had a mental disorder; and

    (b) was incapable of consenting to the intercourse or other act.

(6) A person guilty of an offence under subsection (1) above shall be liable—

    (a) on summary conviction to imprisonment for a term not exceeding 3 months or to a fine not exceeding the statutory maximum or to both;

    (b) on conviction on indictment to imprisonment for life.

(7) A person guilty of aiding, abetting, counselling, procuring or inciting any other person to commit an offence under subsection (1) above shall be liable—

---

[68] For the meaning of "mental disorder", see s.328 (which is set out in n.64 above) of the 2003 Act.

    (a) on summary conviction to imprisonment for a term not exceeding 3 months or to a fine not exceeding the statutory maximum or to both;

    (b) on conviction on indictment to imprisonment for a term not exceeding 2 years or to a fine or to both.

(8) In this section 'sexual act' means any activity which a reasonable person would, in all the circumstances, regard as sexual."

33.11 Section 313 of the Mental Health (Care and Treatment) (Scotland) Act 2003 (asp 13) provides:

"(1) Subject to subsection (3) below, a person who engages in—

    (a) sexual intercourse (whether vaginal or anal); or
    (b) any other sexual act,[69]

with, or towards, a mentally disordered[70] person shall be guilty of an offence if, at the time of the intercourse or other act, the person is one of those specified in subsection (2) below.

(2) Those persons are—

    (a) a person providing care services[71] to the mentally disordered person;
    (b) a person who—

        (i) is an individual employed in, or contracted to provide services in or to; or
        (ii) not being the Scottish Ministers, is a manager of,

a hospital in which the mentally disordered person is being given medical treatment.

(3) Where a person is charged with an offence under subsection (1) above, it shall be a defence for such person to prove that—

    (a) at the time of the intercourse or other act—

        (i) such person did not know, and could not reasonably have been expected to know, that the other person was mentally disordered; or
        (ii) the mentally disordered person was the spouse [or civil partner][71a] of such person; or

    (b) in the case of—

        (i) a person specified in subsection (2)(a) above, immediately before that person began to provide care services to the mentally disordered person; or
        (ii) a person specified in subsection (2)(b) above, immediately before the mentally disordered person was

---

[69] Under s.313(6), "sexual act" is given the same meaning as it has in s.311(8): see para. 33.10, above.
[70] For the meaning of "mental disorder", see s.328 (which is set out in n.64 above) of the 2003 Act.
[71] For "care services", see s.313(5) and (6).
[71a] Words in square brackets inserted by the Civil Partnership Act 2004, Sched. 28, para. 70 (which purports to refer to s.313(5)(a)(ii) of the 2003 Act).

admitted to the hospital referred to in that provision or (where the mentally disordered person has been admitted to that hospital more than once) was last admitted to it,

a sexual relationship existed between them.

(4) A person guilty of an offence under subsection (1) above shall be liable—

(a) on summary conviction to imprisonment for a term not exceeding 3 months or to a fine not exceeding the statutory maximum or to both;
(b) on conviction on indictment to imprisonment for a term not exceeding 2 years or to a fine or to both."

It will be noted that the above offence applies whether or not the mentally disordered person consents, and whether or not that person is capable of consenting.

(3) *By impersonating the woman's husband.* Section 4 of the Criminal Law **33.12** Amendment Act 1885 (now section 7(3) of the Criminal Law (Consolidation) (Scotland) Act 1995) virtually overruled *Wm. Fraser*,[72] and provided that it was rape for A to induce a married woman to permit him to have intercourse with her by impersonating her husband. In *H.M. Advocate v. Montgomery*[73] the woman was at the time married to her second husband, her first being dead, and the accused pretended to be her first husband. This was held to be rape in terms of the section, on the view that if he were indeed her first husband her second marriage would be invalid and the first husband be in law still her husband. The woman was, of course, a married woman, but the *ratio* of the case suggests that "married woman" in the section should be interpreted to include widows.

The effect on the section of the provision that a marriage may be dissolved on the ground of the husband's presumed death[74] has not been considered, but as such a dissolution is unconditional, at any rate unless it is reduced,[75] an accused who pretended that he was a husband in respect of whose presumed death the marriage had been dissolved would not, it is submitted, be guilty of this form of constructive rape.

The section is limited to the single case of impersonation of a particular person, the woman's husband. It does not apply where A merely pretends to be married to the woman, for example, by going through a bigamous form of marriage, or by concealing from the woman that their "marriage" is void for any other reason.

Related offences under the Criminal Law (Consolidation) (Scotland) Act 1995

Section 7(2)(c) of the Criminal Law (Consolidation) (Scotland) Act 1995 **33.13** provides a maximum penalty of two years' imprisonment for anyone who:

---

[72] (1847) Ark. 280.
[73] 1926 J.C. 2.
[74] Presumption of Death (Scotland) Act 1977, s.3.
[75] See Eric M. Clive, *The Law of Husband and Wife in Scotland* (4th ed., 1997), para. 29.008.

"applies or administers to, or causes to be taken by, any woman or girl any drug, matter or thing, with intent to stupefy or overpower so as thereby to enable any person to have unlawful sexual intercourse with such woman or girl".[76]

This section applies to a person drugging a girl in order to have intercourse with her himself.[77]

33.14 It is an offence under section 7(2)(a) of the Criminal Law (Consolidation) (Scotland) Act 1995 to procure or attempt to procure by threats a woman "to have unlawful sexual intercourse", including connection with the procurer.[78]

---

[76] One administration constitutes one offence, however many men have intercourse with the drugged girl: *R. v. Shillingford; R. v. Vanderwall* [1968] 1 W.L.R. 566 (C.A.).
[77] *Cf. R. v. Williams* (1898) 62 J.P. 310; see *infra*, para. 36.29.
[78] See *infra*, para. 36.29.

CHAPTER 34

SODOMY AND BESTIALITY

Sodomy is a "relevant gender-specific offence" for the purposes of s.20 of **34.01** the Gender Recognition Act 2004; and the offences under s.13(5) and (6) of the Criminal Law (Consolidation) (Scotland) Act 1995 (see para. 34.03 of the 3rd edition, as modified below) would also qualify as "gender-specific". For an account of s.20 in the context of the 2004 Act, see para. 33.05, above.

n.3: The reference to "Smith and Hogan" should read "p.494" of the 10th ed.

n.5: Relative to the case of *J.P. Deavy*, the charge (at common law) could not now be one of shameless indecency: see *Webster v. Dominick*, 2003 S.C.C.R. 525, and Chapter 36, below.

In the final line of the text of this paragraph, for "shameless indecency" **34.02** substitute "lewd, indecent or libidinous practices or public indecency, depending on the facts and circumstances": see *Webster v. Dominick*, 2003 S.C.C.R. 525, and Chapter 36, below.

n.7: This footnote should be deleted.

In the first text paragraph, in line 1 on p.520, the following should be **34.03** inserted after "between two": "(or amongst, where there are more than two)"; and, in line 2 on that page, the word "both" should be deleted in the two places where it occurs, "the" being substituted for "both" in the first of these two places. These changes are necessitated by the amendments made by the provision of the Convention Rights (Compliance) (Scotland) Act 2001 (asp 7) mentioned in n.9 (see below).

And in that text paragraph, the words from lines 4–5 (beginning, "A male person") to the end, including footnotes 10 and 11, must be deleted, since s.13(3) of the Criminal Law (Consolidation) (Scotland) Act 1995 is repealed by the Mental Health (Care and Treatment) (Scotland) Act 2003 (asp 13), Sched. 5, Part 1.

n.9: The provision of the Convention Rights (Compliance) (Scotland) Act 2001 (asp 7) mentioned here should be corrected to read "s.10".

In the second text paragraph, in line 7 on p.520, for "both" the word "the" should be substituted.

n.12: The following should be added at the end of this note: "and the Convention Rights (Compliance) (Scotland) Act 2001 (asp 7), s.10(b)".

n.14: *Cartwright v. H.M. Advocate* is now reported at 2003 S.C.C.R. 695.

At the end of this note, the following should be added: "In *Webster v. Dominick*, 2003 S.C.C.R. 525, where a court of five judges held that there was no common law offence of 'shameless indecency', Lord Justice-Clerk Gill (with whom the other four judges agreed), at pp.542G–543A, para.60, said this: 'One significant consequence ... would be that in cases where a statutory prosecution was time-barred (*H.M. Advocate v. Roose* [1999 S.C.C.R. 259]), or where the Crown considered that the statutory penalty was inadequate (*Batty v. H.M. Advocate*), the Crown would no longer have the option of bringing a common law charge of shameless indecency. That is not an unreasonable consequence. Legal principle should not be distorted for the purpose of circumventing strict time-limits or penalties.' It remains to be seen whether the sentiment expressed in the final sentence of this passage represents a general change in policy by the Appeal Court."

After para. 34.03, the following new paragraphs should be inserted.

"Mental Health (Care and Treatment) (Scotland) Act 2003 (asp 13)

34.03A Under section 311(1) and (2) of the Mental Health (Care and Treatment) (Scotland) Act 2003 (asp 13), a person who engages in, *inter alia*, an act of anal sexual intercourse with or towards a mentally disordered person ("mental disorder" being defined in s.328 of the Act) is guilty of an offence if at the time of the act the mentally disordered person does not consent or is, by reason of mental disorder, incapable of consenting to that act. In terms of section 311(3), a mentally disordered person is to be regarded as not consenting if that person is placed in such a state of fear, or is subjected to such threat, intimidation, deceit or persuasion, that any purported consent he or she gives is vitiated; and under subsection (4), such a person is presumed to be incapable of consenting to such an act if that person is unable to understand what the act is, or unable to form a decision as to whether to engage in the act (or as to whether the act should take place), or unable to communicate any such decision. It is a defence for a person charged with such an offence, in relation to a mentally disordered person who is incapable of consenting, to prove that at the material time he did not know and could not reasonably have been expected to know that that mentally disordered person had such a disorder and that he was incapable of consenting to the intercourse: see subsection (5). The maximum penalty for this offence is, on summary conviction, three months and a fine of the statutory maximum, and, on conviction on indictment, life in prison: see subsection (6). It is also an offence for a person to aid, abet, counsel, procure or incite another person to commit such an offence, the maximum penalty being, on summary conviction, three months and a fine of the statutory maximum, and, on conviction on indictment, two years and a fine: see subsection (7). [Section 311 is set out in full at para. 33.10, above; and s.328 is set out at para. 33.09, n.64, above.]

34.03B Section 313(1)–(3) of the Mental Health (Care and Treatment) (Scotland) Act 2003 (asp 13) provides that, subject to certain exceptions and defences, it is an offence for a person providing care services (see subsections (5) and (6)) to a mentally disordered person ('mental disorder' being defined in s.328 of the Act), or employed in (or contracted to provide services in or to) a hospital where a mentally disordered person is receiving treatment, to engage in, *inter alia*, anal sexual intercourse with that mentally disordered person. The maximum penalty for such an offence is, on summary conviction, three months and a fine of the statutory maximum, and, on conviction on indictment, two years and a fine: see subsection (4). [Subsections (1) to (4) of s.313 are set out at para. 33.11, above; and s.328 is set out at para. 33.09, n.64, above.]"

The second sentence of the first text paragraph should be amended so as **34.04** to read: "Under English common law bestiality (buggery) could be committed *per anum* or *per vaginam*[20] and there is no reason for supposing that the same is not the case in Scotland."

n.20: The reference to "Smith and Hogan" should read "p.492" of the 10th ed.; and, the following should be added at the end of this footnote: "The former common law position in England is now reflected in the offence ('Intercourse with an animal') created by s.69 of the Sexual Offences Act 2003."

n.21: At the end of the text of this footnote, the existing full-stop should be replaced by a colon, and the following should be added: "see now s.69 of the Sexual Offences Act 2003. *Cf.* clause 109 ('Sexual Activity with an Animal') of the Draft Scottish Criminal Code; clause 109, which must be read with clauses 60(1)(c) and 110, is broader than s.69 of the Sexual Offences Act 2003."

CHAPTER 35

INCEST

35.02 Following the decision in *Webster v. Dominick*, 2003 S.C.C.R. 525 (see Chapter 36, below), the final words of the second text paragraph (on p.524 of the 3rd edition) must be deleted—*i.e.* the words: "or an example of the common law crime of shamelessly indecent conduct". The accompanying footnote (n.7) must also be deleted.

35.04 In line 9 of the text which appears on p.524 of the 3rd edition, after the words "lawfully married to", insert: ", or in civil partnership with," by virtue of the Civil Partnership Act 2004, Sched. 28, para. 62; and, before the words "A is in a position of trust", insert: "under section 4 of the 2000 Act (as amended by the Regulation of Care (Scotland) Act 2001 (asp 8), Sched. 3, para. 25)".

n.12: In this footnote, the words from "they may, however, be within the reach of" to the end of the text must be deleted, together with the reference to the case of *Batty* and the cross reference to Chapter 36; instead of these words and references, the following should be substituted: "they may, however, be within the reach of the offence under s.313 of the Mental Health (Care and Treatment) (Scotland) Act 2003 (asp 13) if the persons under 18 whom they look after are mentally disordered: see para. 34.03B, above."

In line 1 of the text which appears on p.525 of the 3rd edition, the words "residential care home, nursing home, mental nursing home, or" should be deleted (following amendment by the Regulation of Care (Scotland) Act 2001 (asp 8), Sched. 3, para. 25(2)(a)), and in line 2 there, after the words "private hospital;" the following should be inserted (by virtue of the 2001 Act (asp 8), Sched. 3, para. 25(2)(b)): "(bb) provided by a care home service [within the meaning of section 2(3) of the Regulation of Care (Scotland) Act 2001 (asp 8)];".

n.13: In line 6 of the text of this footnote, after "s.4(9)" there should be added: "as amended by the Regulation of Care (Scotland) Act 2001 (asp 8), Sched. 3, para. 25(3)(a)–(c)".

CHAPTER 36

OTHER SEXUAL OFFENCES

Following the decision in *Webster v. Dominick*, 2003 S.C.C.R. 525, the **36.01**
word "shameless" must be deleted from line 3 of the text of this
paragraph.

n.5: In the citation for *Thomas v. H.M. Advocate*, the year should read **36.02**
"1997" and not 1977.

n.6: In line 3 of the text of this footnote, the word "made" should be **36.03**
substituted for "makes": the past tense must be used since s.6 of the
Sexual Offences Act 1956 is now repealed by Sched. 7 of the Sexual
Offences Act 2003, and there is no exact counterpart of s.6 (nor of the
defences, in s.5(5) of the Scottish 1995 Act, discussed in paras 36.03 *et
seq.*) in the 2003 Act. *Cf.* the 2003 Act, s.9 ("sexual activity with a child").

n.7: Section 6 of the Sexual Offences Act 1956 is repealed by Sched. 7 of
the Sexual Offences Act 2003: but, under Sched. 6, para. 33 of the 2003
Act, s.5(6) of the 1995 Act is amended such that "a like offence" includes
any of the offences in ss.9–14 of that 2003 Act, *i.e.* sexual activity with a
child (s.9); causing or inciting a child to engage in sexual activity (s.10);
engaging in sexual activity in the presence of a child (s.11); causing a child
to watch a sexual act (s.12); child offences committed by children or
young persons (s.13); and arranging or facilitating the commission of a
child sex act (s.14).

n.10: In the last line of this footnote, "of Sched. 1" should be inserted **36.05**
after "of para. 4".

n.13: In line 10 of this footnote, the words "This is" should be replaced by **36.07**
"This was", since ss.5 and 6 of the Sexual Offences Act 1956 are repealed
by the Sexual Offences Act 2003, Sched. 7.

For the existing text, the following should be substituted. **36.08**

"Sexual intercourse etc. with the mentally disordered. Under section
311(1)(b) of the Mental Health (Care and Treatment) (Scotland) Act
2003 (asp 13), a person who engages in vaginal or anal sexual intercourse,
or in any other sexual act, with or towards another person who at that
time is mentally disordered and incapable of consenting due to mental
disorder, is guilty of an offence; and, under section 313 of that Act a
person providing care services is guilty of an offence if he (or she) engages
in sexual intercourse (or any other sexual act) with or towards another
person who is mentally disordered. In the case of both offences, it is a
defence for the accused to prove that he (or she) did not know and could
not reasonably have been expected to know that the other person was

159

mentally disordered (and, in the case of a section 311(1)(b) offence, that that other person was incapable of consenting).[14]"

n.14: For the existing text of this footnote the following should be substituted.

"See paras 33.10 and 33.11, above, where ss.311 and 313 (including definitions and penalties) are set out in detail."

36.09 n.16: Following the decision made, and in particular the view taken of *Batty v. H.M. Advocate,* by the court in *Webster v. Dominick,* 2003 S.C.C.R. 525 at 538D–F, paras 35–36, changes should be made to this footnote: in line 6, delete the word "has"; in line 7, the word "lewd" should be substituted for the words "common law shamelessly indecent"; in line 13, the word "made" should be substituted for "makes"; the final sentence should be deleted; and the undernoted text added at the end.

"In *Webster v. Dominick,* 2003 S.C.C.R. 525, a unanimous court of five judges decided that there was no common law offence of 'shameless indecency', and that prior decisions of the Appeal Court which upheld such a crime (in particular *McLaughlan v. Boyd,* 1934 J.C. 19, and *Watt v. Annan,* 1978 J.C. 84) were wrong to have done so and should be over-ruled. *Webster v. Dominick* also notes that in *Batty v. H.M. Advocate* (contrary to the reports in 1995 J.C. 160 and 1995 S.C.C.R. 525, which treat the case as one of common law shameless indecency) the accused was convicted of five charges of lewd, indecent and libidinous practices, and not of shameless indecency; and, in relation to the question of whether only children below the age of puberty are protected by the common law offence of lewd practices, Lord Justice-Clerk Gill (with whom the remaining members of the court agreed) endorsed the accuracy of Macdonald's proposition (in the 5th ed., at p.149) that 'exposure to, and practices upon, females over 12 years of age, in private places and where the element of assault is absent, are not criminal [at common law]: see 2003 S.C.C.R. at p.534B, para. 19. This may settle the matter in relation to female victims; but given that there is some authority for the view that lewd practices towards consenting boys below or (perhaps) 'about' the age of puberty [see the text of para. 36.09, as amended below] may constitute the offence of lewd, indecent and libidinous practices and behaviour, and that *McLaughlan v. Boyd, supra,* where the male victims were apparently above the age of puberty and (perhaps) over the age of 16 years, is not overruled in its entirety, this issue remains in some doubt, especially since Lord Justice-Clerk Gill in *Webster v. Dominick (supra)* eventually contented himself by stating (at p.540F, para. 49): 'In the modern law, when indecent conduct is directed against a specific victim who is within the class of persons whom the law protects, the crime is that of lewd, indecent and libidinous practices.'"

In the first text paragraph of 36.09, the second and third sentences should be deleted, and the following substituted:

"In *Webster v. Dominick,* 2003 S.C.C.R. 525, it is stated that the crime of lewd, indecent and libidinous practices may be committed by having physical contact with the victim (*e.g.* handling the private parts of a child—see *Lockwood v. Walker* (1910) 6 Adam 124; *H.M. Advocate v. Millbanks*, 2002 S.L.T. 1116; *Brouillard v. H.M. Advocate*, 2004 S.L.T. 726), taking indecent photographs of him or her (see *H.M. Advocate v. Millbanks, supra*), or indecently exposing oneself to the victim (see also *H.M. Advocate v. Millbanks, supra*); or 'by the showing of indecent photographs or videos to the victim; or by other forms of indecent conduct carried out in the presence of the victim' (Lord Justice-Clerk Gill at p.540F–G, para. 49). Such practices may thus include performing sexual acts in presence of a child.[17] Lord Justice-Clerk Gill also suggests in *Webster v. Dominick* (at pp.540G–541A, para. 49) that the offence may be committed 'by means of a lewd conversation with the victim, whether face to face or by a telephone call or through an Internet chat room. In each case, the essence of the offence is the tendency of the conduct to corrupt the innocence of the complainer', which tendency was used as the basis of the decision in *Moynagh v. Spiers*, 2003 S.C.C.R. 765, (see the opinion of the court at p.767B–F, para. 2) where it was held that 'french kissing' a willing female child was within the ambit of lewd practices since, unlike a normal kiss, it was 'calculated to excite deeper sexual desires and lead to closer intimacy' and thus amount to sexual abuse of the child: see also *Boyle v. Ritchie*, 1999 S.C.C.R. 278. A woman may be convicted of using lewd practices towards a girl[18] and presumably also towards a boy: *cf. MacLean v. Bott*, 2003 S.C.C.R. 547—a case of alleged indecent practices by a female towards a 14 year old male pupil, where the charge (which had been one of shameless indecency) was held to be irrelevant by the Appeal Court following its own ruling in *Webster v. Dominick*, 2003 S.C.C.R. 525."

n.17: At the end of this footnote, the following should be added: "*Cf.* the offence of 'engaging in sexual activity in the presence of a child' under s.11 of the Sexual Offences Act 2003: this offence is defined differently depending upon whether the child is under 16 or under 13 at the material time."

In the second text paragraph of 36.09, a full-stop should be substituted for the comma following the words "a statutory offence", and the remainder of the text of this paragraph should be deleted in view of the decision in *Webster v. Dominick*, 2003 S.C.C.R. 525, that there is no such offence as "shameless indecency".

n.20: Section 13(5) of the Criminal Law (Consolidation) (Scotland) Act 1995 is also amended by the Convention Rights (Compliance) (Scotland) Act 2001 (asp 7), s.10(b).

n.21: This footnote falls to be deleted since the text to which it was attached has also been deleted (see above). The general issue discussed in n.21 was, however, mentioned in *Webster v. Dominick*, 2003 S.C.C.R. 525, where Lord Justice-Clerk Gill (with whom the other four judges agreed), after deciding that there was no offence of "shameless indecency" in Scots law, said this (at pp.542G–543A, para. 60): "One significant consequence of the view that I propose would be that in cases where a statutory prosecution was time-barred (*H.M. Advocate v. Roose* [1999 S.C.C.R. 259]), or where the Crown considered that the statutory penalty was inadequate (*Batty v. H.M. Advocate* [1995 S.L.T. 1047]), the

Crown would no longer have the option of bringing a common law charge of shameless indecency. That is not an unreasonable consequence. Legal principles should not be distorted for the purpose of circumventing statutory time limits or penalties." This suggests judicial disapproval of the substitution of a common law offence (of similar or wider ambit) for a statutory one which has become time-barred or which has a limited maximum penalty; but the general issue remains unsettled: see also *Cartwright v. H.M. Advocate*, 2001 S.L.T. 1163; and *cf. R. v. J.* [2004] 3 W.L.R. 1019 (H.L.), where the offences in question were both statutory, and, indeed, were both contained in the same Act. (For general criticism of *Webster v. Dominick*, see Jonathan Burchell and Christopher Gane, "Shamelessness Scotched: the Domain of Decency after Dominick" (2004) 8 Edin.L.R. 231; James Chalmers and Christopher Gane, "The aftermath of shameless indecency" (2003) 8 S.L.P.Q. 310.)

36.10 **n.23:** Section 15 of the Criminal Law (Consolidation) (Scotland) Act 1995 is repealed by s.19(2)(b) of the Criminal Justice (Scotland) Act 2003 (asp 7); and s.14 of the Sexual Offences Act 1956 is repealed by Sched. 7 of the Sexual Offences Act 2003.

36.11 Both in the sub-heading and the text of this paragraph, the word "disordered" should be substituted for "impaired".

n.25: Section 14 of the Sexual Offences Act 1956 is repealed by Sched. 7 of the Sexual Offences Act 2003. *Cf.* Sections 30 (sexual activity with a person with a mental disorder impeding choice), 7 (sexual assault of a child under 13) and 9 (sexual activity with a child) of the 2003 Act.

At the end of 36.11, the following should be added:

"Mentally disordered persons are now protected under the provisions of the Mental Health (Care and Treatment) (Scotland) Act (asp 13). Section 311 of the Act makes it an offence for a person to engage in anal or vaginal intercourse, or any other sexual act (as defined in subsection (8)), with or towards a person who is mentally disordered, if that mentally disordered person does not consent (as further explained in subsection (3)) or is incapable of doing so (as explained in subsection (4)) by reason of mental disorder: it is a defence for the accused to prove that he (or she) did not know and could not reasonably have been expected to know that the person in question had a mental disorder and was incapable of consenting to the intercourse or other sexual act. The maximum penalty, on summary conviction, is three months and a fine of the statutory maximum, and, on conviction on indictment, life in prison (subs. (7)). See also section 313, which makes it an offence for a person providing care services to the mentally disordered to engage in sexual intercourse (whether anal or vaginal) or any other sexual act with or towards any mentally disordered person (subject to defences set out in subsection (3)). [Section 311 and the salient parts of s.313 are set out at paras 33.10 and 33.11, above; "mental disorder" for the purposes of the 2003 Act (asp 13) has the meaning given in s.328, which meaning is partly set out in n.64 of para. 33.09, above.]

n.27: The footnote text beginning "The modern view", in line 5, and **36.12** ending at the end of the footnote is to be deleted (in view of the decision in *Webster v. Dominick*, 2003 S.C.C.R. 525 (see below)).

The second text paragraph of 36.12 is to be deleted, and the following substituted:

"Following the full bench decision in *Webster v. Dominick*, 2003 S.C.C.R. 525, indecent exposure is criminal if it amounts to lewd, indecent and libidinous practices, as will definitely be the case if the exposure is directed to an individual who is a child (male or female) below the age of puberty: whether this would still be true if the victim is 'slightly' over the age of puberty is moot (see the entries for para. 36.09, n.16, above). As Lord Justice-Clerk Gill (with whom the four other judges agreed) stated, at pp.540F–541A, para. 49: '... when indecent conduct [which includes indecent exposure] is directed against a specific victim who is within the class of persons whom the law protects, the crime is that of lewd, indecent and libidinous practices ... [T]he essence of the offence is the tendency of the conduct to corrupt the innocence of the complainer.'
  Where indecent exposure is not directed at a specific victim within the class protected by the offence of lewd practices, the court in *Webster v. Dominick, supra*, opined that such behaviour falls (along with other indecent conduct) to be treated as criminal if it amounts to 'public indecency' (see para. 36.15A, below). As Lord Justice-Clerk Gill opined at p.541B–C, paras 50–51: '[W]here indecent conduct [of which "the paradigm case is that of indecent exposure": Lord Justice-Clerk Gill at p.541E, para. 53] involves no individual victim, it is criminal only where it affronts public sensibility ... In my opinion, this crime, clearly established in Scots law before *McLaughlan v. Boyd* [1934 J.C. 19, the most important relevant prior case being *McKenzie v. Whyte* (1864) 4 Irv. 570], should in modern practice be described as "public indecency". It has a similar place in the law of Scotland to that of the common law offence of public indecency in the law of South Africa.' (For criticism of the use of that South African analogy, see Jonathan Burchell and Christopher Gane, 'Shamelessness Scotched: the Domain of Decency after Dominick' (2004) 8 Edin. L.R. 231, at pp.238–241.) What is not made plain by *Webster v. Dominick, supra*, is the fate of a case of indecent exposure where the accused directs the exposure to an adult victim in circumstances not covered by 'public indecency' (which, in Lord Justice-Clerk Gill's view, 'is an offence that fulfils an appropriate role in the maintenance of public order': *Webster v. Dominick*, at p.542C, para. 58)—*e.g.* where the exposure is directed at an unwilling adult in private: at common law, it may be that such a case is prosecutable only as a breach of the peace, provided that the elements of that offence are otherwise satisfied: see Chapter 41, below; or it may be that it is (or should be) prosecutable as an offence of its own nature, *i.e.* as 'indecent exposure' as such, although *Webster v. Dominick, supra*, provides no support for this—nor does the specimen charge in Schedule 5 of the 1995 Act."

This paragraph should be deleted, in view of the decision in *Webster v.* **36.13** *Dominick*, 2003 S.C.C.R. 525 (see para. 36.15A, below).

36.14 This paragraph should be deleted, in view of the decision in *Webster v. Dominick*, 2003 S.C.C.R. 525 (see para. 36.15A, below).

36.15 In line 6 of the text of this paragraph, the words "shameless indecency" should be deleted and "public indecency" (see para. 36.15A, below) substituted; and, the words from "Cases of this kind" (also in line 6) to the end of the paragraph should be deleted. N.38 should also be deleted.

Following para. 36.15, the following should be inserted:

"Public indecency

36.15A In *Webster v. Dominick*, 2003 S.C.C.R. 525, a full bench held unanimously that at common law there was no such crime as 'shameless indecency', but that there was a crime of 'public indecency' which was identified clearly in Scots law at least as early as the case of *McKenzie v. Whyte* (1864) 4 Irv. 570—particularly by Lord Neaves (at pp.572–573) and Lord Justice-Clerk Inglis (at pp.575 and 577). Consequently, prior case law, which had supported an offence of 'shameless indecency', was overruled (in particular, *McLaughlan v. Boyd*, 1934 J.C. 19, and *Watt v. Annan*, 1978 J.C. 84): see the opinion of Lord Justice-Clerk Gill, with whom the four other judges agreed, at pp.530G–531A, para. 8, 540D, para. 46, and 540E, para. 48. The court also held that 'public indecency' is an offence which fulfils an appropriate role in the maintenance of public order (Lord Justice-Clerk Gill, at p.542D, para. 58), and (thus unlike the now discredited 'shameless indecency') that the depraving or corrupting effect of the conduct in question was an irrelevant consideration (see Lord Justice-Clerk Gill at p.541D, para. 52), that 'shamelessness' was not an element of the offence (see Lord Justice-Clerk Gill at p.542C, para. 57), and that the 'excitation of depraved, inordinate or lustful desires in the lieges' should not be libelled since it played no part in the crime (see Lord Justice-Clerk Gill at p.542D–E, para. 58). As for the *actus reus* of public indecency, the court identified three principal elements—that the conduct in question should be indecent, occur in public, and cause public offence (see Lord Justice-Clerk Gill at pp.540E, para. 48, and 541E, para. 53). Unlike lewd, indecent and libidinous practices, no individual victim is contemplated by this offence.

The court in *Webster v. Dominick, supra*, identified indecent exposure as the paradigm case of indecent conduct for the purposes of public indecency (see Lord Justice-Clerk Gill at p.541E, para. 53), but also indicated that the *actus reus* extends to any other form of indecent behaviour, such as sexual intercourse in public view (an example suggested by Lord Sutherland in *Paterson v. Lees*, 1999 S.C.C.R. 231 at 235F–G), or gestures or actions in a publicly attended stage performance (such as occurred in the South African case of *S. v. F.*, 1977 (2) S.A. 1, where the accused made use of a microphone as if it were his penis and simulated sexual activity by use of it). By contrast with the now discredited offence of 'shameless indecency', it was emphasised by the court that public indecency did not extend to consensual sexual activity in private, the private showing of sexually explicit films, the sale (or exposure for sale) of sexually explicit publications to those who wished to view them, or public performances which portrayed nudity to a consenting audience (as in *Lockhart v. Stephen*, 1987 S.C.C.R. 642 (Sh.Ct.)): see

Lord Justice-Clerk Gill, at p.542B, para. 56. Ultimately, whether or not behaviour is indecent has to be determined by the circumstances of the case 'judged by the social standards that will change from age to age', *i.e.* 'the standards that would be applied by the average citizen in contemporary society': Lord Justice-Clerk Gill, at p.542C–D, para. 58. Whether or not the *actus reus* can extend to non-sexual conduct (as in the English case of *R. v. Gibson* [1990] 2 Q.B. 619, where the public display of earrings, consisting of freeze-dried human foetuses of three to four months gestation, was considered sufficient for conviction of the offence of 'outraging public decency': see Smith & Hogan, pp.757–758) was left unanswered (see Lord Justice-Clerk Gill, at p.541F, para. 54).

As for the 'public' element of the offence, the conduct in question need not occur in a public place, although occurrence in such a place will of course be sufficient. If the conduct occurs in a private place (such as a house or apartment) but can be seen by those who might happen to be present in a public place, then the *actus reus* is (to that extent) fulfilled: see Lord Justice-Clerk Gill at pp.541G–542A, para. 55, where the fact situation in *Usai v. Russell*, 2000 S.C.C.R. 57, is (amongst others) used by way of illustration—*viz.* that the accused stood naked at the window of his house where he could be, and was, seen by persons in the street. It also appears that '[c]onduct fully within the definition could take place on a private occasion if it occurred in the presence of unwilling witnesses' (Lord Justice-Clerk Gill, at pp.541G–542A, para. 55), presumably in the sense that such witnesses are not so much individual victims as members of the public entitled as such not to be offended by the accused's behaviour—although it is difficult to see why public indecency should be an appropriate charge in such a situation which arguably falls within the ambit of breach of the peace (see Chapter 41, below): but *Webster v. Dominick, supra,* did not provide a suitable occasion for working out in any detail the relationship between the two offences.

The indecent conduct must also cause public offence. It seems reasonably clear that actual offence must be spoken to, and spoken to probably by more than one witness. The court in *Webster v. Dominick, supra,* specifically rejected the contention of the Crown that indecent conduct in private could be criminal if a court were to be satisfied that it was of such a nature that were members of the public to become aware of it they would be offended by it (see Lord Justice-Clerk Gill, at p.542B, para. 56); but the court did say this: that public indecency does not extend 'to conduct witnessed only by persons who wish to see it—for example, performances by strippers ... or plays with scenes of nudity ... and the like—except where the conduct is such as to offend even members of a consenting audience. On this view, indecent exposure such as that considered in *Geddes v. Dickson* [2000 S.C.C.R. 1007], which was found to have offended some of those present, would continue to be criminal': Lord Justice-Clerk Gill, at p.542B, para. 56. It is not entirely clear what nuance the court meant to convey by the exception postulated, especially since in *Geddes v. Dickson, supra,* it was found as a fact (2000 S.C.C.R. at p.1011, finding in fact 20) that the possibility of inviting those attending a public disco to show their breasts or penises in return for free drinks had not been intimated to those seeking to attend the event prior to the event itself: *cf.* the fact situation in *Watt v. Annan*, 1978 J.C. 84. Perhaps what the court meant was that public indecency should not extend to conduct which had been consented to by those members of the public who witnessed it in private, provided that that conduct did not exceed (in indecency) what had been consented to; but relating such exception to degrees of individual consent is obviously difficult and potentially leads back to the vagaries of 'shameless indecency' so heavily criticised by the court in *Webster v. Dominick, supra*, itself.

The *mens rea* of public indecency is not considered by the court in *Webster v. Dominick, supra*. What is stated is that '[w]hether or not such indecency is committed for sexual gratification is ... irrelevant to liability, being a matter of motive, but may, on conviction, be a relevant factor in the court's disposal': Lord Justice-Clerk Gill, at p.541F, para. 53. It may be that the court considered the offence to be one of 'strict liability', as is the case with the English common law offence of 'outraging public decency' (see Smith & Hogan, p.758), since after mentioning the leading English authority on that offence, Lord Justice-Clerk Gill (at p.541D–E, para. 52) states (of public indecency) that 'it is sufficient for liability that, on an objective assessment, the conduct complained of should cause public offence'. It would appear, therefore, that if witnesses testify that they were offended by the indecent conduct in question, and the court takes the view that it was reasonable for those witnesses as members of the public to be so offended, the offence will have been committed. Certainly, the *mens rea* position in relation to public indecency must invite comparison with that in relation to breach of the peace (see Chapter 41, para. 41.09)—the other significant public order offence at common law.

There is no evidence that sexual activity with a human corpse was criminal at common law as shameless indecency, but the extensive way in which that crime was perceived would not have ruled out a charge under that head in an appropriate case. Equally, such conduct might now be charged as public indecency if the elements of that offence were otherwise satisfied: there is nothing, however, in Scots criminal law corresponding to the English statutory crime of 'Sexual penetration of a corpse' under section 70 (as read with section 78) of the Sexual Offences Act 2003."

36.15B [The text, including the subheading, and relative footnotes of the paragraph originally numbered 36.23 in the 3rd edition should now appear as para. 36.15B, with the following modifications. The final sentence of the text should be amended, so as to read: "Such a charge might now be brought as one of public indecency if the elements of that offence could be satisfied.[99]" The original text of n.99 should be deleted and the following substituted: "See para. 36.15A, above."]

36.16 To the extent that *McLaughlan v. Boyd*, 1934 J.C. 19, would have supported the criminalisation of homosexual practices as shameless indecency, it is overruled by the full bench decision in *Webster v. Dominick*, 2003 S.C.C.R. 525: but homosexual practices between adults short of sodomy might be prosecutable at common law as public indecency where the elements of that crime can be satisfied: see para. 36.15A, above.

36.17 **n.42:** Section 13 of the Criminal Law (Consolidation) (Scotland) Act 1995 is further amended by the Mental Health (Care and Treatment) (Scotland) Act 2003 (asp 13), Sched. 5, Pt 1, which repeals subsection (3).

In the definition of "homosexual act" given in s.13(4) of the Criminal Law (Consolidation) (Scotland) Act 1995, the reference to "shameless indecency" is now problematic since shameless indecency was declared not to be a common law offence by a full bench in *Webster v. Dominick*, 2003 S.C.C.R. 525. That case confirmed that indecent conduct was criminal at common law either as lewd, indecent and libidinous practices or as public indecency—but not as shameless indecency. It remains to be seen, therefore, what content (if any) is now to be given to "an act of shameless indecency by one male person with another male person".

In the second text paragraph of 36.17, at lines 3–4, the words "which would be prosecuted as shamelessly indecent conduct[44]" should be deleted, following the decision in *Webster v. Dominick*, 2003 S.C.C.R. 525.

n.44: This footnote should be deleted, since paras 36.20 to 36.22 are to be deleted.

n.46: English law is now governed by the Sexual Offences Act 2003, which no longer refers to acts of "gross indecency" and indeed repeals s.11 of the Criminal Law Amendment Act 1885 under which the two cases referred to in this note were decided (see Sched. 7 of the 2003 Act).

The second text paragraph of 36.17 on p.535 of the 3rd edition (beginning: "Male persons who are mentally handicapped") should now be deleted, since s.13(3) of the Criminal Law (Consolidation) (Scotland) Act 1995 is repealed by the Mental Health (Care and Treatment) (Scotland) Act 2003 (asp 13), Sched. 5, Pt 1.

36.18 The whole of this paragraph falls to be deleted (as does n.51) since the Mental Health (Scotland) Act 1984 has been repealed by the Mental Health (Care and Treatment) (Scotland) Act 2003 (asp 13), Sched. 5, Pt 1. The 2003 Act contains substituted offences under ss.311 and 313 (which are set out, in so far as relevant, in the substituted Chapter 33, at paras 33.10 and 33.11 above: the meaning of "mental disorder" for the purposes of those sections is set out in s.328 of the 2003 Act).

36.20–36.22 These paragraphs, together with their initial heading "Shameless indecency" and notes 54–95, must now be deleted, following the full bench decision in *Webster v. Dominick*, 2003 S.C.C.R. 525, that there is no common law offence of shameless indecency: see para. 36.15A, above.

36.23 This paragraph, as amended, is renumbered 36.15B: see para. 36.15, above.

36.27 **n.20:** The reference to the Criminal Law (Consolidation) (Scotland) Act 1995 should read "s.8(3)(b)" rather than s.(3)(b).

36.28 **n.21:** Section 23 of the Sexual Offences Act 1956 is repealed by the Sexual Offences Act 2003, Sched. 7.

36.30 This paragraph (together with nn.29–31) should be deleted since the Mental Health (Scotland) Act 1984 is wholly repealed by the Mental

Health (Care and Treatment) (Scotland) Act 2003 (asp 13), Sched. 5, Pt 1. There is no provision in the 2003 Act (asp 13) analogous to s.106(1)(b) of the 1984 Act.

36.34 This paragraph (together with nn.39–48) should be deleted since s.8(1) and (2) of the Criminal Law (Consolidation) (Scotland) Act 1995 are repealed (and not replaced) by the Criminal Justice (Scotland) Act 2003 (asp 7), s.19(2).

36.36 The words *"or mentally impaired women"* should be deleted from the heading to this paragraph: see the entry for para. 36.37, below.

36.37 This paragraph (together with nn.55–57) should be deleted, since the Mental Health (Scotland) Act 1984 is wholly repealed by the Mental Health (Care and Treatment) (Scotland) Act 2003 (asp 13), Sched. 5, Pt.1. There is no equivalent to s.106(1)(c) of the 1984 in the 2003 Act (asp 13).

36.40 The "corresponding English provision" (s.32 of the Sexual Offences Act 1956) mentioned in this paragraph (at lines 4–5 on p.550 of the 3rd edition) was repealed by the Sexual Offences Act 2003, Sched. 7.

n.71: Section 13(4) of the Criminal Law (Consolidation) (Scotland) Act 1995 (meaning of "homosexual act") includes an act of "shameless indecency"; but, in *Webster v. Dominick*, 2003 S.C.C.R. 525, it was held that shameless indecency was not a crime at common law in Scotland. It is uncertain, therefore, what an act of shameless indecency now means in this statutory context.

36.41 In this paragraph, at line 3, the words "sections 8(1)–(5) and 9" should now read "sections 8(3)–(5) and 9", since s.8(1) and (2) of the Criminal Law (Consolidation) (Scotland) Act 1995 were repealed by the Criminal Justice (Scotland) Act 2003 (asp 7), s.19(2)(a).

36.44 n.76a: The citation for *Reid v. H.M. Advocate* should read: "1999 S.C.C.R. 19".

36.47 After this paragraph, the following new paragraph should be inserted.

36.47A *"Trafficking in prostitution (etc.).* Section 22 of the Criminal Justice (Scotland) Act 2003 (asp 7) provides:

'(1) A person commits an offence who arranges or facilitates—

(a) the arrival in the United Kingdom of, or travel there (whether or not following such arrival) by, an individual and—

(i) intends to exercise control over prostitution by the individual or to involve the individual in the making or production of obscene or indecent material; or

(ii) believes that another person is likely to exercise such control or so to involve the individual, there or elsewhere; or

(b) the departure from there of an individual and—

(i) intends to exercise such control or so to involve the individual; or

(ii) believes that another person is likely to exercise such control or so to involve the individual,

outwith the United Kingdom.

(2) For the purposes of subsection (1), a person exercises control over prostitution by an individual if the person exercises control, direction or influence over the prostitute's movements in a way which shows that the person is aiding, abetting or compelling the prostitution.

(3) A person guilty of an offence under this section is liable—

(a) on conviction on indictment, to imprisonment for a term not exceeding fourteen years, to a fine or to both; or

(b) on summary conviction, to imprisonment for a term not exceeding six months, to a fine not exceeding the statutory maximum or to both.

(4) Subsection (1) applies to anything done—

(a) in the United Kingdom; or

(b) outwith the United Kingdom—

(i) by an individual to whom subsection (6) applies; or

(ii) by a body incorporated under the law of a part of the United Kingdom.

(5) If an offence under this section is committed outwith the United Kingdom, proceedings may be taken in any place in Scotland; and the offence may for incidental purposes be treated as having been committed in that place.

(6) This subsection applies to—

(a) a British citizen;

(b) a British overseas territories citizen;

(c) a British National (Overseas);

(d) a British Overseas citizen;

(e) a person who is a British subject under the British Nationality Act 1981 (c.61); and

(f) a British protected person within the meaning of that Act.

(7) In this section, "material" has the same meaning as in section 51 of the Civic Government (Scotland) Act 1982 (c.45) and includes a pseudo-photograph within the meaning of section 52 of that Act, a copy of a pseudo-photograph and data stored on a computer disc or by any other electronic means which is capable of conversion into a photograph or pseudo-photograph.'"

n.97: In the text of this note, the words "shamelessly indecent conduct" **36.48** should be deleted and the following substituted: "public indecency".

CHAPTER 37

TREASON AND ALLIED OFFENCES

37.24 Any lingering suggestion that s.3 of the Treason Felony Act 1848 could be used to prosecute a person who published "any printing or writing" advocating a peaceful change from monarchical to republican government in the United Kingdom has been ridiculed by the House of Lords in *R (Rusbridger) v. Attorney General* [2004] 1 A.C. 357. In that case, the editor of the Guardian newspaper (and one of its journalists) sought from a civil court a declaration that s.3 should be read so as not to criminalise any published advocation of such peaceful change or, alternatively, a declaration that s.3 (to the extent that it did so criminalise such advocation) was incompatible with Article 10 (freedom of expression) of the European Convention on Human Rights (see the Human Rights Act 1998, Sched. 1). Although the House was divided (*cf.* Lord Steyn—with whom Lord Scott of Foscote and Lord Walker of Gestingthorpe agreed—at p.368G, para. 25, Lord Hutton, at p.371, para. 35, and Lord Rodger of Earlsferry, at p.377, para. 57) on the question of whether the claimants had demonstrated the "exceptional circumstances" which are required if a civil court is to entertain an action for a declaration against the Crown that proposed action would be lawful, their Lordships accepted (for example) that the view "that a total legislative ban on republican discourse in print could be compatible with Article 10 of the Convention would stretch judicial gullibility to breaking point" (Lord Steyn at p.364B–C, para. 8); that the "part of section 3 of the 1848 Act which appears to criminalise the advocacy of republicanism is a relic of a bygone age and does not fit into the fabric of our modern legal system" (Lord Steyn at p.369, at para. 28); that "section 3 of the 1848 Act is a dead letter so far as advocacy of political change by peaceful and constitutional means is concerned" (Lord Scott of Foscote, at p.373E, para. 44); and, that to the extent that it permitted prosecution of the publishers of republican, and thus anti-monarchy, advocacy s.3 was "obsolete" (see Lord Walker of Gestingthorpe, at pp.377G–378B, paras 60–61). In relation to this statutory provision, and others like it which "have become out-of-date and which should be repealed or amended but which linger on untouched since, in a crowded Parliamentary timetable, governments have had other priorities", Lord Rodger of Earlsferry was content to rely on the good sense of prosecutors to gauge correctly the public interest, and thus refrain from prosecuting: should that sense of the public interest elude them, "any resulting prosecution is liable to provoke public criticism or even ridicule, while placing a martyr's crown on the defendant's head" (Lord Rodger of Earlsferry at p.375B–E, para. 52). In England, should private prosecutions under s.3 be attempted by extreme monarchists, procedure exists to prevent their onward progress (see Lord Rodger of Earlsferry at p.375F–G, para. 53); in Scotland, such private prosecutions would be (at best) theoretical (see Renton & Brown, paras 3–01 and 3–09 to 3–15) bearing in mind that this offence is statutory and (apparently) triable only on indictment.

n.68: Section 42 of the Police (Scotland) Act 1967 is also amended by the **37.27** Anti-terrorism, Crime and Security Act 2001, Sched. 7, para. 5(2), (3), by the Railways and Transport Safety Act 2003, Sched. 5, para. 4(1), and by the Energy Act 2004, s.68(4).

The meaning of "prohibited place" is extended by Sched. 17, para. 2 of **37.40** the Communications Act 2003, which provides: "For the purposes of the Official Secrets Act 1911 (c.28), any electronic communications station or office belonging to, or occupied by, the provider of a public electronic communications service shall be a prohibited place." For the meaning of "electronic communications service", see s.32(2) of the 2003 Act.

In *R. v. Shayler* [2002] 2 All E.R. 477, the House of Lords decided that a **37.47** defendant charged under ss.1(1) and 4(1) of the Official Secrets Act 1989 could not mount a defence of "public or national interest" relative to disclosures which he had admittedly made contrary to the provisions of the Act. It was also held that those provisions, bearing in mind their rationale and significance, were not incompatible with Article 10 ("Freedom of expression") of the European Convention on Human Rights; although the provisions in question did restrict the defendant's rights under that Article, such restriction was justified by the legitimate objectives secured by the legislation (which did, in any event, permit lawful ways by which persons such as the defendant might bring their concerns over security issues to the notice of the authorities without disclosing restricted matters (as in this case) to a Sunday newspaper)

n.11: The entries under Sched. 3 of the Official Secrets Act 1989 (Pre- **37.54** scription) Order 1990 (S.I. 1990 No. 200) are substituted by those found in Sched. 2 to the Official Secrets Act 1989 (Prescription) (Amendment) Order 2003 (S.I. 2003 No. 1918).

n.20: For the reference to "Sched. 12" of the Pollution Prevention and **37.60** Control Act 1999, read "Sched. 2".

Section 34(2) of the Legal Aid (Scotland) Act 1986 is extended by para.9 **37.62** of Sched. 6 to the Scottish Public Services Ombudsman Act 2002 (asp 11), such that the following new paragraph is added:

"(d) for the purpose of any investigation by the Scottish Public Services Ombudsman under the Scottish Public Services Ombudsman Act 2002 (asp 11)."

CHAPTER 38

OFFENCES OF DISHONESTY AGAINST THE STATE

38.01 Section 6(5)(a) of the European Communities Act 1972 is also amended by reg. 3(e) of the Intervention Board for Agricultural Produce (Abolition) Regulations 2001 (S.I. 2001 No. 3686).

38.02 **n.2:** Section 170 of the Customs and Excise Management Act 1979 is also amended by s.293(4) of the Criminal Justice Act 2003.

n.12: In line 2 of this footnote, after the year "1985", the following should be inserted: "and by Sched. 28, para. 2 to the Criminal Justice Act 2003"; and, in line 3, after "Class B" there should be inserted: "or Class C".

Section 170 of the Customs and Excise Management Act 1979 is amended by s.293(4) of the Criminal Justice Act 2003 such that subsection (4A) of the 1979 Act is replaced by the following:

"(4A) In the case of—

(a) an offence under subsection (2) or (3) above committed in Great Britain in connection with a prohibition or restriction on the importation or exportation of any weapon or ammunition that is of a kind mentioned in section 5(1)(a), (ab), (aba), (ac), (ad), (ae), (af) or (c) or (1A)(a) of the Firearms Act 1968 [on which, see para. 30.30 and the entry for that para. above],

(b) [offences in Northern Ireland], or

(c) any such offence committed in connection with the prohibitions contained in sections 20 and 21 of the Forgery and Counterfeiting Act 1981,

subsection (3)(b) above shall have effect as if for the words '7 years' there were substituted the words '10 years'."

Relative to the first text paragraph of 38.02 on p.588 of the 3rd edition, in *R. v. Forbes* [2001] 3 W.L.R. 428 (H.L.), the defendant imported through Heathrow Airport two video films which he believed to be "The Exorcist" and "Kidz". He further believed that the import of those particular films was prohibited: had the films been what he believed them to be, they would not have fallen within any prohibited category. Unknown to the defendant, however, the films he in fact imported were films containing indecent photographs of young boys and thus were prohibited for that reason. The defendant claimed to be entitled to be acquitted of charges under s.170(2)(b) of the 1979 Act on the principle established in *R. v. Taffe* [1984] A.C. 539; but the House of Lords confirmed his conviction for the offences since, as in *R. v. Hennessey* (1978) 68 Cr.App.R. 419, the defendant believed the materials to be prohibited goods, the materials were prohibited goods, and the steps taken by the defendant at Amsterdam Airport to conceal the identity of the materials demonstrated that he was knowingly concerned in the fraudulent evasion of the relevant prohibition.

n.41: Section 136 of the Customs and Excise Management Act 1979 is **38.11** also amended by reg. 6(7)(b) of the Intervention Board for Agricultural Produce (Abolition) Regulations 2001 (S.I. 2001 No. 3686).

Section 50 of the Customs and Excise Management Act 1979 is amended **38.13** by s.293(2) of the Criminal Justice Act 2003, such that subsection (5A) of the 1979 Act is replaced by the following:

"(5A) In the case of—

(a) an offence under subsection (2) or (3) above committed in Great Britain in connection with a prohibition or restriction on the importation of any weapon or ammunition that is of a kind mentioned in section 5(1)(a), (ab), (aba), (ac), (ad), (ae) (af) or (c) or (1A)(a) of the Firearms Act 1968 [on which, see para. 30.30 and the entry for that para. above],
(b) [offences in Northern Ireland], or
(c) any such offence committed in connection with the prohibition contained in section 20 of the Forgery and Counterfeiting Act 1981,

subsection (4)(b) above shall have effect as if for the words '7 years' there were substituted the words '10 years'."

n.43: Section 50 of the 1979 Act is also amended by s.293(2) of the Criminal Justice Act 2003, as noted immediately above.

n.45: Subsection (5A) of s.50 of the 1979 Act is now replaced by virtue of s.293(2) of the Criminal Justice Act 2003; see above.

n.48: In the citation for *R. v. Whitehead*, for "[1892]", read "[1982]".

It should be noted that subsection (3) of s.67 of the Customs and Excise **38.14** Management Act 1979 has become intermingled with subsection (2) on p.595 of the 3rd edition.

In s.17(1)(a) of the Alcoholic Liquor Duties Act 1979, for "office" read: **38.19** "officer".

n.70: Section 36 of the Value Added Tax Act 1994 is further amended by **38.21** the Finance Act 2002, Sched. 40, Pt 2(1).

Subsection 11 of s.72 of the Value Added Tax Act 1994 is amended by s.17(5) of the Finance Act 2003, such that after the word "supplies" there are to be added the words: "or is supplied with".

n.75: Paragraph 4(2) of Schedule 11 to the Value Added Tax Act 1994 is now substituted by new subparagraphs (2)–(5) by virtue of s.17(4) of the Finance Act 2003.

38.22 **n.76:** To the list of statutes mentioned at the beginning of this footnote there should be added the Local Governance (Scotland) Act 2004 (asp 9). The statutory instruments, 1999 No. 787 and 2001 No. 1399, referred to in this footnote are revoked by art. 2 of the Scottish Parliament (Elections etc.) Order 2002 (S.I. 2002 No. 2779), which is currently the leading instrument relative to Scottish Parliamentary elections. With respect to European Parliamentary elections, see the European Parliamentary Elections Act 2002 (as amended by the European Parliamentary Elections Act 2003) and the Local and European Elections (Registration of Citizens of Accession States) Regulations 2003 (S.I. 2003 No. 1557).

38.23 **n.81:** The modification of penalties for Scottish Parliamentary elections is now authorised by the Scottish Parliament (Elections etc.) Order 2002 (S.I. 2002 No. 2779), Sched. 6, Pt 1 (entry for s.168).

38.24 **n.84:** The reference to the Scottish Parliament in s.160(4) of the Representation of the People Act 1983 is now authorised by the Scottish Parliament (Elections etc.) Order 2002 (S.I. 2002 No. 2779), Sched. 6, Pt 1 (entry for s.160): that Order revokes S.I. 1999 No. 787 and S.I. 2001 No. 1399.

n.92: In line 2 of this footnote, for "s.59" read: "s.159".

38.32 Section 159 of the Representation of the People Act 1983 is amended by para. 7 of Sched. 17 to the Political Parties, Elections and Referendums Act 2000.

38.34 **n.19:** See the entry for para. 38.24, n.84, above.

38.35 Section 93 of the Representation of the People Act 1983 is substituted by s.144 of the Political Parties, Elections and Referendums Act 2000, such that, *inter alia*, there is now no reference to illegal practices in this context. (The substituted section is itself amended by the Communications Act 2003, Sched. 17, para. 62(2), (3)(a) and (3)(b).) Consequently, the text of para. 38.35 from "BROADCASTING" to the end (including nn.26 and 27) should be deleted.

38.36 Sections 81 and 82 of the Representation of the People Act 1983 are amended by the Political Parties, Elections and Referendums Act 2000, Sched. 18, paras 7 and 8.

n.28: Not all amendments effected by Sched. 18 to the Political Parties, Elections and Referendums Act 2000 are now excluded from local government elections in Scotland: see Local Governance (Scotland) Act 2004 (asp 9), s.14, esp. (2) and (3).

n.31: Section 92 of the Representation of the People Act 1983 is amended by the Communications Act 2003, Sched. 17, para. 61.

38.38 Section 175(2) of the Representation of the People Act 1983 is amended by the Political Parties, Elections and Referendums Act 2000, Sched. 21, para. 6(6), such that the words "illegal payment, employment or hiring" now read: "illegal payment or employment".

n.36: Section 175(1) of the Representation of the People Act 1983 is amended in a similar way to s.175(2): see the immediately preceding entry.

In the second line of the quoted text of s.106(5), the word "withdrawal" **38.39** should be inserted after the word "candidate's".

n.41: Section 62(1) of the Representation of the People Act 1983 is **38.43** modified for the purposes of European elections by the European Parliamentary Elections (Franchise of Relevant Citizens of the Union) Regulations 2001 (S.I. 2001 No. 1184), Sched., Pt 1.

In the text of this paragraph, at line 4, for the words "any postmaster" **38.44** there should be substituted: "any official designated by a universal postal service provider", for the purposes of the Postal Services Act 2000 (Consequential Modifications No. 1) Order 2001 (S.I. 2001 No. 1149), Sched. 1, para. 57(2), which modifies to this extent s.63(3)(d) of the Representation of the People Act 1983.

Sections 148 and 149 of the Representation of the People Act 1983 apply **38.46** only to local government elections in Scotland: see Political Parties, Elections and Referendums Act 2000, Sched. 17, para. 5(1) and (2).

n.52: Section 37(1)(a) of the British Nationality Act 1981 is amended by **38.47** the British Overseas Territories Act 2002, Sched. 1, para. 4. (The amendment presupposes knowledge of the prior amendment of the section by s.4(3) of the British Nationality (Falkland Islands) Act 1983.)

CHAPTER 39

SEDITION AND ALLIED OFFENCES

39.09 Terrorism offences are principally governed by the Terrorism Act 2000 and the Anti-terrorism, Crime and Security Act 2001; but for the sake of completeness, reference should also be made to the Prevention of Terrorism Act 2005: s.1 of the 2000 Act provides the core meaning of "terrorism" for the 2005 Act (see the 2005 Act, s.15(1)).

The main provisions of the Prevention of Terrorism Act 2005 (ss.1–9), unless previously repealed or extended under s.13, will expire 12 months after the date on which the Act received the Royal Assent (*i.e.* 12 months after March 11, 2005). The purpose of the Act is to permit the Secretary of State, or a court (where the order involves the imposition of obligations incompatible with the right to liberty under Article 5 of the European Convention on Human Rights), to make "control orders" against individuals with a view to protecting the public from a risk of terrorism. Control orders impose such obligations as are considered necessary to prevent or restrict involvement by the individuals subject to them in terrorism-related activity (as defined in s.1(9)). Under s.9(1) of the Act, it is an offence for a person, without reasonable excuse, to contravene an obligation imposed on him by a control order: maximum penalty is, on summary conviction, imprisonment for six months and a fine, and on conviction on indictment, imprisonment for five years and a fine (s.9(4)(a), (c)).

n.19: For the most recent additions to proscribed organisations under the Terrorism Act 2000, see the Terrorism Act 2000 (Proscribed Organisations) (Amendment) Order 2001 (S.I. 2001 No. 1261), art. 2, and the Terrorism Act 2000 (Proscribed Organisations) (Amendment) Order 2002 (S.I. 2002 No. 2724), arts 2 and 3.

39.10 n.21: This note should read: "*Cf.* s.118 of the 2000 Act" since s.118 does not apply to the defence under s.11(2).

In line 1 of the second text paragraph on p.623 of the 3rd edition, after "for a person" the following words should be inserted: "in a public place"; and, at the end of that paragraph, the following should be added: "In *Rankin v. Murray*, 2004 S.C.C.R. 422, the appeal court emphasised that section 13 (notwithstanding the side note 'uniform') did not restrict the ambit of 'article' in any way. Thus, even if the appellant, who had been observed by the police at a ferry terminal at Troon, had, as he maintained, never been a member or supporter of the proscribed organisation in question, his wearing in a public place items of jewellery bearing the clearly visible initials of that organisation was sufficient to arouse reasonable suspicion of such membership or support, and that was all that the offence required."

n.35: The text of this note should read: "*Cf.* s.118.", since s.118 does not **39.11**
apply to the defence under s.18(2).

n.39: The text of this note should read: "*Cf.* s.118.", since s.118 does not
apply to the defence under s.21(5).

n.42: Section 19 does not now apply "if the information came to the
person in the course of a business in the regulated sector" (see s.19(1A),
inserted by the Anti-terrorism, Crime and Security Act 2001, Sched. 2,
para. 5(3)). For the meaning of "business in the regulated sector", see
Sched. 3A of the 2000 Act (as inserted by the 2001 Act, Sched. 2, para. 6).
"Failure to disclose" on the part of a person involved in a business in the
regulated sector is now an offence in terms of s.21A (see also s.21B) of the
2000 Act: ss.21A and 21B were inserted by the 2001 Act, Sched. 2, para.
5(2).

Also, in lines 3 and 4 of the text of n.42, "(see s.118)" should read: "(*cf.*
s.118)", since s.118 is not applicable to s.19(3) or (4).

After the subheading "OFFENCES IN CONNECTION WITH TER- **39.12**
RORIST INVESTIGATIONS", the following should be inserted:

"Section 38B (inserted by section 117(2) of the Anti-terrorism, Crime and
Security Act 2001) of the 2000 Act provides:

'(1) This section applies where a person has information which he
knows or believes might be of material assistance—

(a) in preventing the commission by another person of an act of
terrorism, or
(b) in securing the apprehension, prosecution or conviction of
another person, in the United Kingdom, for an offence
involving the commission, preparation or instigation of an
act of terrorism.

(2) The person commits an offence if he does not disclose the
information as soon as reasonably practicable in accordance with
subsection (3).

(3) Disclosure is in accordance with this subsection if it is made—

(a) ...
(b) in Scotland, to a constable...
(c) ...

(4) It is a defence for a person charged with an offence under
subsection (2) to prove that he had a reasonable excuse for not
making the disclosure.

(5) A person guilty of an offence under this section shall be
liable—

(a) on conviction on indictment, to imprisonment for a term
not exceeding five years, or to a fine or to both, or
(b) on summary conviction, to imprisonment for a term not
exceeding six months, or to a fine not exceeding the statutory maximum or to both.

(6) Proceedings for an offence under this section may be taken, and the offence may for the purposes of those proceedings be treated as having been committed, in any place where the person to be charged is or has at any time been since he first knew or believed that the information might be of material assistance as mentioned in subsection (1).' "

In s.39(3) of the 2000 Act, there should be inserted "or 38B" at the end, this amendment being required by the Anti-terrorism, Crime and Security Act 2001, s.117(3).

n.43: In line 3 of this note, for "n.39.09" read: "para. 39.09".

39.13 **n.47:** Section 54(1) and (2) of the 2000 Act now extend to "radioactive materials or weapons designed or adapted for the discharge of any radioactive material": see s.54(1)(aa) and s.54(2)(aa), inserted by the 2001 Act s.120(1); and, "biological weapons" are redefined, and a definition of "radioactive material" is provided, by s.55 of the 2000 Act, as amended by the 2001 Act, s.120(2)(a),(b): the original definition of "nuclear weapon" has been dropped—2001 Act, s.120(2)(c).

n.64: Section 64 of the 2000 Act was repealed by the Extradition Act 2003, Sched. 4, consequent on the repeal of the Extradition Act 1989 by that Sched.

Section 52 of the Crime (International Co-operation) Act 2003 adds to the Terrorism Act 2000 a series of new provisions (ss.63A to 63E) which allow extra territorial jurisdiction for certain offences in the 2000 Act, including those under s.54 and ss.56–61.

After paragraph 39.13, the following should be inserted:

"The Anti-terrorism, Crime and Security Act 2001

39.13A USE OF SUBSTANCES ETC. TO INFLUENCE THE GOVERNMENT OR INTIMIDATE THE PUBLIC. Section 113 of the 2001 Act provides:

'(1) A person who takes any action which—

(a) involves the use of a noxious substance [see para. 39.13C, *infra*] or other noxious thing;
(b) has or is likely to have an effect falling within subsection (2); and
(c) is designed to influence the government or to intimidate the public or a section of the public,

is guilty of an offence.
(2) Action has an effect falling within this subsection if it—

(a) causes serious violence against a person anywhere in the world;
(b) causes serious damage to real or personal property anywhere in the world;
(c) endangers human life or creates a serious risk to the health or safety of the public or a section of the public; or

(d) induces in members of the public the fear that the action is likely to endanger their lives or create a serious risk to their health or safety;

but any effect on the person taking the action is to be disregarded.
(3) A person who—

(a) makes a threat that he or another will take any action which constitutes an offence under subsection (1); and
(b) intends thereby to induce in a person [see para. 39.13C, *infra*] anywhere in the world the fear that the threat is likely to be carried out,

is guilty of an offence.
(4) A person guilty of an offence under this section is liable—

(a) on summary conviction, to imprisonment for a term not exceeding six months or a fine not exceeding the statutory maximum (or both); and
(b) on conviction on indictment, to imprisonment for a term not exceeding fourteen years or a fine (or both).

(5) In this section—
"the government" means the government or the United Kingdom, of a part of the United Kingdom or of a country other than the United Kingdom; and
"the public" includes the public of a country other than the United Kingdom.'

By virtue of section 113A, section 113 applies to conduct done outside the United Kingdom if that conduct is done to advance 'a political, religious or ideological cause' and is effected by a United Kingdom national or a United Kingdom resident, or by any person to (or in relation to) a United Kingdom national, a United Kingdom resident or a protected person, or by any person in circumstances falling within section 63D(1)(b) and (c) or (3)(b) and (c) of the Terrorism Act 2000. (For 'United Kingdom national', 'United Kingdom resident' and 'protected person', see ss.63A(2), (3) and 63C(3) of the 2000 Act: ss.63A, 63C and 63D were added to the 2000 Act by the Crime (International Co-operation) Act 2003, s.52; and s.113A was added to the 2001 Act by s.53 of the 2003 Act.

HOAXES INVOLVING NOXIOUS SUBSTANCES OR THINGS. Section 114 of the **39.13B** 2001 Act provides:

'(1) A person is guilty of an offence if he—

(a) places any substance [see para. 39.13C, *infra*] or other thing in any place; or
(b) sends any substance or other thing from one place to another (by post, rail or any other means whatever);

with the intention of inducing in a person [see para. 39.13C, *infra*] anywhere in the world a belief that it is likely to be (or contain) a noxious substance or other noxious thing and thereby endanger human life or create a serious risk to human health.

(2) A person is guilty of an offence if he communicates any information which he knows or believes to be false with the intention of inducing in a person anywhere in the world a belief that a noxious substance or other noxious thing is likely to be present (whether at the time the information is communicated or later) in any place and thereby endanger human life or create a serious risk to human health.

(3) A person guilty of an offence under this section is liable—

(a) on summary conviction, to imprisonment for a term not exceeding six months or a fine not exceeding the statutory maximum (or both); and

(b) on conviction on indictment, to imprisonment for a term not exceeding seven years or a fine (or both).'

39.13C Sections 113 and 114 of the 2001 Act are qualified by section 115 which provides:

'(1) For the purposes of sections 113 and 114 "substance" includes any biological agent and any other natural or artificial substance (whatever its form, origin or method of production).

(2) For a person to be guilty of an offence under section 113(3) or 114 it is not necessary for him to have any particular person in mind as the person in whom he intends to induce the belief in question.' "

39.19 nn.82 and 85: In England, the size of a public assembly has been reduced to two or more persons: see the Anti-social Behaviour Act 2003, s.57. *Cf.* ss.19–22 of the Antisocial Behaviour etc. (Scotland) Act 2004 (asp 8), which refer to the dispersal of groups "of two or more persons in a public place": see para. 41.14B, *infra*.

39.20 Section 14A of the Public Order Act 1986 is amended by the Land Reform (Scotland) Act 2003 (asp 2), Sched. 2, para. 9, such that subsection (9A) is inserted: that subsection provides—

"In relation to Scotland, the references in this section to the public's rights (or limited rights) of access do not include any right which the public or any member of the public may have by way of access rights within the meaning of the Land Reform (Scotland) Act 2003 (asp 3)."

For "access rights", see the entry for para. 15.43, *supra*.

39.22 Section 17 of the Public Order Act 1986 is amended by Part 4 of Sched. 8 to the Anti-terrorism, Crime and Security Act 2001, such that the words "in Great Britain" are to be omitted.

On p.632 of the 3rd edition, the final sentence of this paragraph should be deleted and the following substituted: "Where a 'programme service' is referred to in those sections, what is to be understood is 'programme service' within the meaning of section 201 of the Broadcasting Act 1990 as amended by the Communications Act 2003, section 360(1) and (2). (For the meanings of 'programme service' and 'electronic

communications network' referred to in section 201 as so amended, reference should be made to section 405(1) of the 2003 Act.)"
Footnotes 99, 1 and 2 on that page should be deleted.

The text of s.241(1)(a) of the Trade Union and Labour Relations Act **39.32** 1992 should be amended (by virtue of the Civil Partnership Act 2004, Sched. 27, para. 145) so that for the word "wife" there is substituted: "spouse or civil partner".

In s.244(1) of the 1992 Act, it has been considered sufficient for a "trade **39.37** dispute" to exist that a dispute should be about a term *or* a condition of employment, the use of the composite expression in the subsection showing "that it was intended to be given a broad meaning": see *P. v. NASUWT* [2003] 1 All E.R. 993 (H.L.) at 1001b, para. 24, *per* Lord Hoffmann.

CHAPTER 40

MOBBING

40.14 n.62: The text of this footnote should be replaced by the following:

"*Coleman v. H.M. Advocate*, 1999 S.C.C.R. 87. In *Coleman*, Lord Justice-Clerk Cullen, at p.103B, and Lord Coulsfield, at p.112C, indicated that their respective opinions depended on the application of the law of mobbing and rioting and not on what had been said in *Brown v. H.M. Advocate*, 1993 S.C.C.R. 382, in relation to concert. Nevertheless, the Appeal Court in *Coleman* may have been influenced by *Brown*, the soundness of which that court was not prepared, or indeed in a position, to reconsider. What was said in *Brown* relative to art and part guilt, at least in relation to antecedent concert, was subsequently disapproved by a court of five judges in *McKinnon v. H.M. Advocate*, 2003 S.L.T. 281 (see the entry for Chapter 5, para. 5.16, *supra*). Following *McKinnon*, therefore, it is a matter for consideration whether *Coleman* is correctly decided in relation to mobbing."

CHAPTER 41

BREACH OF THE PEACE, OBSCENE PUBLICATIONS AND BLASPHEMY

n.5: Convicting a person for breach of the peace in relation to his conduct **41.01** at a peaceful political demonstration or protest may well interfere with his right of freedom of expression (Article 10(1) of the European Convention on Human Rights: see the Human Rights Act 1998, Sched. 1) and/or his right to freedom of peaceful assembly and association with others (Article 11(1)): but these rights are not absolute. Under Articles 10(2) and 11(2), restriction may be placed on the expression of these rights if the restriction is "prescribed by law" and is necessary in a democratic society in the interests of any of the matters specified in those sub-articles—which matters include "public safety" and "the prevention of disorder". Breach of the peace, as defined in *Smith v. Donnelly*, 2001 S.L.T. 1007, is certainly prescribed by law: see the admissibility case of *Lucas v. U.K.*, European Court of Human Rights, March 18, 2003, Applic. No. 39013/02, the decision of the court there being conveniently set out in the commentary to *Jones v. Carnegie; Tallents v. Gallacher; Barrett v. Carnegie; Carberry v. Currie; Park v. Frame*, 2004 S.C.C.R. 361 at 377E–383C.

For cases where convictions for breach of the peace were held to be justified and proportionate, notwithstanding Articles 10(1) and 11(1), see *Jones v. Carnegie*, 2004 S.L.T. 609, appeals of Jane Tallents (at pp.614J–616I, paras 15–28), where the appellant had been convicted for disrupting the proceedings at the Scottish Parliament Chamber in Edinburgh, and Gaynor Barrett (at pp.616J–617J, paras 29–36), where the conviction related to a protest in the roadway outside the main gate of a naval base. See also *Quinan v. Carnegie*, 2005 S.C.C.R. 267, where *Jones v. Carnegie* was applied by the Appeal Court in affirming the conviction of a member of the Scottish Parliament for breach of the peace at an anti-nuclear demonstration.

n.11: In *McGraw v. H.M. Advocate*, 2004 S.C.C.R. 637, it was held that **41.02** "disorderly conduct" is not of the essence of a charge of breach of the peace, and that a jury verdict which convicted the accused of such a charge under deletion of the express reference to such conduct could not for that reason be an incompetent verdict.

And, in *Jones v. Carnegie*, 2004 S.L.T. 609, a court of five judges did not overrule *Butcher v. Jessop*, 1989 S.C.C.R. 119, on the question of the adequacy of the bare statutory style of charge for breach of the peace; but the court did make the following observation, at p.618K, para. 45: "[W]e would note that the Solicitor General accepted that, notwithstanding the decision in *Butcher v. Jessop*, it would normally be proper for the prosecutor to specify the conduct which was said to form a breach of the peace rather than to rely on the statutory form of charge."

41.04 Following the reassessment of the offence by the Appeal Court in *Smith v. Donnelly*, 2001 S.L.T. 1007 (see para. 41.05 of the 3rd edition), it is clear that conduct which causes mere embarrassment or upset is not sufficient for conviction of breach of the peace: see *Borwick v. Urquhart*, 2003 S.C.C.R. 243.

n.19: *Cf.* also *McMillan v. Higson*, 2003 S.L.T. 573, where the court held (Lord Cameron of Lochbroom dissenting) that there was insufficient evidence to justify the sheriff's conclusion that deliberately blocking the egress of the complainer's vehicle was sufficiently provocative, in the circumstances of the case, to demonstrate the necessary potential for alarm and disturbance.

41.05 The account of breach of the peace proffered in *Smith v. Donnelly*, 2001 S.L.T. 1007, was considered by the European Court of Human Rights in the admissibility case of *Lucas v. U.K.*, March 18, 2003, Applic. No. 39013/02. The Court noted there, with evident approval, that the test for breach of the peace "set down in Scottish law has the objective standard of the reasonable person"; the Court also noted that, given "the need to avoid excessive rigidity and to keep pace with changing circumstances, many laws are inevitably couched in terms which, to a greater or lesser extent, are vague" but that this in itself did "not disclose a violation of the certainty required by the Convention (in relation to Article 7)"—or indeed in relation to Article 5, the alleged breach of which, along with Articles 10 and 11, comprised the basis of the appellant's case. The Court's conclusion, in this aspect of its decision, was "that the current definition is formulated with the degree of precision required by the Convention and it provides sufficient guidance to individuals as to the consequences of their actions."

n.28: On the compatibility of particular types of breach of the peace with Articles 10 and 11 of the European Convention on Human Rights, see the entry for paragraph 41.01, n.5, *supra*.

n.45: *Cf.* McDonald v. Heywood, 2002 S.C.C.R. 92.

n.46: In *Jones v. Carnegie*, 2004 S.L.T. 609 at 614G, para. 12, a court of five judges, whilst refraining from casting any doubts on the soundness of the actual result in *Young v. Heatly*, 1959 J.C. 66, made the following observation: "... we would caution that where conduct complained of took place in private there requires to be evidence that there was a realistic risk of the conduct being discovered".

41.07 In *Jones v. Carnegie*, 2004 S.L.T. 609 (court of five judges), counsel for the appellant, Jones, submitted that prior authorities had been wrong to conclude that evidence of actual alarm was unnecessary: but the court affirmed that the prior authorities had not been wrong to so conclude. Indeed, the court observed (at p.614H–I, para. 13), that if breach of the peace were to be limited to cases where there was actual alarm "this would represent an unfortunate and unjustifiable narrowing of the common law" the safeguard against any undue expansion of the law being "the need ... for the condut to be genuinely alarming and disturbing to any reasonable person". The court also observed (there) that it was not persuaded "that the adoption of a subjective test would provide a satisfactory basis for applying the law [since] ... even if there were evidence of alarm, this would not be conclusive. Conversely, it may be said with some force that the protection of a neighbourhood against breach of the peace should not be inhibited merely because a bystander displayed an over-stoical reaction to the conduct in question."

See also the observation of the court (of five judges) in *Jones v. Carnegie*, **41.10** 2004 S.L.T. 609 at 614G, para. 12, which is set out in the entry for paragraph 41.05, n.46, *supra*.

Section 43 of the Telecommunications Act 1984 is repealed by the **41.13** Communications Act 2003, Sched. 19(1): consequently, the existing text of this paragraph, together with nn.71 and 72, falls to be deleted, and the following should be substituted:

"*Communications Act 2003*. Section 127 of this Act provides: **41.13**

'(1) A person is guilty of an offence if he—

    (a) sends by means of a public electronic communications network a message or other matter that is grossly offensive or of an indecent, obscene or menacing character; or
    (b) causes any such message or matter to be so sent.

(2) A person is guilty of an offence if, for the purpose of causing annoyance, inconvenience or needless anxiety to another, he—

    (a) sends by means of a public electronic communications network, a message that he knows to be false,
    (b) causes such a message to be sent; or
    (c) persistently makes use of a public electronic communications network.

(3) A person guilty of an offence under this section shall be liable, on summary conviction, to imprisonment for a term not exceeding six months or to a fine not exceeding level 5 on the standard scale, or to both.

(4) Subsections (1) and (2) do not apply to anything done in the course of providing a programme service (within the meaning of the Broadcasting Act 1990 (c.42).'

A 'public electronic communications network' has the meaning set out in section 151(1) of the 2003 Act, *viz.* 'an electronic communications network provided wholly or mainly for the purpose of making electronic communications services available to members of the public'."

Section 31 of the Fire Services Act 1947 is repealed by the Fire (Scotland) **41.14** Act 2005 (asp 5), Sched. 4. Section 85 of the 2005 Act now provides:

"(1) A person who knowingly gives or causes to be given to a person acting on behalf of a relevant authority [as defined in s.6] a false alarm of—

    (a) fire;

  (b) a road traffic accident; or
  (c) an emergency of another kind,

shall be guilty of an offence.
  (2) A person guilty of an offence under subsection (1) shall be liable on summary conviction—

  (a) to a fine not exceeding level 5 on the standard scale;
  (b) to imprisonment for a term not exceeding 3 months; or
  (c) to both."

After this paragraph, the following should be inserted.

"Antisocial Behaviour etc. (Scotland) Act 2004 (asp 8).

41.14A BREACH OF AN ANTISOCIAL BEHAVIOUR ORDER. Under section 4 of the Act, where a person, who is at least 12 years of age, has engaged in 'antisocial behaviour' towards a relevant person (as defined in s.4(13)), a 'local authority' or a 'registered social landlord' may apply to a sheriff for the making of an 'antisocial behaviour order' against that person. If the sheriff grants the order, or makes an interim order under section 7, it is an offence for the person subject to it to do, without reasonable excuse, anything that the order prohibits him from doing (see s.9(1)). The maximum penalty for such an offence is, on summary conviction, six months in prison and a fine of the statutory maximum; and, on conviction on indictment, the maximum is five years in prison and a fine (see s.9(2)). 'Antisocial behaviour' and other terms used in the Act are defined in section 143, which, *inter alia*, provides:

  '(1) For the purposes of this Act ..., a person ("A") engages in antisocial behaviour if A—

  (a) acts in a manner that causes or is likely to cause alarm or distress; or
  (b) pursues a course of conduct that causes or is likely to cause alarm or distress,

to at least one person who is not of the same household as A; and "antisocial behaviour" shall be construed accordingly.
  (2) In this Act, unless the context otherwise requires—
  "conduct" includes speech; and a course of conduct must involve conduct on at least two occasions;
  "local authority" means a council constituted under section 2 of the Local Government etc. (Scotland) Act 1994 (c.39)...
  "registered social landlord" means a body registered in the register maintained under section 57 of the Housing (Scotland) Act 2001 (asp 10)...'

Under section 9(3) of the Act, if what the person has done in breach of an antisocial behaviour order amounts to a separate offence, and he is charged with that separate offence, he is not to be proceeded against for an offence contrary to section 9(1); but, if he is convicted of that separate offence, the fact that he committed that offence when subject to that order must be taken into account in the determination by the court of an appropriate sentence (see s.9(4)).

KNOWINGLY CONTRAVENING A DIRECTION UNDER SECTION 21 OF THE **41.14B**
ACT. Under section 19(1) (see also s.20) of the Act, a police officer of or
above the rank of superintendent may authorise the exercise of powers
conferred by section 21 in a particular locality (see s.19(3)) during a
specified period (see s.19(2) and (4)) if he has reasonable grounds for
believing—

> '(a) that any members of the public have been alarmed or dis-
> tressed as a result of the presence or behaviour of groups of
> two or more persons in public places in any locality in the
> officer's police area (the "relevant locality"); and
> (b) that antisocial behaviour is a significant, persistent and
> serious problem in the relevant locality.'

And section 21 provides:

> '(1) Where a constable has reasonable grounds for believing that
> the presence or behaviour of a group of two or more persons in any
> public place in the relevant locality is causing or is likely to cause
> alarm or distress to any members of the public, the constable may
> exercise a power mentioned in subsection (3).
> (2) In determining whether to exercise a power mentioned in
> subsection (3) a constable shall have regard to whether the exercise
> of the power would be likely to result in the persons in the group
> causing less alarm and distress to members of the public in the
> relevant locality than if the power were not exercised.
> (3) Subject to subsection (5), the constable may give—

> (a) a direction requiring the persons in the group to disperse;
> (b) a direction requiring any of those persons whose place of
> residence is not within the relevant locality to leave the
> relevant locality or any part of the relevant locality;
> (c) a direction prohibiting any of those persons whose place of
> residence is not within the relevant locality from returning
> to the relevant locality or part of the relevant locality during
> such period (not exceeding 24 hours) from the giving of the
> direction as the constable may specify.

> (4) The constable may require a direction under paragraph (a) or
> (b) of subsection (3) to be complied with—

> (a) immediately or by such time as the constable may specify;
> (b) in such way as may be so specified.

> (5) A direction under subsection (3) may not be given in respect of
> a group of persons—

> (a) who are engaged in conduct which is lawful under section
> 220 of the Trade Union and Labour Relations (Con-
> solidation) Act 1992 (c.52); or
> (b) who are taking part in a procession in respect of which—

> (i) written notice has been given in accordance with sub-
> sections (2) and (3) of section 62 of the Civic Gov-
> ernment (Scotland) Act 1982 (c.45);
> (ii) by virtue of subsection (6) or (7) of that section such
> notice is not required to be given.'

Directions may be given orally, and to a single person or two or more persons together (see s.22(1)); and section 22(2) provides:

'A person who, without reasonable excuse, knowingly contravenes a direction given to that person under section 21 shall be guilty of an offence and liable on summary conviction to—

    (a) a fine not exceeding level 4 on the standard scale; or
    (b) imprisonment for a term not exceeding 3 months,

or to both.'

Relevant definitions are given in section 25, which provides:

'(1) In this Part [Part 3—"Dispersal of Groups"]—
"public place" means any place to which the public have access at the material time (whether on payment of a fee or otherwise); and includes—

    (a) the doorways or entrances of premises abutting on any such place;
    (b) a road (as defined in section 151(1) of the Roads (Scotland) Act 1984 (c.54));
    (c) any common passage, close, court, stair or yard pertinent to any tenement or group of separately owned houses; and
    (d) any place to which the public do not have access but to which persons have unlawfully gained access; and

"relevant locality" has the meaning given by section 19(1)(a).
(2) In this Part, any reference to the presence or behaviour of a group of persons includes a reference to the presence or behaviour of any one or more persons in the group.'

41.14C FAILING TO COMPLY WITH AN ORDER TO STOP A VEHICLE (*and related matters*). Section 126 of the Act provides:

'(1) Where—

    (a) regulations under section 127 are in force [*i.e.* regulations made by the Scottish Ministers as to the removal and retention of motor vehicles seized under section 126, and release or disposal of such vehicles]; and
    (b) subsection (2) applies,

a constable in uniform may exercise the powers mentioned in subsection (3).
(2) This subsection applies where the constable has reasonable grounds for believing that a motor vehicle—

    (a) is being used on any occasion in a manner which—

        (i) contravenes section 3 or 34 of the Road Traffic Act 1988 (c.52) (careless and inconsiderate driving and prohibition of off-road driving); and
        (ii) is causing, or is likely to cause, alarm, distress or annoyance to members of the public; or

    (b) has been used on any occasion in a manner which—

        (i) contravened either of those sections of that Act; and
        (ii) caused or was likely to cause, such alarm, distress or annoyance.

(3) The powers are—

    (a) if the motor vehicle is moving, power to order the person driving it to stop the vehicle;
    (b) subject to subsection (4), power to seize and remove the motor vehicle;
    (c) for the purposes of exercising a power falling within paragraph (a) or (b), power to enter any premises (other than a private dwelling house) on which the constable has reasonable grounds for believing the motor vehicle to be;
    (d) power to use reasonable force, if necessary, in the exercise of a power conferred by any of paragraphs (a) to (c).

(4) Subject to subsection (5), the constable shall not seize the motor vehicle unless—

    (a) where the case falls within subsection (2)(a)—

        (i) the constable has warned the person who is using the motor vehicle in the manner mentioned in that subsection that if the use continues the constable will seize the vehicle; and
        (ii) it appears to the constable that, after the warning, the use has continued; or

    (b) where the case falls within subsection (2)(b)—

        (i) the constable has warned the person who used the motor vehicle in the manner mentioned in that subsection that if the use is repeated, the constable will seize the vehicle; and
        (ii) it appears to the constable that, after the warning, the use has been repeated.

(5) Subsection (4) does not require a warning to be given by a constable on any occasion on which the constable would otherwise have the power to seize a motor vehicle under this section if—

    (a) the circumstances make it impracticable for the constable to give the warning;
    (b) the constable has already on that occasion given a warning under that subsection in respect of any use of that motor vehicle or of another motor vehicle by that person or any other person; or
    (c) the constable has reasonable grounds for believing—

        (i) that such a warning has been given on that occasion otherwise than by that constable; or
        (ii) that the person whose use of that motor vehicle on that occasion would justify the seizure is a person to whom a warning under that subsection has been given (whether or not by that constable or in respect of the same

vehicle or the same or similar use) on a previous
occasion in the previous 12 months.

(6) A person who fails to comply with an order under subsection
(3)(a) shall be guilty an offence.

(7) A person guilty of an offence under subsection (6) shall be
liable on summary conviction to a fine not exceeding level 3 on the
standard scale.

(8) In this section—

"driving" has the same meaning as in the Road Traffic Act 1988
(c.52);

"motor vehicle" means any mechanically propelled vehicle, whether or not it is intended or adapted for use on roads; and

"private dwelling house" does not include—

(a) any garage or other structure occupied with the dwelling
house; or

(b) any land appurtenant to the dwelling house.' "

41.16 Following the decision of a full bench in *Webster v. Dominick*, 2003
S.L.T. 975, there is no such offence as "shameless indecency" at common
law, and thus this paragraph falls to be deleted from the 3rd edition. The
opinion of the court there (see pp.984K–L, para. 53 and 985H, para. 59)
provides no support for any view that the selling or exposing for sale of
indecent publications can now be prosecuted as "public indecency". (For
"public indecency" see the entries for Chapter 36, *supra*).

41.17 The final sentence of this paragraph now falls to be deleted, since one
cannot conspire to commit, or be art and part in the commission of, what
is not an offence: see *Webster v. Dominick*, 2003 S.L.T. 975 (court of five
judges), where it was declared that there was no such offence as "shameless indecency" at common law.

n.90: This footnote should now be read subject to what is stated in the
entry for para. 41.16, *supra, quoad* shameless indecency.

41.18 n.96: Paragraph 11 of Sched. 10 to the Broadcasting Act 1996 is now
repealed by the Communications Act 2003, Sched. 19(1); and s.201 of the
Broadcasting Act 1990, which carries the relevant definition of "programme service" is amended by s.360 of, and Sched. 19(1) to, the 2003
Act: see s.202 of the 1990 Act for the relevant definition of "programme".

41.19 n.98: For the reference to pp.720–735 of "Smith and Hogan", there
should now be substituted a reference to pp.739–754 of the 10th edition.

With respect to s.7(2) of the Theatres Act 1968, for the current meaning
of "programme service" under the 1990 Act, see the entry for para. 41.18,
n.96, *supra*.

41.20 The first sentence of the text of this paragraph (together with footnote 2)
now falls to be deleted: see the entry for para. 41.16, *supra, mutatis
mutandis*.

n.4: The meaning of "film exhibition" in s.21(1) of the Cinemas Act 1985 is now (by virtue of the Communications Act 2003, Sched. 17, para 76) as follows: "any exhibition of moving pictures other than an exhibition of items included in a programme service (within the meaning of the Communications Act 2003) that is being simultaneously received (or virtually so) by the exhibitor".

In the text of s.52(1)(a) of the Civic Government (Scotland) Act 1982, the **41.21** phrase "(meaning in this section a person under the age of 16)" should be deleted, since this deletion was required by the Criminal Justice and Public Order Act 1994, s.84(6)(a)(ii); and in s.52(2) of the 1982 Act, for the words "under the age of 16" (in both places where they appear) there should be substituted: "under the age of 18"—this amendment being required by s.16(1) and (2) of the Protection of Children and Prevention of Sexual Offences (Scotland) Act 2005 (asp 9). See also new para. 41.22A, below.

n.8: The maximum penalty on indictment has been increased from 3 to 10 years by the Criminal Justice (Scotland) Act 2003 (asp 7), s.19(1)(a).

n.10: *Ogilvie v. H.M. Advocate* is now reported at 2001 S.C.C.R. 792. See also on sentencing, *Gair v. H.M. Advocate*, 2002 S.C.C.R. 54, and *McGaffney v. H.M. Advocate*, 2004 S.C.C.R. 384.

n.12: Section 52A of the 1982 Act is also amended by the Criminal Justice **41.22** (Scotland) Act 2003 (asp 7), s.19(1)(b), such that s.52A(3) now reads as follows:

> "A person shall be liable (a) on summary conviction of an offence under this section to imprisonment for a period not exceeding 6 months or to a fine not exceeding level 5 on the standard scale or to both; (b) on conviction on indictment of such an offence to imprisonment for a period not exceeding 5 years or to a fine or to both."

In *Arnott v. McFadyen*, 2002 S.C.C.R. 96, it was held that the Crown did not have to prove, in relation to an indecent photograph of a child possessed by an accused person, that that person knew that the photograph was that of a child.

After this paragraph, the following new paragraph should be added:

The offences created by sections 52(1)(a)–(c) and 52A are subject to the **41.22A** exceptions specified in section 52B of the 1982 Act, section 52B having been inserted by section 16(3) of the Protection of Children and Prevention of Sexual Offences (Scotland) Act 2005 (asp 9). The exceptions relate to situations where the photograph in question was of the child aged 16 or over (or the accused reasonably believed that to be so); at the time of the offence charged or at the time when the accused obtained the photograph, the accused and the child were married to or civil partners of each other, or were partners in an established relationship; and, either the child consented to the photograph being taken or made (or, as the case may be, being in the accused's possession), or the accused reasonably believed that to be so. If the offence charged is one under section 52(1)(b), the exception additionally requires that the showing or distributing of the photograph was only to the child; and if the offence charged is one under section 52(1)(c), the additional requirement is that the accused had the photograph in his possession with a view to its being distributed or shown only to the child. The exceptions apply (see section 52B(9)) "whether the photograph showed the child alone or with the accused, but not if it showed any other person". Certain evidential matters in connection with these exceptions are provided for by section 52C of the 1982 Act, that section also being inserted by section 16(3) of the 2005 Act.

41.23 n.14: *Ingram v. Macari* was, however, a case involving the now discredited common law offence of shameless indecency: relative to "public indecency", *cf.* what was said by the court in *Webster v. Dominick*, 2003 S.L.T. 975 at 984J, para. 52.

41.25 Prior to the words "The Indecent Displays (Control) Act 1981 provides:", there should be inserted: "Section 1 of".

For s.1(4)(d) of the Indecent Displays (Control) Act 1981, there is now substituted (by virtue of the Licensing Act 2003, Sched. 6, para. 80(a)):

> "included in a performance of a play (within the meaning of paragraph 14(1) of Schedule 1 to the Licensing Act 2003) in England and Wales or of a play (within the meaning of the Theatres Act 1968) in Scotland;"

And, in s.1(4)(e) of the 1981 Act, for the words "included in a film exhibition as defined in the Cinemas Act 1985" there is substituted (by virtue of the 2003 Act, Sched. 6, para. 80(b)): "included in the exhibition of a film within the meaning of paragraph 15 of Schedule 1 to the Licensing Act 2003, in England and Wales, or a film exhibition, as defined in the Cinemas Act 1985, in Scotland."

Following the narration of s.1 of the Indecent Displays (Control) Act 1981, in the second line of the penultimate text paragraph at the foot of p.669 of the 3rd edition, the words "shameless indecency or" should be deleted, since the court in *Webster v. Dominick*, 2003 S.L.T. 975 (court of five judges) decided that there was no such common law offence as "shameless indecency".

CHAPTER 43

DANGEROUS DRUGS

n.1: The whole of Part V (which includes s.41) of the Criminal Law **43.01**
(Consolidation) (Scotland) Act 1995 was repealed by the Proceeds of
Crime Act 2002, Sched. 12. Drug trafficking offences are no longer
treated separately for the purposes of confiscation of the benefits of
criminal conduct or a criminal lifestyle. Reference should be made to the
complex provisions of the 2002 Act (especially Part 3) for the precise
position on confiscation under Scots law.

Cannabis and cannabis resin have been reclassified as Class C drugs: see **43.05**
the Misuse of Drugs Act 1971 (Modification) (No. 2) Order 2003 (S.I.
2003 No. 3201), art. 2. For more recent additions to Class A and Class C
drugs, see the Misuse of Drugs Act 1971 (Modification) Order 2003 (S.I.
2003 No. 1243). A very recent addition to Class A drugs (in Part 1 of
Sched. 2 to the Misuse of Drugs Act 1971) is "Fungus (of any kind) which
contains psilocin or an ester of psilocin": see s.21 of the Drugs Act 2005.

Text and **n.19:** The Misuse of Drugs Regulations 1985 (S.I. 1985 No.
2066) were revoked by the Misuse of Drugs Regulations 2001 (S.I. 2001
No. 3998), Sched. 7. Poppy-straw is excluded from ss.4(1) and 5(1) under
the 2001 Regulations, reg. 4(4).

n.21: The Misuse of Drugs Regulations 1985 (S.I. 1985 No. 2066) were **43.06**
revoked by the Misuse of Drugs Regulations 2001 (S.I. 2001 No. 3998),
Sched. 7: see now reg. 4 of the 2001 Regulations.

n.22: The maximum penalty for conviction on indictment of a s.4(2) or **43.07**
4(3) offence, where a Class C drug is concerned, is now 14 years'
imprisonment and a fine: Criminal Justice Act 2003, Sched. 28, para. 1(2),
(3)(a),(b).

n.24: In *Clark v. H.M. Advocate*, 2002 S.C.C.R. 675 at 681G, para.12, the
appeal court shared "the doubts expressed by Lord Justice-General
Rodger in *Salmon v. H.M. Advocate* at p.763B, as to the appropriateness
of trying to apply the concept of concert in cases under section 4(3)(b)".
  Relative to the required elements of "being concerned in the supply of
drugs", see also *Sharkey v. H.M. Advocate*, 2001 S.C.C.R. 290, which was
distinguished in *Smith (S) v. H.M. Advocate*, 2002 S.C.C.R. 1059; and,
for the effect of s.28(2) on, *inter alia*, that offence, see *Henvey v. H.M.
Advocate*, 2005 S.C.C.R. 282, where certain dicta in *Salmon v. H.M.
Advocate* were not followed by a court of five judges.

After this paragraph, the following new paragraph and footnote should
be inserted.

43.07A Section 4A[30a] provides:

> "(1) This section applies if—
>
>   (a) a court is considering the seriousness of an offence under section 4(3) of this Act, and
>   (b) at the time the offence was committed the offender had attained the age of 18.
>
> (2) If either of the following conditions is met the court—
>
>   (a) must treat the fact that the condition is met as an aggravating factor (that is to say, a factor that increases the seriousness of the offence), and
>   (b) must state in open court that the offence is so aggravated.
>
> (3) The first condition is that the offence was committed on or in the vicinity of school premises at a relevant time.
>
> (4) The second condition is that in connection with the commission of the offence the offender used a courier who, at the time the offence was committed, was under the age of 18.
>
> (5) In subsection (3), a relevant time is—
>
>   (a) any time when the school premises are in use by persons under the age of 18;
>   (b) one hour before the start and one hour after the end of any such time.
>
> (6) For the purposes of subsection (4), a person uses a courier in connection with an offence under section 4(3) of this Act if he causes or permits another person (the courier)—
>
>   (a) to deliver a controlled drug to a third person, or
>   (b) to deliver a drug related consideration to himself or a third person.
>
> (7) For the purposes of subsection (6), a drug related consideration is a consideration of any description which—
>
>   (a) is obtained in connection with the supply of a controlled drug, or
>   (b) is intended to be used in connection with obtaining a controlled drug.
>
> (8) In this section—
>
> 'school premises' means land used for the purposes of a school excluding any land occupied solely as a dwelling by a person employed at the school; and
> 'school' has the same meaning—
>
>   (a) ...
>   (b) in Scotland, as in section 135(1) of the Education (Scotland) Act 1980; ....."

n.30a: Inserted by s.1(1) of the Drugs Act 2005.

43.08 The following new subsections (inserted by s.2(2) of the Drugs Act 2005) should be added after s.5(4) of the Misuse of Drugs Act 1971:

"(4A) In any proceedings for an offence under subsection (3) above, if it is proved that the accused had an amount of a controlled drug in his possession which is not less than the prescribed amount [*i.e.* prescribed by regulations made by the Secretary of State: see the 1971 Act, s.37(1)], the court or jury must assume that he had the drug in his possession with the intent to supply it as mentioned in subsection (3).

(4B) Subsection (4A) above does not apply if evidence is adduced which is sufficient to raise an issue that the accused may not have had the drug in his possession with that intent.

(4C) Regulations under subsection (4A) above have effect only in relation to proceedings for an offence committed after the regulations come into force."

n.31: The maximum penalty for conviction on indictment of a s.5(3) offence, where a Class C drug is involved, is now 14 years' imprisonment and a fine: Criminal Justice Act 2003, Sched. 28, para. 1(2), (3)(a),(b).

The Misuse of Drugs Regulations 1985 (S.I. 1985 No. 2066) were revoked by the Misuse of Drugs Regulations 2001 (S.I. 2001 No. 3998), Sched. 7: see now reg. 6(6) and (7) of the 2001 Regulations.

n.50: The maximum penalty for conviction on indictment of a s.8 offence, where a Class C drug is involved, is now 14 years' imprisonment and a fine: Criminal Justice Act 2003, Sched. 28, para. 1(2), (3)(d). **43.12**

Section 14 of the Criminal Justice (International Co-operation) Act 1990 was repealed by Sched. 12 to the Proceeds of Crime Act 2002. The 2002 Act is concerned with the confiscation of the proceeds of criminal conduct in general, and contains a suite of offences of comparable width: see in particular the offences contained in ss.327 to 334 (as also the interpretation provisions in s.340). The 2002 Act also repeals Part V (which includes ss.36, 37 and 38) of the Criminal Law (Consolidation) (Scotland) Act 1995: see now s.342 of the 2002 Act. **43.14**

Section 39 of the Criminal Law (Consolidation) (Scotland) Act 1995 is included in Part V of that enactment, and Part V is repealed by the Proceeds of Crime Act 2002, Sched. 12: see the entry for para. 43.14, *supra*. **43.15**

It has now been accepted by a court of five judges in Scotland that s.28 of the 1971 Act imposes an evidential rather than a persuasive burden: see *Henvey v. H.M. Advocate*, 2005 S.C.C.R. 282. **43.17**

n.91: The Misuse of Drugs Regulations 1985 (S.I. 1985 No. 2066) were revoked by the Misuse of Drugs Regulations 2001 (S.I. 2001 No. 3998) which are now the principal relevant regulations: regs 6–11 remain the appropriate regulations for the purposes of this footnote—save that it should be noted that reg. 6A was inserted by the Misuse of Drugs (Amendment) (No. 2) Regulations 2003 (S.I. 2003 No. 1653), reg. 2(2), and amendments were made to regs 6–10 (together with the addition of Sched. 8 to which they refer) by the Misuse of Drugs (Amendment) (No. 3) Regulations 2003 (S.I. 2003 No. 2429); minor amendments were made **43.18**

to regs. 6 and 11 of the principal regulations by the Health Act 1999 (Consequential Amendments) (Nursing and Midwifery) Order 2004 (S.I. 2004 No. 1771), Sched., para. 24.

Text and **n.92:** The Misuse of Drugs (Designation) Order 1986 (S.I. 1986 No. 2331) was revoked by the Misuse of Drugs (Designation) Order 2001 (S.I. 2001 No. 3997), which is now the principal order.

43.19 **n.94:** The maximum penalty for conviction on indictment of an offence involving a Class C drug under s.12(6) or 13(3) has been raised from 5 years to 14 years by the Criminal Justice Act 2003, Sched. 28, para. 1.

43.21 After this paragraph, the following should be inserted.

"SMOKING TOBACCO ETC.

43.22 With respect to the smoking of tobacco, other substances or mixtures, the Smoking, Health and Social Care (Scotland) Act 2005 (asp 13) provides:

'**1.**—(1) A person who, having the management or control of no-smoking premises, knowingly permits another to smoke there commits an offence.

(2) A person accused of an offence under this section is to be regarded as having knowingly permitted another to smoke in no-smoking premises if that person ought to have known that the other person was smoking there.

(3) It is a defence for an accused charged with an offence under this section to prove—

(a) that the accused (or any employee or agent of the accused) took all reasonable precautions and exercised all due diligence not to commit the offence; or

(b) that there were no lawful and reasonable practicable means by which the accused could prevent the other person from smoking in the no-smoking premises.

(4) A person guilty of an offence under this section is liable, on summary conviction, to a fine not exceeding level 4 on the standard scale. [See also s.6 and Sched. 1, which relate to fixed penalties for this offence.]

2.—(1) A person who smokes in no-smoking premises commits an offence.

(2) It is a defence for an accused charged with an offence under this section to prove that the accused did no know, and could not reasonably be expected to have known, that the place in which it is alleged that the accused was smoking was no-smoking premises.

(3) A person guilty of an offence under this section is liable, on summary conviction, to a fine not exceeding level 3 on the standard scale. [See also s.6 and Sched. 1, which relate to fixed penalties for this offence.]

3.—(1) If notices are not conspicuously displayed—

(a) in, on or near no-smoking premises so as to be visible to and legible by persons in and persons approaching the premises; and

(b) stating—

    (i) that the premises are no-smoking premises; and

    (ii) that it is an offence to smoke there or knowingly to permit smoking there,

the person having the management or control of the premises commits an offence.

(2) It is a defence for an accused charged with an offence under this section to prove that the accused (or any employee or agent of the accused) took all reasonable precautions and exercised all due diligence not to commit the offence.

(3) The Scottish Ministers may, after consulting such persons as they consider appropriate, by regulations provide further as to the manner of display, form and content of the notices referred to in subsection (1) and that any such provision is to be treated, for the purposes of that subsection, as if incorporated in it.

(4) A person guilty of an offence under this section is liable, on summary conviction, to a fine not exceeding level 3 on the standard scale. [See also s. 6 and Sched. 1, which relate to fixed penalties.]

4.—(1) In this Part [Part 1], "smoke" means smoke tobacco, any substance or mixture which includes it or any other substance or mixture; and a person is to be taken as smoking if the person is holding or otherwise in possession or control of lit tobacco, of any lit substance or mixture which includes tobacco or of any other lit substance or mixture which is in a form or in a receptacle in which it can be smoked.

(2) In this Part, "no-smoking premises" means such premises or such classes of premises, being premises of a kind mentioned in subsection (4), as are prescribed by regulations made by the Scottish Ministers after consulting such persons as they consider appropriate on a draft of the regulations.

(3) Regulations under subsection (2) may prescribe premises or parts of premises or classes of premises or parts of premises which are excluded from the definition of "no-smoking premises".

(4) The kind of premises referred to in subsection (2) is premises which are wholly or substantially enclosed and—

(a) to which the public or a section of the public has access;

(b) which are being used wholly or mainly as a place of work;

(c) which are being used by and for the purposes of a club or other unincorporated association; or

(d) which are being used wholly or mainly for the provision of education or of health or care services.

(5) In subsection (4)(b), the reference to work includes work undertaken for no financial advantage.

(6) Regulations under subsection (2) may, for the purposes of that subsection, define or elaborate the meaning of any of the expressions—

(a) "premises";

197

(b) "wholly or substantially enclosed";
(c) "the public"; and
(d) "has access".

(7) Regulations under subsection (2) may define or elaborate the meaning of "premises"—

(a) by reference to the person or class of person who owns or occupies them;
(b) so as to include vehicles, vessels, trains and other means of transport (except aircraft), or such, or such classes, of them as are specified in the regulations.

(8) The Scottish Ministers may, by regulations, after consulting such persons as they consider appropriate on a draft of the regulations, modify subsection (4) so as—

(a) to add a kind of premises to; or
(b) remove a kind of premises (but not the kind referred to in paragraph (a) of that subsection) from,

those in that subsection.

(9) Regulations made by virtue of subsection (7)(b) may provide as to how the statement referred to in section 3(1)(b) is to be expressed in the case of each of the means of transport referred to in the regulations and that any such provision is to be treated, for the purposes of that section, as if incorporated in it.'"

CHAPTER 44

OFFENCES IN CONNECTION WITH OFFICIALS

Text, at line 6 on p.692 of the 3rd edition: delete the full-stop following **44.03**
the word "standing".

Section 68(1) of the Criminal Justice (Scotland) Act 2003 (asp 7)
provides:

> "In determining whether actings which consist of offering or
> accepting a bribe constitute a crime at common law, it is immaterial
> that the functions of the person who receives or is offered the bribe—
>
> > (a) have no connection with;
> > (b) are carried out in a country or territory outwith,
>
> the United Kingdom."

This provision in effect makes s.108(1) of the Anti-terrorism, Crime and
Security Act 2001 applicable to Scotland.
   See also s.69 of the 2003 Act, which extends the jurisdiction of the
Scottish courts in respect of anything done outwith the United Kingdom
by a United Kingdom national, Scottish partnership or incorporated
body, if what was done would constitute, *inter alia*, the common law
crime of "bribery or accepting a bribe" had it been done in Scotland: in
such cases, s.11(3) of the 1995 Act applies.

Under s.69 of the Criminal Justice (Scotland) Act 2003 (asp 7), the jur- **44.04**
isdiction of the Scottish courts in respect of anything done outwith the
United Kingdom by a United Kingdom national, Scottish partnership or
incorporated body is extended if what was done would constitute, *inter
alia*, an offence under s.1 of the Public Bodies Corrupt Practices Act 1889
if done in Scotland: in such cases, s.11(3) of the 1995 Act applies.

In a charge which alleged a contravention of s.1(2) of the 1889 Act, it was **44.05**
held not to be necessary to show with any precision in what way or ways
the member of a community council, who allegedly had been bribed, was
to show favour in respect of a matter or transaction in which that
community council was concerned, namely an actual or proposed
application for a betting office licence for premises in which the accused
was interested—given that that member of the community council was
not a member of the relevant licensing authority: see *King v. Williams*,
2004 S.C.C.R. 493.

In *King v. Williams*, 2004 S.C.C.R. 493, it was taken as clear that a **44.06**
community council was a public body for the purposes of the Public
Bodies Corrupt Practices Act 1889: see the opinion of the court at
p.496E, para.9.

Under s.4(2) of the Prevention of Corruption Act 1916, "local and public authorities of all descriptions" now include "authorities existing in a country or territory outside the United Kingdom" by virtue of s.68(2) of the Criminal Justice (Scotland) Act 2003 (asp 7), which extends to Scotland various statutory amendments made by s.108(2)–(4) of the Anti-terrorism, Crime and Security Act 2001, in view of the jurisdictional extra-territoriality accorded to certain bribery and corruption offences by the 2001 Act and now, *quoad* Scotland, by the Act of 2003.

n.23: It has been held in England that a "public body" under the 1889 Act and 1916 Acts does not include a government department or the Crown: *R. v. Natji* [2002] 1 W.L.R. 2337 (C.A.).

nn.23 and **24:** Section 7 of the Public Bodies Corrupt Practices Act 1889 has been amended such that the limitation to public bodies in the United Kingdom no longer applies: see the Anti-terrorism, Crime and Security Act 2001, s.108(3), which is made applicable to Scotland by the Criminal Justice (Scotland) Act 2003, s.68(2) and which provides that "public body" "includes any body which exists in a country or territory outwith the United Kingdom" and which is equivalent to any body described in s.7.

CHAPTER 45

BIGAMY

n.8: The cross-reference should read: "*supra*, para. 19.113" rather than **45.01**
19.13.

After this paragraph, the following should be added: **45.13**

"The Civil Partnership Act 2004

Under section 1(1) of the Civil Partnership Act 2004, a civil partnership is **45.14**
defined as a relationship between two people of the same sex which is
formed when they register as civil partners of each other in any part of
the United Kingdom or outside it under the terms of an appropriate
Order in Council; such a relationship may also be treated as having been
formed by virtue of the registration of an overseas relationship. Such a
partnership, contracted between two people who are eligible to do so (see
s.86 of the Act), is intended to be the equivalent of marriage, at least in
most respects (*cf.* Kenneth McK. Norrie, 'What the Civil Partnership Act
2004 does not do', 2005 S.L.T. (News) 35); but since it is not marriage as
such, common law bigamy cannot be applicable. For that reason, section
100(1) provides as follows:

'A person ("A") commits an offence who registers in Scotland as the
civil partner of another person ("B") knowing that either or both—

  (a) A is already married to or in civil partnership with a person
      other than B, or
  (b) B is already married to or in a civil partnership with a
      person other than A.'

The maximum penalty for an offence under section 100(1) is, on summary
conviction, three months in prison and a fine of level 3 on the standard
scale, and on conviction on indictment, two years in prison and a fine (see
s.100(3))."

CHAPTER 46

POLLUTION

46.01 **n.1:** Section 75(5)(a) of the 1990 Act is amended (by substitution of more general terms for "nursing home") by the Regulation of Care (Scotland) Act 2001 (asp 8), Sched. 3, para. 17: see the entry for n.7, *infra*.

n.7: In the definition of "household waste" in s.75(5) of the 1990 Act, for the words "nursing home" there are to be substituted: "which are used to provide a care home service (as defined by section 2(3) of the Registration of Care (Scotland) Act 2001 (asp 8))". See the 2001 Act (asp 8), Sched. 3, para. 17.

In subsection (9)(a) of s.33 of the 1990 Act (maximum penalty on summary conviction), the figure £20,000 must now be read as "£40,000": see the Antisocial Behaviour etc. (Scotland) Act 2004 (asp 8), Sched. 2, para. 4(3).

46.04 A person is not guilty of a contravention of s.30F(1) of the 1974 Act if the relevant act, in respect of fish other than salmon, is done for a scientific purpose or for protecting, improving or developing stocks of fish, and that person has prior permission in writing of the Scottish Ministers: s.28(1),(2)(c) of the Salmon and Freshwater Fisheries Etc. (Scotland) Act 2003 (asp 15).

The maximum fine under s.30F(6)(a) of the 1974 Act is increased from £20,000 to £40,000 by the Antisocial Behaviour etc. (Scotland) Act 2004 (asp 8), Sched. 2, Part 1, para. 2(2).

46.05 **n.31:** See further the Energy Act 2004, Part 2, Chapter 3 (ss.105–114) for requirements as to "decommissioning programmes" relative to renewable energy installations and "electric lines" in waters in a "Renewable Energy Zone".

46.09 **n.38:** The reference to "s.131(5)" at line 4 of the text of this note—maximum penalty for an offence under s.135—should read: "s.135(5)".

46.11 **nn.51–55:** Sections 137 to 141 of the Merchant Shipping Act 1995 are repealed by the Marine Safety Act 2003. The 2003 Act makes new provision for directions by the Secretary of State relative to ships, following accidents or otherwise, where there is risk of, or in order to prevent or reduce, pollution by adding new Schedule 3A to the 1995 Act. Under paragraph 5(a) of that Schedule, a person to whom such a direction is given must comply with it. It is an offence under paragraph 6(1) to contravene paragraph 5(a): maximum penalty is, on summary conviction, a fine of £50,000, and on indictment, a fine (see para. 8). Paragraph 6(2) provides: "It is a defence for a person charged with an offence under sub-paragraph (1) to prove—(a) that he tried as hard as he could to comply with the relevant direction, or (b) that he reasonably believed that compliance with the direction would involve a serious risk to human life." It is also an offence (see paragraph 7) intentionally to obstruct a person who is acting on behalf of the Secretary of State in connection with the giving of a direction under the Schedule or who is complying with such a direction, or acting by virtue of paragraph 4 ("action in lieu of a direction"): the maximum penalties are the same as those which apply to an offence under paragraph 6 (see para. 8).

Paragraphs (c) and (d) of s.32(1) of the Radioactive Substances Act 1993 **46.12** receive minor amendment by virtue of the Energy Act 2004, Sched. 15, para. 11.

As a result of amendments required by the Water Industry (Scotland) Act **46.14** 2002 (Consequential Provisions) Order 2003 (S.S.I. 2003 No. 331), Sched., para. 4, s.62(2)(a) (as amended by the Fire (Scotland) Act 2005 (asp 5), Sched. 3, para. 6) now reads as follows:

"(2) Subsection (1) of this section shall not apply to the operation of a loudspeaker—

(a) for police or ambulance purposes, for or in connection with the exercise of any function of a relevant authority (as defined in section 6 of the Fire (Scotland) Act 2005 (asp 5)), by Scottish Water in the exercise of any of its core functions (within the meaning of section 70(2) of the Water Industry (Scotland) Act 2002 (asp 3)), or by a local authority within its area."

n.67: Section 54(3) of the Civic Government (Scotland) Act 1982 is amended by the Water Industry (Scotland) Act 2002 (asp 3), Sched. 7, para. 13, such that in the list of exceptions to the offence, for "a water authority" one must now read "Scottish Water".

Section 63 of the Criminal Justice and Public Order Act 1994 is amended by the Anti-social Behaviour Act 2003, Sched. 3, such that "in the open air" is to be deleted from the description of the offence.

See also the Antisocial Behaviour etc. (Scotland) Act 2004 (asp 8), s.45 (which makes it an offence for a person to be responsible for exceeding the "permitted level of noise" from property after service of a warning notice under s.44).

CHAPTER 47

PERJURY AND ALLIED OFFENCES

47.01 n.1: In line 3 of the text of this note, the cross-reference should read "para. 47.40" rather than para. 47.41.

47.03 Any statement given on oath in a nominated court in Scotland for transmission by live television link or by telephone to a court conducting criminal proceedings outside the United Kingdom is to be treated for the purposes of the common law crime of perjury as made in proceedings before that nominated court: Crime (International Co-operation) Act 2003, ss.30(5)(c) and 31(6)(c); see also Sched. 2, Parts 1 and 2.

n.6: Section 6 of the Explosive Substances Act 1883 has been amended by virtue of para. 1 of Sched. 27 to the Civil Partnership Act 2004.

47.22 Any statement given on oath in a nominated court in Scotland for transmission by live television link or by telephone to a court conducting criminal proceedings outside the United Kingdom is to be treated for the purposes of ss.44 to 46 of the Criminal Law (Consolidation) (Scotland) Act 1995 as made in proceedings before that nominated court: Crime (International Co-operation) Act 2003, ss.30(5)(c) and 31(6)(c); see also Sched. 2, Parts 1 and 2.

47.38 n.2: The reference to "Smith and Hogan" should now be stated as "pp.310–312 of the 10th ed.".

47.44 In the text of s.172(1)(c) of the Road Traffic Act 1988, the words "except an offence under paragraph 8 of Schedule 1 to the Road Traffic (Driver Licensing and Information Systems) Act 1989," should be deleted: see the Statute Law (Repeals) Act 2004, Sched. 1, Part 14.

n.40: After the reference to *Bingham v. Bruce* [1962] 1 W.L.R. 70, but before the full stop, insert: ": see also *Brown v. Frame*, 2005 S.L.T. 744".

CHAPTER 48

ESCAPES FROM LAWFUL CUSTODY

After amendment by s.24(1) of the Criminal Justice (Scotland) Act 2003 **48.10**
(asp 7), s.13 of the Prisons (Scotland) Act 1989 now reads as follows
(footnotes 29 and 30 remaining as they appear in the 3rd edition):

"Without prejudice to section 295 of the Criminal Procedure
(Scotland) Act 1995 (c.46) (legal custody of persons generally), a
prisoner is in legal custody—

(a) while he is confined in or being taken to or from any prison
in which he may lawfully be confined; or

(b) while he is working or is, for any other reason, outside the
prison in the custody or under the control of an officer of
the prison [or prisoner custody officer[29] performing custodial duties at the prison or a prison officer temporarily
attached to the prison][30], a constable ('constable' having the
same meaning as it has, by virtue of paragraph 17(1) and (2)
of Schedule 1 to the Crimes (Sentences) Act 1997 (c.43), in
section 40(1) of this Act) or a police custody and security
officer; or

(c) while he is being taken to any place to which he is required
or authorised by or under this Act to be taken; or

(d) while he is kept in custody in pursuance of such requirement
or authorisation."

Section 295 of the 1995 Act is amended by s.24(2) of the Criminal Justice
(Scotland) Act 2003 (asp 7); and, for the meaning of "police custody and
security officer", see s.76 of the Criminal Justice (Scotland) Act 2003 (asp
7) which amends the Police (Scotland) Act 1967 to make provision for
this new type of officer.

n.31: The Mental Health (Scotland) Act 1984 is repealed in its entirety by
Part 1 of Schedule 5 to the Mental Health (Care and Treatment) (Scotland) Act 2003 (asp 13); no equivalent to s.120(1) of the 1984 Act is
enacted in the Act of 2003. Section 295 of the 1995 Act is amended by
s.24(2) of the Criminal Justice (Scotland) Act 2003 (asp 7).

The Mental Health (Scotland) Act 1984 is repealed in its entirety by Part **48.12**
1 of Schedule 5 to the Mental Health (Care and Treatment) (Scotland)
Act 2003 (asp 13); no equivalent to s.120 of the 1984 Act is enacted in the
Act of 2003. This paragraph, together with footnote 33, should therefore
be deleted from the text of the 3rd edition.

Since the Mental Health (Scotland) Act 1984 has been repealed in its **48.13**
entirety by Part 1 of Schedule 5 to the Mental Health (Care and

Treatment) (Scotland) Act 2003 (asp 13), the existing sub-heading and text of this paragraph should be deleted and the following substituted:

"MENTALLY DISORDERED PERSONS DETAINED IN HOSPITALS. The Mental Health (Care and Treatment) (Scotland) Act 2003 (asp 13) does not contain any provisions making it an offence for a patient to abscond from a hospital where he is detained by virtue of a court order whether or not that order contains a restriction order."

n.34: The existing text of this footnote should be deleted, and the following substituted:

"Under s.310 of the Mental Health (Care and Treatment) (Scotland) Act 2003 (asp 13), regulations are to be made as to the circumstances under which mentally disordered persons who are subject to, *inter alia*, detention in a hospital by virtue of orders made by courts under the 1995 Act or the 2003 Act (asp 13) and who have absconded may be taken into custody 'by specified persons'."

48.14 Since the Mental Health (Scotland) Act 1984 has been repealed in its entirety by Part 1 of Schedule 5 to the Mental Health (Care and Treatment) (Scotland) Act 2003 (asp 13), the existing sub-heading and text of this paragraph should be deleted and the following substituted:

"INDUCING OR ASSISTING PATIENTS TO ABSCOND. Section 316 of the Mental Health (Care and Treatment) (Scotland) Act 2003 (asp 13) provides:

'(1) A person who knowingly—

(a) induces or assists a patient to do or fail to do anything which results in the patient's being liable under [regulations made under s.310 of this Act: see subs. (4)] to be taken into custody and dealt with under [section 310]; or
(b) ... [see para. 48.18, below]

shall be guilty of an offence."

The maximum penalties for a contravention of section 316(1) are, on summary conviction, six months and a fine of the statutory maximum, and, on conviction on indictment, two years and a fine (see s.316(3))."

nn.35 and 36: These footnotes should be deleted.

48.15 The original text of s.41(2)(a) of the Police (Scotland) Act 1967, which is reproduced at the top of p.743 of the 3rd edition, should be corrected so that for the words "to execute" there are substituted the words "in the execution of"; the text of paragraph (a) is amended by s.76(5)(b) of the Criminal Justice (Scotland) Act 2003 (asp 7) so that the paragraph now reads as follows:

"(a) who is in the lawful custody of a constable[38] or police custody and security officer or any person assisting a constable or any such officer, in the execution of his duty".

(For the meaning of "police custody and security officer", see s.76 of the Criminal Justice (Scotland) Act 2003 (asp 7) which amends the Police (Scotland) Act 1967 to make provision for this new type of officer.)

n.38: References in s.41(1) and (2) of the Police (Scotland) Act 1967 to "a constable in the execution of his duty" are now to be read as if they included references to a member of the Civil Nuclear Constabulary who "(a) is exercising any of the powers or privileges conferred on him by section 56 [of the Energy Act 2004]; or (b) is otherwise performing his duties under the direction and control of the chief constable or as an employee of the Police Authority". For the Civil Nuclear Constabulary, see Part 1, Chapter 3 (ss.51–71) of the Energy Act 2004.

Under subsection (4) of s.41 of the Police (Scotland) Act 1967 (that subsection having been inserted by s.104(2) of the Police Reform Act 2002), reference to "a person assisting a constable in the execution of his duty" is to include a reference to "any person who is neither a constable nor in the company of a constable but who—(a) is a member of an international joint investigation team [as defined in subsection (5), which is also inserted by s.104(2) of the 2002 Act] that is led by a constable of a police force or by a member of the National Criminal Intelligence Service or of the National Crime Squad; and (b) is carrying out his functions as a member of that team".

Since the Mental Health (Scotland) Act 1984 has been repealed in its **48.18** entirety by Part 1 of Schedule 5 to the Mental Health (Care and Treatment) (Scotland) Act 2003 (asp 13), the existing sub-heading and text of this paragraph should be deleted and the following substituted:

"*Mentally disordered patients.* Section 316 of the Mental Health (Care and Treatment) (Scotland) Act 2003 (asp 13) provides:

'(1) A person who knowingly—

    (a) induces or assists a patient to do or fail to do anything which results in the patient's being liable under [regulations made under s.310 of this Act: see subs. (4)] to be taken into custody and dealt with under [section 310]; or

    (b) harbours a patient who has, with that result, done or failed to do anything,

shall be guilty of an offence.

(2) Where a person is charged with an offence under subsection (1)(b) above, it shall be a defence for such person to prove that the doing of that with which the person is charged—

    (a) did not obstruct the discharge by any person of a function conferred or imposed on that person by virtue of this Act; and

    (b) was intended to protect the interests of the patient.'

The maximum penalties for a contravention of s.316(1) are, on summary conviction, six months and a fine of the statutory maximum, and, on conviction on indictment, two years and a fine (see s.316(3))."

CHAPTER 49

OFFENCES IN CONNECTION WITH JUDICIAL OFFICIALS

49.02 Following amendment by section 76(5)(a) of the Criminal Justice (Scotland) Act 2003 (asp 7), section 41(1)(a) of the Police (Scotland) Act 1967 now provides:

> "Any person who assaults, resists, obstructs, molests or hinders a constable or police custody and security officer in the execution of his duty or a person assisting such a constable or any such officer ... shall be guilty of an offence."

For "police custody and security officer" see the 1967 Act, s.9, as amended, and s.9A, as inserted, by s.76 of the 2003 Act (asp 7).

n.3: A "constable in the execution of his duty" now includes a member of the Civil Nuclear Constabulary "who (a) is exercising any of the powers or privileges conferred on him by section 56 [of the Energy Act 2004]; or (b) is otherwise performing his duties under the direction and control of the chief constable or as an employee of the Police Authority". For the "Civil Nuclear Constabulary" see Part 1, Chapter 3 (ss.51–71) of the Energy Act 2004.

A person assisting a constable in the execution of his duty now includes "any person who is neither a constable nor in the company of a constable but who—(a) is a member of an international joint investigation team that is led by a constable of a police force or by a member of the National Criminal Intelligence Service or of the National Crime Squad; and (b) is carrying out his functions as a member of that team": Police (Scotland) Act 1967, s.41(4), as inserted by the Police Reform Act 2002, s.104(2). For the meaning of "international joint investigation team", see the 1967 Act, s.41(5), which is also inserted by s.104(2) of the 2002 Act.

n.4: In *Walsh v. McFadyen*, 2002 J.C. 93, the Appeal Court stopped short of deciding that "hinders" in s.41(1)(a) of the Police (Scotland) Act 1967 did not necessarily require any physical element on the part of the accused; but the Court, in applying "the principle applied by the High Court in *Skeen v. Shaw*", stated as follows (at p.96E–I, para. 8): "A person who deliberately performs some action with his body so as to place some difficulty in the way of the police constables who are trying to take a sec [sic] 14(1) [of the 1995 Act] detainee to a police station, and especially if he does so in a way calculated to cause the constables to resort to the use of force to effect their purpose, is clearly hindering them in the execution of their duty. If it be the case that the word 'hinders' requires a physical aspect or physical element then ... that physical element was provided in the present case by the deliberate decision of the appellant to sit on the couch and to remain inert, thus rendering it necessary for the police constables to use force ... He deliberately placed a serious difficulty in their way by choosing to turn himself into a limp dead weight."

"Constables" under s.42(1) of the Police (Scotland) Act 1967 now include **49.03** constables of the British Transport Police Force (see the Anti-terrorism, Crime and Security Act 2001, Sched. 7, para. 5(2)) and "members of the Civil Nuclear Constabulary" (see the 1967 Act, s.42(3), as inserted by the Energy Act 2004, s.68(4)); for the "Civil Nuclear Constabulary", see Part 1, Chapter 3 (ss.51–71) of the Energy Act 2004.

Section 44(2) of the Police (Scotland) Act 1967, as amended by s.76(7)(a) **49.06** of the Criminal Justice (Scotland) Act 2003 (asp 7), now reads: "Any constable or police custody and security officer who neglects or violates his duty shall be guilty of an offence." For "police custody and security officer" see the 1967 Act, s.9, as amended, and s.9A, as inserted, by s.76 of the 2003 Act (asp 7).

CHAPTER 50

CONTEMPT OF COURT

50.01 In *Mayer v. H.M. Advocate*, 2004 S.L.T. 1251, the petitioner argued, *inter alia*, that what was observed in *H.M. Advocate v. Airs*, 1975 J.C. 64, and *Wylie v. H.M. Advocate*, 1966 S.L.T. 149 (put simply, that contempt was not classified as a crime but as something *sui generis* in Scots law, and that alleged contempt at a trial was best dealt with on the spot by the trial judge) required to be reconsidered; that (in the words of the opinion of the court at p.1255A, para. 16) "in terms of art. 6 of the European Convention on Human Rights the conduct held [by the trial judge, Lord Hardie] to be contempt was criminal and should be dealt with accordingly; and that the scope for a dual approach in Scots law, distinguishing conduct amounting to contempt that was otherwise within the scope of the general criminal law from conduct of an administrative or disciplinary character, was limited given the exposure to significant custodial penalties in all cases". In the event, the court decided that the matter held as contempt by the trial judge in this case was essentially one that fell under the disciplinary category (on the second of the tests used in the jurisprudence of the European Court of Human Rights for assessing whether or not proceedings were criminal and thus attracted the protections of Article 6), that it was an unusual form of contempt, and that the petitioner's position would be adequately protected by remit of the issue raised by him to a member of the court other than the original trial judge—the procedure to be adopted being first put out for discussion. The court recognised, however, that *stante* the tests used by the European Court of Human Rights where the application of Article 6 was in dispute (especially perhaps the third of these, in terms of the degree of severity of the penalty which the person concerned risks incurring), and in an appropriate case, the general observations made in *Wylie* (*supra*) might require to be revisited (*Mayer, supra*, opinion of the court at pp.1262L–1263A, para. 66). The court in *Mayer* (at p.1263D, para 68) declined to remit the "new and difficult questions" raised by the debate in the case to a larger court for an authoritative ruling, since "given the wide scope and varied nature of contempt of court under Scots law, a comprehensive solution to all such questions cannot reasonably be anticipated upon such a remit". And the court concluded (also at p.1263D, para. 68) that "[i]f the law on contempt of court is to be revisited and possibly modified in the light of the Convention and the pertinent European jurisprudence, it is more appropriate that this should be done in the context of a case which is more typical of the forms of contempt of court with which the courts regularly require to deal".

The criteria evolved by the European Court of Human Rights for the applicability of Article 6 to proceedings, where whether these are criminal or not is in dispute, are set out in a number of cases: see, *e.g. Ravnsborg v. Sweden* (1994) 18 E.H.R.R. 38 at p.45 (opinion of the Commission), para. 48, and at p.50 (opinion of the Court), para. 30 *et seq.* Guidance as to the procedure to be adopted by a judge when considering an issue of contempt was issued by the Lord Justice-General in April 2003 (see 2003 S.L.T. (News) 118), but was modified on February 20, 2004 following the case of *Kyprianou v Cyprus*, Applic. no. 73797/01, January 27, 2004: see *Mayer v. H.M. Advocate*, 2004 S.L.T. 1259G–K, paras 47 and 48.

Kyprianou was a case in which a lawyer representing a person accused of murder had been found in contempt because of statements made to, and his demeanour towards, the trial judges: the same judges who made the finding of contempt sentenced him, *inter alia*, to five days imprisonment. Under the applicable domestic law, there was no doubt that such a contempt of which the applicant had been found guilty was classified as an offence (misdemeanour), for which the maximum penalty was one month in prison. The Government of Cyprus therefore did not dispute that the contempt in question was a crime to which Article 6 of the Convention applied. Whilst noting that there was no dispute between the parties as to this issue, the European Court of Human Rights (Second Section), at para. 31, observed: "In any event, the Court finds that the criminal nature of the offence of contempt of court in this case cannot be disputed. Applying the criteria established by the case-law of the Court ..., namely a) the domestic classification of the offence, b) the nature of the offence, and c) the degree of severity of the penalty that the person concerned risks incurring, it is clear that the offence in question was criminal. The offence was classified in domestic law as criminal, it was not confined to the applicant's status as a lawyer, the maximum possible sentence was one month's imprisonment and the sentence actually imposed on the applicant was 5 days' imprisonment ... Therefore, the requirements of Article 6 of the Convention in respect of the determination of any criminal charge, and the defence rights of everyone charged with a criminal offence, apply fully in the present case." (As noted in *Mayer, supra, Kyprianou's* case has been referred to the Grand Chamber.)

n.34: See now *Ashworth Hospital Authority v. MGN Ltd* [2002] 1 W.L.R. **50.05** 2033, H.L., especially the opinion of Lord Woolf, C.J., at p.2042E, para. 37, *et seq.*

n.39: See also *H.M. Advocate v. Dickie*, 2002 S.C.C.R. 312, where, at **50.06** p.321A–B, para. 20, Lord Hardie considered that the necessary wilfulness might have been inferred from the conduct of a solicitor who failed timeously to obtain alternative representation for his client at a High Court trial, and also failed timeously to forward the relevant papers to counsel when alternative representation had eventually been obtained, since "in assessing whether there has been any defiance of the authority of the court by a solicitor one must assume that he is aware of his professional responsibilities [to the court]". Lord Hardie concluded, however, that the circumstances of this case could also have led to the inference of sheer incompetence on the part of the solicitor, who thus was given the benefit of the doubt.

n.55: That the modern approach involves a test close to that favoured in **50.12** *Stuurman v. H.M. Advocate*, 1980 J.C. 111, is also confirmed by *Beggs v. H.M. Advocate*, 2001 S.C.C.R. 836: see the opinion of the court there at p.848F, para. 3.

n.62: See also *Beggs v. H.M. Advocate*, 2001 S.C.C.R. 836.

50.13 n.72: It seems that the saving for the common law under s.6(c) of the Contempt of Court Act 1981 is unlikely to be taken advantage of very often, if at all: in *Beggs v. H.M. Advocate*, 2001 S.C.C.R. 836, where press publicity was (in the words of the court at p.855E, para. 29) "extensive and highly prejudicial to the applicant" prior to proceedings becoming active under the 1981 Act, the court stated (at p.853F, para. 24):

> "It is true that the statute reserves common law liability in respect of conduct intended to prejudice the administration of justice but it would require a clear case to justify the exercise of any residual power outwith the limits which were laid down by parliament and clearly designed to provide a regime balanced to be fair to all the public interests involved."

50.15 n.83: See also *H.M. Advocate v. Dickie*, 2002 S.C.C.R. 312 at 320F–321A, para. 20, where Lord Hardie (with reference to *McMillan v. Carmichael*, 1993 S.C.C.R. 943) concludes (at p.321A) that "even the gross recklessness in this case cannot in law amount to contempt of court"; at p.321A, however, Lord Hardie notes that "the court in *McMillan v. Carmichael* also concluded that a finding of contempt of court might be inferred" and that he might have been prepared to infer the necessary "wilful failure in defiance of the authority of the court" on the part of a solicitor in the circumstances of this case, since in assessing whether or not to make such an inference one must assume that a solicitor is aware of his professional responsibilities to the court.

50.16 In *H.M. Advocate v. Beggs (No. 2)*, 2001 S.C.C.R. 879 at 886E–887A, para. 20, Lord Osborne at a High Court trial decided that the meaning of "publication" advanced in s.2(1) of the Contempt of Court Act 1981 was not comprehensive, and that a "publication" might extend, therefore, to prejudicial material posted by newspapers on an archival basis on their websites since such sites were "created with a view to the communication of information to the public, or at least a section of it". It was also necessary for Lord Osborne to consider whether prejudicial material first published in a newspaper before proceedings became active but thereafter posted to that newspaper's website, and maintained on that site during the time when proceedings were active, fell within the terms of s.2(3) of the 1981 Act: and his Lordship (at p.887D–F, para. 22) decided (by preferring the view advanced by the panel) that s.2(3) was satisfied in this case in that the "the expression 'the time of publication' was capable of referring to a period of time during which the material was accessible on the website, commencing with the moment when it first appeared and ending when it was withdrawn. During that whole period, the material was accessible to members of the public and ought to be regarded as being published throughout." Nevertheless, Lord Osborne held (at pp.888C–890B, paras 23–26) that the strict liability rule did not in this case apply to the material objected to since, in terms of s.2(2) of the 1981 Act, a substantial risk was not created that the course of justice would be seriously impeded or prejudiced.

In respect of s.6(c) of the Contempt of Court Act 1981 see *Beggs v. H.M.* **50.19**
Advocate, 2001 S.C.C.R. 836, opinion of the court at p.853F, para. 24—
as this is set out at para. 50.13, n. 72, above.

In relation to s.4(2) of the Contempt of Court Act 1981, and an order **50.22**
pronounced thereunder by Lord Hardie in the course of proceedings
relative to a plea in bar of trial and postponement of a trial diet, which
order referred to "these proceedings", Lord Osborne (the presiding judge
at the subsequent trial) concluded that (*H.M. Advocate v. Beggs (No. 1)*,
2001 S.C.C.R. 869 at 873E–F): "[w]hile the words 'these proceedings'
might be thought to be capable of embracing the whole proceedings
following on the indictment, it appears to me inherently improbable that
the judge dealing with a minute of postponement intended to make an
order under section 4(2) of the Act of 1981 extending to a trial with which
he had no legitimate concern". If, however, the order was capable of
extending to the trial, Lord Osborne considered that he was entitled to
review that order with a view to its termination. (A fresh application for a
s.4(2) order covering the trial was refused, since counsel for the panel
confirmed that his concern was not with fair and accurate reporting of the
trial proceedings, but rather with what such report might engender—
s.4(2), of course, being "intended to deal with fair and accurate reports of
proceedings which should none the less be postponed, not with material
outwith the scope of such reports, to which the strict liability rule could
apply under section 2(2) of the Act of 1981": *H.M. Advocate v. Beggs
(No. 1)*, *supra*, Lord Osborne at p.874F, repeating what was said by Lord
Justice-General Rodger in *Galbraith v. H.M. Advocate*, 2000 S.C.C.R.
935 at 939E, para. 10.)

n.7: *Scottish Criminal Cases Review Commission, Petitioners*, is now **50.24**
reported at 2001 S.C.C.R. 775.

On the question whether s.8 of the Contempt of Court Act 1981 binds the
Appeal Court in Scotland, a matter reserved in the *Scottish Criminal
Cases Review Commission, Petitioners, supra*, (see pp.783A–784A, paras
13–15 thereof), see now *R. v. Mirza* [2004] 1 A.C. 1118 (H.L.): there, it
was held that s.8 of the 1981 Act was not intended to apply to a trial
court nor to an appeal court hearing an appeal in the case, but that courts
were in general restricted in their enquiries as to what pertained in the
jury room by a longstanding rule of English common law, as to the
confidentiality of jury deliberations—see opinions of Lord Slynn of
Hadley, at p.1146C–D, para. 57; Lord Hope of Craighead, at pp.1155C–
G, paras 92–93, 1166E, para. 129; Lord Hobhouse of Woodburgh, at
p.1170G, para. 142, *et seq.* (*cf.* pp.1169H–1170A); and Lord Rodger of
Earlsferry, at p.1181D–G, para. 172.

In line 2 of the text of this paragraph, the phrase "(as applied to Scot- **50.25**
land)" should be deleted, following repeal of s.1(5) of the Judicial Proceedings (Regulation of Reports) Act 1926 by the Civil Partnership Act
2004, Sched. 27, para. 8(3); in the text of s.1(1) of the 1926 Act, paragraph (a) should be corrected so that the words "matter or indecent" are
inserted between "any indecent" and "medical"; and, also in the text of
s.1(1) of the 1926 Act, the initial part of paragraph (b), following
amendment by para. 8(2) of Sched. 27 to the Civil Partnership Act 2004,

should now read: "in relation to any proceedings under Part II of the Family Law Act 1996 or otherwise in relation to any proceedings for dissolution of marriage, for nullity of marriage, or for judicial separation or for the dissolution or annulment of a civil partnership or for the separation of civil partners, any particulars other than the following, that is to say—".

n.8: Delete the word "And", and substitute "As" for "as".

50.26 In *Frame v. Aberdeen Journals Limited*, July 8, 2005, 2005HCJAC79, unreported, the Appeal Court upheld a decision of the sheriff that a newspaper article, which had clearly identified a person under 16 as the person who had been arrested and charged with murder by police (who had been acting under a previously granted petition warrant) on the preceding day, had not contravened s.47(1) of the 1995 Act, that article not having contained "a report of any proceedings in a court".

50.27 Section 44 of the Children (Scotland) Act 1995 is amended by s.52(a) of the Criminal Justice (Scotland) Act 2003 (asp 7), such that subsection (1) now provides:

"(1) No person shall publish any matter in respect of a case about which the Principal Reporter has from any source received information or any matter in respect of proceedings at a children's hearing, or before a sheriff on an application under section 57, section 60(7), section 65(7) or (9), section 76(1) or section 85(1) of this Act, or on any appeal under this Part of this Act, which is intended to, or is likely to, identify—

    (a) the child concerned in, or any other child connected (in any way) with, the case, the proceedings or appeal;

    (b) an address or school as being that of any such child."

After paragraph 50.27, the following new paragraph should be inserted:

50.27A "*Proceedings relating to parenting orders.* Section 111 of the Antisocial Behaviour etc. (Scotland) Act 2004 (asp 8) provides:

'(1) Subject to subsection (2), a person shall be guilty of an offence if the person publishes [which, under subsection (7), includes "causing to be published" and "publishing in a programme service"], anywhere in the world, any matter in respect of relevant proceedings [as defined in subsection (7)] which is intended, or likely to, identify—

    (a) the parent concerned in the proceedings (the "person concerned");

    (b) any address as being that of the person concerned;

    (c) the child concerned in the proceedings;

    (d) any other child—

        (i) who is a member of the same household as the person concerned; or

        (ii) of whom the person concerned is a parent; or

(e) any—

> (i) address; or
> (ii) school,

as being that of a child mentioned in paragraph (c) or (d).

(2) In relevant proceedings [as defined in subsection (7)], the court may, in the interests of justice, order that subsection (1) shall not apply to the proceedings to such extent as the court considers appropriate.

(3) A person guilty of an offence under subsection (1) shall be liable on summary conviction to a fine not exceeding level 4 on the standard scale.

(4) It shall be a defence for a person charged with an offence under subsection (1) to show that the person—

(a) did not know; and
(b) had no reason to suspect,

that the published matter was intended, or was likely, to identify the person concerned, child, address or school (as the case may be).'

For 'parenting orders', see the 2004 Act (asp 8), Part 9 (ss.102–110)."

nn.13 and 14: Section 8 of the Magistrates' Courts Act 1980 is repealed by **50.28** the Criminal Justice Act 2003, Sched. 3, para. 51(3) and Sched. 37, Part 4. The 2003 Act introduces new procedures and offences: see, *e.g.* s.311.

n.14: Section 38 of the Criminal Procedure and Investigations Act 1996 is amended by the Criminal Justice Act 2003, s.311(7).